Reflections on the Great Depression

To my parents, Richard and Paula Parker; "See you 'round some time Dickie"

Reflections on the Great Depression

Randall E. Parker
Associate Professor of Economics, East Carolina University, Greenville, North Carolina, USA

Edward Elgar
Cheltenham, UK • Northampton, MA, USA

Published by
Edward Elgar Publishing Limited
Glensanda House
Montpellier Parade
Cheltenham
Glos GL50 1UA
UK

Edward Elgar Publishing, Inc.
136 West Street
Suite 202
Northampton
Massachusetts 01060
USA

A catalogue record for this book
is available from the British Library

ISBN 1 84064 745 0

Printed and bound in Great Britain by Biddles Ltd, *www.biddles.co.uk*

Contents

Acknowledgements

I would like to thank several individuals who were responsible for the completion of this book:

My wife Monica for her love, friendship and unquestioned support.

My entire family. I have never walked alone. May we all lead contemplative lives.

Philip A. Rothman, valued colleague, world-class time series econometrician, and great friend.

Gucharan S. Laumas, my friend and source of encouragement. I'm not sure I can ever repay what I owe.

James S. Fackler and W. Douglas McMillin, thanks for all you have done for me. There are debts here as well that I am not sure I can repay.

Ben Bernanke and James Hamilton. You fellows may not know it, but you are everything good people and great scientists should be.

The economists of the interwar generation who so graciously agreed to speak with me.

Foreword

Ben S. Bernanke
Howard Harrison and Gabrielle Snyder Beck Professor of Economics, Princeton University

I have always been impressed by the reading public's appetite for history and historical biography. What is it that moves people with no professional or academic stake in historical interpretation to want to know about events far removed from their own experience? Here is one answer: History is a highbrow form of gossip. The stories of individuals swept up in – and occasionally influencing – the tide of world events are intrinsically fascinating, in no small part because they so often display the eternal verities of the human condition. Most fascinating of all are accounts of human reactions under great stress – hence the seemingly disproportionate attention of popular historians to warfare and battle.

The Great Depression of the 1930s was not a period of active warfare – it was, rather, a period of temporary cease-fire in a worldwide struggle that lasted from 1914 to 1945. But the 1930s were nevertheless an enormously difficult time in which to live, and not only because of the privation and economic hardship that the Depression created around the world. The era was traumatic also because no one – not the political leaders, not the "experts" – really understood what was happening or what was in store for the world. Would it all end in revolution? And if so, from the left or from the right? In warfare, at least, one knows who the enemy is and what needs to be done in order to prevail. During the Depression, nobody knew either. From such conditions come both fascinating history and engaging individual stories.

The interviews with famous senior economists contained in this enjoyable book achieve two important, and quite distinct, goals. First, they provide invaluable insights into the history of theorizing about the Depression. A point that is made repeatedly in the interviews is that hindsight can make anyone seem wise. Much more difficult is to know what to do when all hell is breaking loose around you. In these conversations we see the struggles of the brightest young economists of their generation to reconcile old paradigms of the efficiency and optimality of free markets with the hard facts of mass

vii

unemployment and economic collapse they saw around them in the 1930s. In their attempts to find new answers we see the roots of current ideas and debates in economics. We also see firsthand how messy and nonlinear the search for new paradigms can be. These interviews do an excellent job of recapturing the sense of uncertainty, the feeling of grappling with an intractable puzzle, that almost every one of these economists experienced.

The second achievement of these interviews is to provide, well, first-rate highbrow gossip. The interviewees are outstanding economists but they are also an exceptional group of people. They hail from around the world, from a variety of cultural and socioeconomic backgrounds. Each, in one way or the other, found his or her way to professional prominence, often in the face of substantial adversity. Victor Zarnowitz grew up in the town that was to become infamous as the site of the Auschwitz death camp and spent 19 months in Russian labor camps. Anna Schwartz was a rare example of a woman achieving professional eminence in economics in the United States in the first half of the twentieth century. And Charles Kindleberger had his phone calls bugged by the FBI in the 1930s and barely escaped Prague ahead of the Nazi invaders. Their experiences reflected in microcosm the experiences of millions during the Depression, and their personal stories, almost as much as their professional careers, convey to us a flavor of that very difficult time.

Enjoy the gossip.

Preface

This book is about the most prominent economic explanations of the Great Depression and how the events of this period affected the lives, experiences, and subsequent thinking of the leading economists of the twentieth century who lived through that era. I confess, as Ben Bernanke does in his recent book *Essays on the Great Depression*, that I consider myself to be a Great Depression buff. It all goes back to my father. The stories and lessons in life he would teach me were all punctuated with what happened to him and his family during the Depression. As a young child, I was intrigued with the historical record and the adjectives my father used to describe the desperation so many people were living under. In my studies of economics as both an undergraduate and graduate student, my fascination with the largest slide in the history of the business cycle intensified.

Macroeconomics has always been my area of concentration and I observed three things in particular regarding the economic literature of the Depression early in my career (the second half of the 1980s). First, an active and fruitful research agenda could be pursued in testing the validity of modern macro theories using interwar data, that is, scrutinizing the robustness and plausibility of contemporary theory viewed through the lens of history. There existed strands of the literature where modern macro theories were judged by how well they explained the Depression. I thought the combination of macroeconomics and economic history was an interesting line of research in which to be a participant.

Second, there appeared to be a good number of important macroeconomic events, policies, and behaviors of prices and quantities during the interwar era that remained unexplained. Even though many years had passed, there still were considerable questions that remained unanswered, and similarly an active and fruitful research agenda could be pursued in this area.

Third, and most importantly, I was struck by how little consensus there was regarding the economic explanations for either the causes, or depth, or protracted length of the Depression in the literature. Explaining the Depression, it seemed to me, was the leading task for macroeconomists. If understanding business cycle fluctuations was one of the goals of macroeconomists, what other period of time could supplant the Depression in terms of the magnitude and persistence of its cyclical downturn? The economic misery during that time was worldwide, deep, and prolonged. The profession needed to have good explanations for why the Depression happened and what could be done to prevent it from recurring. Apparently the literature was a long way from achieving anything close to general agreement. Moreover, I was taken aback by how intensely most of the major contributors to this literature insisted on the exclusive correctness of their own singular "pet" theory, or so-called monocausal explanation, of the Great Depression. I thought surely there was room for more than just one explanation in so dramatic a worldwide economic downturn. However, the more I read of the earlier literature (pre-Bernanke, 1983), the more I recognized that the literature had ceased to advance our understanding of the Depression as it had evolved into a stand-off of monocausal explanations all pitted against each other. Regarding monocausal explanations, Victor Zarnowitz (1992) has written, "As was recognized early by the 'classics,' the sharp dichotomies and monocausal theories tend to be invalidated by experience." But yet, more than 50 years after the depth of the Great Depression, monocausal explanations did not appear to be invalidated in the works that comprised the literature on the Depression and this literature was still sharply divided. If explaining the Depression was the main task of macroeconomists, we were failing. I did not find this to be very satisfactory.

I decided, together with my colleague Jim Fackler of the University of Kentucky, to empirically test the explanatory power of the most prominent monocausal theories of the Depression. We felt that in order to validate a monocausal theory, it should be capable of explaining the major turning points of the business cycle and the cyclical bottom of the Depression in March 1933, or at least a major part of it. We decided to have an econometric horse race. Recent advances in the profession's understanding of the Depression (particularly Bernanke, 1983 and Hamilton, 1987), as well as Bernanke's (1986) advance in the estimation of structural vector autoregressions, made this horse race a natural experiment. The results, published in Fackler and Parker (1994), showed that none of the theories considered, on their own, was able to capture the actual movements of output or the depth of the Depression within its explanatory path and constructed 95 percent confidence bands. Rather, it required a combination of several of the many existing theories of the Depression to produce an empirically satisfactory accounting of the depth and path of output during this time period. Moreover, along with the work of McCallum (1990), we were the first to show, using counterfactual historical simulations, that if the Federal Reserve would have kept the money supply growing at the rate of growth that prevailed in the 1920s, the Depression could have been largely averted. So, two points were confirmed: monocausal theories are inadequate to account for the Depression and money really did matter.

We had hoped that our paper made some scholarly contribution, however small, toward building a consensus view of the Depression and emphasizing the need to eschew monocausal explanations. But something kept telling me there was more to the story than the scholarly literature itself. While the literature was very important, there were other pieces to the puzzle of the Depression, a personal side, that we needed to hear about. I realized that I wanted to get a record of the reflections on the Great Depression of the leading economists of the twentieth century who lived through and were trained during this era, on a personal interview basis before I, and the profession, missed the chance. Such reflections did not exist in print and I felt it important (perhaps mistakenly) to provide such a record. There certainly is a long list of research (see, for example, Leijonhufvud, 1968) regarding what Keynes might have meant or could have meant in certain passages of *The General Theory* and other works. He passed away and so did the chance to ask him. I decided not to have the same set of circumstances prevail for the participants in the development of the literature on the Great Depression. I wanted to know what they really thought. Here was my chance to find out. I wanted to go right to the source 60 years or so after the Depression. I wanted these individuals to reflect on their lives and the impact the Depression had on them, both personally and professionally. Sometimes people say things in an interview that they would not ordinarily say, or that would not be published in a scholarly paper. There is an essence to a one-on-one interview that cannot be and is not captured in the pages of a scholarly publication. I wanted to find out for myself if there was any such "essence" to be captured in the reflections on the Great Depression.

In this book I do not pretend to cover all of the important issues or schools of thought, nor have I interviewed all of the important economists that made contributions to the literature on the Great Depression. When I began this project, I set out to find the people who are considered to have been, and in many cases still are, the most important economists of the interwar generation and talk to them whether or not they have written any work specifically on the Depression. I wanted Lester Chandler, Martin Bronfenbrenner and Gottfried Haberler to be included. I quickly found out that I conceived this idea a little late, as they had passed away. The fact that I got to speak with Moses Abramovitz, Albert Hart, Wassily Leontief and Herbert Stein, all of whom have passed away since our respective interview, shows I was not too late.

In the 11 interviews conducted for this book there were a number of standard questions regarding the Depression that I asked all of the individuals with whom I spoke. However, each one of these individuals had a particular and unique experience and I wanted to see if and how the Depression had an impact on their thinking and how it molded their lives. I also wanted to spend some time asking other interesting questions related to macroeconomics in the areas of each individual's particular expertise. But more than this, these are people of uncommon intellect and substantial wit. So, I also took the liberty of asking related questions and let the conversation go where it would. If the ensuing discussion was scholarly in tone, maybe the reader will learn something from these interviews or at least have what was already known reinforced in their mind. If it was humorous and the conversation became lighter, maybe the reader will share in some of the fun I had putting this book together. My sincere hope is that these interviews give you a healthy dose of the former and a happy dose of the latter.

Randall E. Parker

An Overview of the Great Depression

It has been said in many places, and without controversy, that the Great Depression provided the fertile ground from which modern macroeconomics sprouted. In addition, the Depression produced the economists of the twentieth century who began and nurtured the economic literature on the Great Depression in particular, and the development of modern macroeconomics in general. This book contains interviews with 11 of the leading economists of the twentieth century who lived through and were trained during the Depression era: Paul Samuelson, Milton Friedman, Moses Abramovitz, Albert Hart, Charles Kindleberger, Anna Schwartz, James Tobin, Wassily Leontief, Morris Adelman, Herbert Stein, and Victor Zarnowitz. The purpose of this book is to provide a record of their reflections on the Great Depression. If, as Ben Bernanke (1995) has said, understanding the Great Depression is "the Holy Grail of macroeconomics," we have the opportunity to pose questions on these matters to some of the very first individuals who began the search for the Holy Grail and lived the events. There are many questions of interest and each person has a story to tell regarding how the Depression affected them. We will turn our attention to these individuals in the interviews that follow. Before we do, however, it is important to provide some historical and theoretical background for the interviews.

This chapter provides an overview of selected events and economic explanations of the interwar era, so that the reader can put the substance of the interviews into proper context. What follows is not intended to be a detailed and exhaustive review of the literature on the Great Depression, or of any one theory in particular. Rather, I will attempt to describe what I consider to be the "big picture" events and topics of interest. In doing so, I hope to highlight the content and importance of the questions and answers contained in the 11 interviews. For the reader who wishes more extensive analysis and detail, references to additional materials are also included.

THE 1920s

The Great Depression, and the economic catastrophe that it was, is perhaps properly scaled in reference to the decade that preceded it, the 1920s. By conventional macroeconomic measures, this was a decade of brisk economic growth in the United States. Perhaps the moniker "the roaring twenties" summarizes this period most succinctly. The disruptions and shocking nature of World War I had been survived and it was felt the United States was entering a "new era." In January 1920, the Federal Reserve seasonally adjusted index of industrial production, a standard measure of aggregate economic activity, stood at 81 (1935–39 = 100). When the index peaked in July 1929 it was at 114, for a growth rate of 40.6 percent over this period. Similar rates of growth over the 1920–29 period equal to 47.3 percent and 42.4 percent are computed using annual real gross national product data from Balke and Gordon (1986) and Romer (1988), respectively. Further computations using the Balke and Gordon (1986) data indicate an average annual growth rate of real GNP over the 1920–29 period equal to 4.6 percent. In addition, the relative international economic strength of this country was clearly displayed by the fact that nearly one-half of world industrial output in 1925–29 was produced in the United States (Bernanke, 1983).

The decade of the 1920s also saw major innovations in the consumption behavior of households. The development of installment credit over this period led to substantial growth in the consumer durables market (Bernanke, 1983). Purchases of automobiles, refrigerators, radios and other such durable goods all experienced explosive growth during the 1920s as small borrowers, particularly households and unincorporated businesses, utilized their access to available credit (Persons, 1930; Bernanke, 1983; Soule, 1947).

Economic growth during this period was mitigated only somewhat by three recessions. According to the National Bureau of Economic Research (NBER) business cycle chronology, two of these recessions were from May 1923 through July 1924 and October 1926 through November 1927. Both of these recessions were very mild and unremarkable. In contrast, the 1920s began with a recession lasting 18 months from the peak in January 1920 until the trough of July 1921. Original estimates of real GNP from the Commerce Department showed that real GNP fell 8 percent between 1919 and 1920 and another 7 percent between 1920 and 1921 (Romer, 1988). The behavior of prices contributed to the naming of this recession "the Depression of 1921," as the implicit price deflator for GNP fell 16 percent and the Bureau of Labor Statistics wholesale price index fell 46 percent between 1920 and 1921. Although thought to be severe, Romer (1988) has demonstrated that the so-called "postwar depression" was not as severe as once thought. While the deflation from war-time prices was substantial, revised estimates of real GNP show falls in output of only 1 percent between 1919 and 1920 and 2 percent between 1920 and 1921. Romer (1988) also argues that the behaviors of output and prices are inconsistent with the conventional explanation of the Depression of 1921 being primarily driven by a decline in aggregate demand.

Rather, the deflation and the mild recession are better understood as resulting from a decline in aggregate demand together with a series of positive supply shocks, particularly in the production of agricultural goods, and significant decreases in the prices of imported primary commodities. Overall, the upshot is that the growth path of output was hardly impeded by the three minor downturns, so that the decade of the 1920s can properly be viewed economically as a very healthy period.

Friedman and Schwartz (1963) label the 1920s "the high tide of the Reserve System." As they explain, the Federal Reserve became increasingly confident in the tools of policy and in its knowledge of how to use them properly. The synchronous movements of economic activity and explicit policy actions by the Federal Reserve did not go unnoticed. Taking the next step and concluding there was cause and effect, the Federal Reserve in the 1920s began to use monetary policy as an implement to stabilize business cycle fluctuations. "In retrospect, we can see that this was a major step toward the assumption by government of explicit continuous responsibility for economic stability. As the decade wore on, the System took – and perhaps even more was given – credit for the generally stable conditions that prevailed, and high hopes were placed in the potency of monetary policy as then administered" (Friedman and Schwartz, 1963).

The giving/taking of credit to/by the Federal Reserve has particular value pertaining to the recession of 1920–21. Although suggesting the Federal Reserve probably tightened too much, too late, Friedman and Schwartz (1963) call this episode "the first real trial of the new system of monetary control introduced by the Federal Reserve Act." It is clear from the history of the time that the Federal Reserve felt as though it had successfully passed this test. The data showed that the economy had quickly recovered and brisk growth followed the recession of 1920–21 for the remainder of the decade.

Moreover, Eichengreen (1992) suggests that the episode of 1920–21 led the Federal Reserve System to believe that the economy could be successfully deflated or "liquidated" without paying a severe penalty in terms of reduced output. This conclusion, however, proved to be mistaken at the onset of the Depression. As argued by Eichengreen (1992), the Federal Reserve did not appreciate the extent to which the successful deflation could be attributed to the unique circumstances that prevailed during 1920–21. The European economies were still devastated after World War I, so the demand for United States' exports remained strong many years after the War. Moreover, the gold standard was not in operation at the time. Therefore, European countries were not forced to match the deflation initiated in the United States by the Federal Reserve (explained below pertaining to the gold standard hypothesis).

The implication is that the Federal Reserve thought that deflation could be generated with little effect on real economic activity. Therefore, the Federal

Reserve was not vigorous in fighting the Great Depression in its initial stages. It viewed the early years of the Depression as another opportunity to successfully liquidate the economy, especially after the perceived speculative excesses of the 1920s. However, the state of the economic world in 1929 was not a duplicate of 1920–21. By 1929, the European economies had recovered and the interwar gold standard was a vehicle for the international transmission of deflation. Deflation in 1929 would not operate as it did in 1920–21. The Federal Reserve failed to understand the economic implications of this change in the international standing of the United States' economy. The result was that the Depression was permitted to spiral out of control and was made much worse than it otherwise would have been had the Federal Reserve not considered it to be a repeat of the 1920–21 recession. It is in this sense that I ask several of the interviewees if they see any parallels between the recession of 1920–21 and the Great Depression.

THE BEGINNINGS OF THE GREAT DEPRESSION

In January 1928 the seeds of the Great Depression, whenever they were planted, began to germinate. For it is around this time that two of the most prominent explanations for the depth, length, and worldwide spread of the Depression first came to be manifest. Without any doubt, the economics profession would come to a firm consensus around the idea that the economic events of the Great Depression cannot be properly understood without a solid linkage to both the behavior of the supply of money together with Federal Reserve actions on the one hand and the flawed structure of the interwar gold standard on the other. I shall have more to say about these below.

It is well documented that many public officials, such as President Herbert Hoover and members of the Federal Reserve System in the latter 1920s, were intent on ending what they perceived to be the speculative excesses that were driving the stock market boom. Moreover, as explained by Hamilton (1987), despite plentiful denials to the contrary, the Federal Reserve assumed the role of "arbiter of security prices." Although there continues to be debate as to whether or not the stock market was overvalued at the time (White, 1990; DeLong and Schleifer, 1991), the main point is that the Federal Reserve believed there to be a speculative bubble in equity values. Hamilton (1987) describes how the Federal Reserve, intending to "pop" the bubble, embarked on a highly contractionary monetary policy in January 1928. Between December 1927 and July 1928 the Federal Reserve conducted $393 million of open market sales of securities so that only $80 million remained in the Open Market account. Buying rates on bankers' acceptances were raised from 3 percent in January 1928 to 4.5 percent by July, reducing Federal Reserve holdings of such bills by $193 million, leaving a total of only $185 million of these bills on balance. Further, the discount rate was increased from 3.5 percent to 5 percent, the highest level since the recession of 1920–21. "In short, in terms of the magnitudes consciously controlled by the Fed, it would be difficult to design a more contractionary policy than that initiated in January 1928" (Hamilton, 1987).

The pressure did not stop there, however. The death of Federal Reserve Bank President Benjamin Strong and the subsequent control of policy ascribed to Adolph Miller of the Federal Reserve Board insured that the fall in the stock market was going to be made a reality. Miller believed the speculative excesses of the stock market were hurting the economy, and the Federal Reserve continued attempting to put an end to this perceived harm (Cecchetti, 1998). The amount of Federal Reserve credit that was being extended to market participants in the form of broker loans became an issue in 1929. The Federal Reserve adamantly discouraged lending that was collateralized by equities. The intentions of the Board of Governors of the Federal Reserve were made clear in a letter dated February 2, 1929 sent to Federal Reserve banks. In part the letter read:

> The board has no disposition to assume authority to interfere with the loan practices of member banks so long as they do not involve the Federal reserve banks. It has, however, a grave responsibility whenever there is evidence that member banks are maintaining speculative security loans with the aid of Federal reserve credit. When such is the case the Federal reserve bank becomes either a contributing or a sustaining factor in the current volume of speculative security credit. This is not in harmony with the intent of the Federal Reserve Act, nor is it conducive to the wholesome operation of the banking and credit system of the country. (Board of Governors of the Federal Reserve 1929: 93–94, quoted from Cecchetti, 1998)

The deflationary pressure to stock prices had been applied. It was now a question of when the market would break. Although the effects were not immediate, the wait was not long.

THE ECONOMY STUMBLES

The NBER business cycle chronology dates the start of the Great Depression in August 1929. For this reason many have said that the Depression started on Main Street and not Wall Street. Be that as it may, the stock market plummeted in October of 1929. The bursting of the speculative bubble had been achieved and the economy was now headed in an ominous direction. The Federal Reserve's seasonally adjusted index of industrial production stood at

114 (1935–39 = 100) in August 1929. By October it had fallen to 110 for a decline of 3.5 percent (annualized percentage decline = 14.7 percent). After the crash, the incipient recession intensified, with the industrial production index falling from 110 in October to 100 in December 1929, or 9 percent (annualized percentage decline = 41 percent). In 1930, the index fell further from 100 in January to 79 in December, or an additional 21 percent.

While popular history treats the crash and the Depression as one and the same event, economists know that they were not. But there is no doubt that the crash was one of the things that got the ball rolling. Several authors have offered explanations for the linkage between the crash and the recession of 1929–30. Mishkin (1978) argues that the crash and an increase in liabilities led to a deterioration in the household balance sheet. The reduced liquidity led consumers to defer consumption of durable goods and housing and thus contributed to a fall in consumption. Temin (1976) suggests that the fall in stock prices had a negative wealth effect on consumption, but attributes only a minor role to this given that stocks were not a large fraction of total wealth; the stock market in 1929, although falling dramatically, remained above the value it had achieved in early 1928, and the propensity to consume from wealth was small during this period. Romer (1990) provides evidence suggesting that if the stock market were thought to be a predictor of future economic activity, then the crash can rightly be viewed as a source of increased consumer uncertainty that depressed spending on consumer durables and accelerated the decline that had begun in August 1929. Flacco and Parker (1992) confirm Romer's findings using different data and alternative estimation techniques.

Looking back on the behavior of the economy during the year of 1930, industrial production declined 21 percent, the consumer price index fell 2.6 percent, the supply of high-powered money (that is, the liabilities of the Federal Reserve that are usable as money, consisting of currency in circulation and bank reserves; also called the monetary base) fell 2.8 percent, the nominal supply of M1 (the product of the monetary base multiplied by the money multiplier) dipped 3.5 percent and the ex post real interest rate turned out to be 11.3 percent, the highest it had been since the recession of 1920–21 (Hamilton, 1987). In spite of this, when put into historical context, there was no reason to view the downturn of 1929–30 as historically unprecedented. Its magnitude was comparable to that of many recessions that had previously occurred. Perhaps there was justifiable optimism in December 1930 that the economy might even shake off the negative movement and embark on the path to recovery, rather like what had occurred after the recession of 1920–21 (Bernanke, 1983). As we know, the bottom would not come for another 27 months.

THE ECONOMY CRUMBLES

During 1931, there was a "change in the character of the contraction" (Friedman and Schwartz, 1963). Beginning in October 1930 and lasting until December 1930, the first of a series of banking panics now accompanied the downward spasms of the business cycle. Although bank failures had occurred throughout the 1920s, the magnitude of the failures that occurred in the early 1930s was of a different order altogether (Bernanke, 1983). The absence of any type of deposit insurance resulted in the contagion of the panics being spread to sound financial institutions and not just those on the margin. Moreover, institutional arrangements that had existed in the private banking system designed to provide liquidity to fight bank runs before 1913 were not exercised after the creation of the Federal Reserve System. For example, during the panic of 1907, the effects of the financial upheaval had been contained through a combination of lending activities by private banks, called clearinghouses, and the suspension of deposit convertibility into currency. While not preventing bank runs and the financial panic, their economic impact was lessened to a significant extent by these countermeasures enacted by private banks, as the economy quickly recovered in 1908. The aftermath of the panic of 1907 and the desire to have a central authority to combat the contagion of financial disruptions was one of the factors that led to the establishment of the Federal Reserve System. After the creation of the Federal Reserve, clearinghouse lending and suspension of deposit convertibility by private banks were not undertaken. Believing the Federal Reserve to be the "lender of last resort," it was apparently thought that the responsibility to fight bank runs was the domain of the central bank (Friedman and Schwartz, 1963; Bernanke, 1983). Unfortunately, when the banking panics came in waves and the financial system was collapsing, being the "lender of last resort" was a responsibility that the Federal Reserve either could not or would not assume.

The economic effects of the banking panics were devastating. Aside from the obvious impact of the closing of failed banks and the subsequent loss of deposits by bank customers, the growth rate of the money supply accelerated its downward spiral. Although the economy had flattened out after the first wave of bank failures in October–December 1930, with the industrial production index steadying from 79 in December 1930 to 80 in April 1931, the remainder of 1931 brought a series of shocks from which the economy was not to recover for some time.

In May, the failure of Austria's largest bank, the Kredit-anstalt, touched off financial panics in Europe. In September 1931, having had enough of the distress associated with the international transmission of economic depression, Britain abandoned its participation in the gold standard. Further, just as the United States' economy appeared to be trying to begin recovery, the second wave of bank failures hit the financial system in June and did not abate until December. In addition, the Hoover administration in December 1931, adhering to its principles of limited government, embarked on a campaign to balance the federal budget. Tax increases resulted the following June, just as the economy was to hit the first low point of its so-called "double bottom" (Hoover, 1952).

The results of these events are now evident. Between January and December 1931 the industrial production index declined from 78 to 66, or 15.4 percent, the consumer price index fell 9.4 percent, the nominal supply of M1 dipped 5.7 percent, the ex post real interest rate remained at 11.3 percent, and although the supply of high-powered money actually increased 5.5 percent (we will see that this is a crucial point in the conversation with Paul Samuelson), the currency–deposit and reserve–deposit ratios began their upward ascent, and thus the money multiplier started its downward plunge (Hamilton, 1987). If the economy had flattened out in the spring of 1931, then by December output, the money supply, and the price level were all on negative growth paths that were dragging the economy deeper into depression.

The economic difficulties were far from over. The economy displayed some evidence of recovery in late summer/early fall of 1932. However, in December 1932 the third, and largest, wave of banking panics hit the financial markets and the collapse of the economy arrived with the business cycle hitting bottom in March 1933. Industrial production between January 1932 and March 1933 fell an additional 15.6 percent. For the combined years of 1932 and 1933, the consumer price index fell a cumulative 16.2 percent, the nominal supply of M1 dropped 21.6 percent, the nominal M2 money supply fell 34.7 percent, and although the supply of high-powered money increased 8.4 percent, the currency–deposit and reserve–deposit ratios accelerated their upward ascent. Thus the money multiplier continued on a downward plunge that was not arrested until March 1933. Similar behaviors for real GDP, prices, money supplies and other key macroeconomic variables occurred in many European economies as well (Snowdon and Vane, 1999; Temin, 1989).

An examination of the macroeconomic data in August 1929 compared to March 1933 provides a stark contrast. The unemployment rate of 3 percent in August 1929 was at 25 percent in March 1933. The industrial production index of 114 in August 1929 was at 54 in March 1933, or a 52.6 percent decrease. Given, as mentioned above, that the United States produced one-half of world industrial production in 1925–29, the United States accounted for one-fourth of the fall in world industrial output. The money supply had fallen 35 percent, prices plummeted by about 33 percent, and more than one-third of banks in the United States were either closed or taken over by other banks. The "new era" ushered in by "the roaring twenties" was over. Roosevelt took office in March 1933, a nationwide bank holiday was declared from March 6 until March 13, and the United States abandoned the international gold standard in April 1933. Recovery commenced immediately and the economy began its long path back to the pre-1929 secular growth trend.

CONTEMPORARY EXPLANATIONS

The economics profession during the 1930s was at a loss to explain the Depression. The most prominent conventional explanations were of two types. First, some observers at the time firmly grounded their explanations on the two pillars of classical macroeconomic thought, Say's Law and the belief in the self-equilibrating powers of the market. Many argued that it was simply a question of time before wages and prices adjusted fully enough for the economy to return to full employment and achieve the realization of the putative axiom that "supply creates its own demand." Second, the Austrian school of thought argued that the Depression was the inevitable result of overinvestment during the 1920s. The best remedy for the situation was to let the Depression run its course so that the economy could be purified from the negative effects of the false expansion. Government intervention was viewed by the Austrian school as a mechanism that would simply prolong the agony and make any subsequent depression worse than it would ordinarily be.

The Hoover administration and the Federal Reserve Board also contained several so-called "liquidationists." These individuals basically believed that economic agents should be forced to re-arrange their spending proclivities and alter their alleged profligate use of resources. If it took mass bankruptcies to produce this result and wipe the slate clean so that everyone could have a fresh start, then so be it. The liquidationists viewed the events of the Depression as an economic penance for the speculative excesses of the 1920s. Thus, the Depression was the price that was being paid for the misdeeds of the previous decade. This is perhaps best exemplified in the well-known quotation of Treasury Secretary Andrew Mellon, who advised President Hoover to "Liquidate labor, liquidate stocks, liquidate the farmers, liquidate real estate." Mellon continued, "It will purge the rottenness out of the system. High costs of living and high living will come down. People will work harder, live a more moral life. Values will be adjusted, and enterprising people will pick up the wrecks from less competent people" (Hoover, 1952). Hoover apparently followed this advice as the Depression wore on. He continued to reassure the public that if the principles of orthodox finance were faithfully followed, recovery would surely be the result.

The business press at the time was not immune from such liquidationist prescriptions either. The *Commercial and Financial Chronicle*, in an August 3, 1929 editorial entitled "Is Not Group Speculating Conspiracy, Fostering Sham Prosperity?" complained of the economy being replete with profligate spending including:

> (a) The luxurious diversification of diet advantageous to dairy men ... and fruit growers ...; (b) luxurious dressing ... more silk and rayon ...; (c) free spending for automobiles and their accessories, gasoline, house furnishings and equipment, radios, travel, amusements and sports; (d) the displacement from the farms by tractors and autos of produce-consuming horses and mules to a number aggregating 3,700,000 for the period 1918–1928 ... (e) the frills of education to thousands for whom places might better be reserved at bench or counter or on the farm. (Quoted from Nelson, 1991)

Persons, in a paper which appeared in the November 1930 *Quarterly Journal of Economics*, demonstrates that some academic economists also held similar liquidationist views.

Although certainly not universal, the descriptions above suggest that no small part of the conventional wisdom at the time believed the Depression to be a penitence for past sins. In addition, it was thought that the economy would be restored to full employment equilibrium once wages and prices adjusted sufficiently. Say's Law will ensure the economy will return to health, and supply will create its own demand sufficient to return to prosperity, if we simply let the system work its way through. In his memoirs published in 1952, 20 years after his election defeat, Herbert Hoover continued to steadfastly maintain that if Roosevelt and the New Dealers would have stuck to the policies his administration put in place, the economy would have made a full recovery within 18 months after the election of 1932. We have to intensify our resolve to "stay the course." All will be well in time if we just "take our medicine." In hindsight, it challenges the imagination to think up worse policy prescriptions for the events of 1929–33.

MODERN EXPLANATIONS

As the interviews reveal, there remains considerable debate regarding the economic explanations for the behavior of the business cycle between August 1929 and March 1933. This section describes the main hypotheses that have been presented in the literature attempting to explain the causes for the depth, protracted length, and worldwide propagation of the Great Depression.

The United States' experience, considering the preponderance of empirical results and historical simulations contained in the economic literature, can largely be accounted for by the monetary hypothesis of Friedman and Schwartz (1963) together with the nonmonetary/financial hypotheses of Bernanke (1983) and Fisher (1933). That is, most, but not all, of the characteristic phases of the business cycle and depth to which output fell from

1929 to 1933 can be accounted for by the monetary and nonmonetary/financial hypotheses. The international experience, well documented in Choudri and Kochin (1980), Hamilton (1988), Temin (1989), Bernanke and James (1991), and Eichengreen (1992), can be properly understood as resulting from a flawed interwar gold standard. Each of these hypotheses is explained in greater detail below.

It should be noted that I do not include a section covering the nonmonetary/nonfinancial theories of the Great Depression. These theories, including Temin's (1976) focus on autonomous consumption decline, the collapse of housing construction contained in Anderson and Butkiewicz (1980), the effects of the stock market crash, the uncertainty hypothesis of Romer (1990), and the Smoot–Hawley Tariff Act of 1930, are all worthy of mention and can rightly be apportioned some of the responsibility for initiating the Depression. However, any theory of the Depression must be able to account for the protracted nonneutralities associated with the punishing deflation imposed on the United States and the world during that era. While the nonmonetary/nonfinancial theories go a long way accounting for the impetus for, and first year of the Depression, my reading of the empirical results of the economic literature indicates that they do not have the explanatory power of the three other theories mentioned above to account for the depths to which the economy plunged.

The Monetary Hypothesis

In reviewing the economic history of the Depression above, it was mentioned that the supply of money fell by 35 percent, prices dropped by about 33 percent, and one-third of all banks vanished. Milton Friedman and Anna Schwartz, in their 1963 book *A Monetary History of the United States, 1867–1960*, call this massive drop in the supply of money "The Great Contraction."

Friedman and Schwartz (1963) discuss and painstakingly document the synchronous movements of the real economy with the disruptions that occurred in the financial sector. They point out that the series of bank failures that occurred beginning in October 1930 worsened economic conditions in two ways. First, bank shareholder wealth was reduced as banks failed. Second, and most importantly, the bank failures were exogenous shocks and led to the drastic decline in the money supply. The persistent deflation of the 1930s follows directly from this "great contraction."

However, this raises an important question: Where was the Federal Reserve while the money supply and the financial system were collapsing? If the Federal Reserve was created in 1913 primarily to be the "lender of last resort" for troubled financial institutions, it was failing miserably. Friedman and Schwartz pin the blame squarely on the Federal Reserve and the failure of monetary policy to offset the contractions in the money supply. As the money multiplier continued on its downward path, the monetary base, rather than being aggressively increased, simply progressed slightly upwards on a gently positive sloping time path. As banks were failing in waves, was the Federal Reserve attempting to contain the panics by aggressively lending to banks scrambling for liquidity? The unfortunate answer is "no." When the panics were occurring, was there discussion of suspending deposit convertibility or suspension of the gold standard, both of which had been successfully employed in the past? Again the unfortunate answer is "no." Did the Federal Reserve consider the fact that it had an abundant supply of free gold, and therefore that monetary expansion was feasible? Once again the unfortunate answer is "no." The argument can be summarized by the following quotation:

> At all times throughout the 1929–33 contraction, alternative policies were available to the System by which it could have kept the stock of money from falling, and indeed could have increased it at almost any desired rate. Those policies did not involve radical innovations. They involved measures of a kind the System had taken in earlier years, of a kind explicitly contemplated by the founders of the System to meet precisely the kind of banking crisis that developed in late 1930 and persisted thereafter. They involved measures that were actually proposed and very likely would have been adopted under a slightly different bureaucratic structure or distribution of power, or even if the men in power had had somewhat different personalities. Until late 1931 – and we believe not even then – the alternative policies involved no conflict with the maintenance of the gold standard. Until September 1931, the problem that recurrently troubled the System was how to keep the gold inflows under control, not the reverse. (Friedman and Schwartz, 1963)

The inescapable conclusion is that it was a failure of the policies of the Federal Reserve System in responding to the crises of the time that made the Depression as bad as it was. If monetary policy had responded differently, the economic events of 1929–33 need not have been as they occurred. This assertion is supported by the results of Fackler and Parker (1994). Using counterfactual historical simulations, they show that if the Federal Reserve had kept the M1 money supply growing along its pre-October 1929 trend of 3.3 percent annually, most of the Depression would have been averted. McCallum (1990) also reaches similar conclusions employing a monetary base feedback policy in his counterfactual simulations.

Friedman and Schwartz trace the seeds of these regrettable events to the death of Federal Reserve Bank of New York President Benjamin Strong in 1928. Strong's death altered the locus of power in the Federal Reserve System and left it without effective leadership. Friedman and Schwartz maintain that

Strong had the personality, confidence and reputation in the financial community to lead monetary policy and sway policy makers to his point of view. Friedman and Schwartz believe that Strong would not have permitted the financial panics and liquidity crises to persist and affect the real economy. Instead, after Governor Strong died, the conduct of open market operations changed from a five-man committee dominated by the New York Federal Reserve to that of a 12-man committee of Federal Reserve Bank governors. Decisiveness in leadership was replaced by inaction and drift. Others (Temin, 1989; Wicker, 1965) reject this point, claiming the policies of the Federal Reserve in the 1930s were not inconsistent with the policies pursued in the decade of the 1920s.

Meltzer (1976) also points out errors made by the Federal Reserve. His argument is that the Federal Reserve failed to distinguish between nominal and real interest rates. That is, while nominal rates were falling, the Federal Reserve did virtually nothing, since it construed this to be a sign of an "easy" credit market. However, in the face of deflation, real rates were rising and there was in fact a "tight" credit market. Failure to make this distinction led money to be a contributing factor to the initial decline of 1929.

Cecchetti (1992) and Nelson (1991) bolster the monetary hypothesis by demonstrating that the deflation during the Depression was anticipated at short horizons, once it was under way. The result, using the Fisher equation, is that high ex ante real interest rates were the transmission mechanism that led from falling prices to falling output. In addition, Cecchetti (1998) and Cecchetti and Karras (1994) argue that if the lower bound of the nominal interest rate is reached, then continued deflation renders the opportunity cost of holding money negative. In this instance the nature of money changes. Now the rate of deflation places a floor on the real return nonmoney assets must provide to make them attractive to hold. If they cannot exceed the rate on money holdings, then agents will move their assets into cash and the result will be negative net investment and a decapitalization of the economy.

The monetary hypothesis, however, is not without its detractors. As we shall see in the interviews, Paul Samuelson observes that the monetary base did not fall during the Depression. Moreover, expecting the Federal Reserve to have aggressively increased the monetary base by whatever amount was necessary to stop the decline in the money supply is hindsight. A course of action for monetary policy such as this was beyond the scope of discussion prevailing at the time. In addition, others, like Moses Abramovitz, point out that the money supply had endogenous components that were beyond the Federal Reserve's ability to control. Namely, the money supply may have been falling as a result of declining economic activity, or so-called "reverse causation." Moreover the gold standard, to which the United States continued to adhere until March 1933, also tied the hands of the Federal Reserve in so far as gold outflows that occurred required the Federal Reserve to contract the supply of money. These views are also contained in Temin (1989) and Eichengreen (1992), as discussed below.

Bernanke (1983) argues that the monetary hypothesis: (i) is not a complete explanation of the link between the financial sector and aggregate output in the 1930s; (ii) does not explain protracted non-neutrality; and (iii) is quantitatively insufficient to explain the depth of the decline in output. Bernanke (1983) not only resurrected and sharpened Fisher's (1933) debt deflation hypothesis, but also made further contributions to what has come to be known as the nonmonetary/financial hypothesis.

The Nonmonetary/Financial Hypothesis

Bernanke (1983), building on the monetary hypothesis of Friedman and Schwartz (1963), presents an alternative interpretation of the way in which the financial crises may have affected output. The argument involves both the effects of debt deflation and the impact that bank panics had on the ability of financial markets to efficiently allocate funds from lenders to borrowers. These nonmonetary/financial theories hold that events in financial markets other than shocks to the money supply can help to account for the paths of output and prices during the Great Depression.

Fisher (1933) asserted that the dominant forces that account for "great" depressions are (nominal) over-indebtedness and deflation. Specifically, he argued that real debt burdens were substantially increased when there were dramatic declines in the price level and nominal incomes. The combination of deflation, falling nominal income and increasing real debt burdens led to debtor insolvency, lowered aggregate demand, and thereby contributed to a continuing decline in the price level and thus further increases in the real burden of debt.

Bernanke (1983), in what is now called the "credit view," provided additional details to help explain Fisher's debt deflation hypothesis. He argued that in normal circumstances, an initial decline in prices merely reallocates wealth from debtors to creditors, such as banks. Usually, such wealth redistributions are minor in magnitude and have no first-order impact on the economy. However, in the face of large shocks, deflation in the prices of assets forfeited to banks by debtor bankruptcies leads to a decline in the nominal value of assets on bank balance sheets. For a given value of bank liabilities, also denominated in nominal terms, this deterioration in bank assets threatens insolvency. As banks reallocate away from loans to safer government securities, some borrowers, particularly small ones, are unable to obtain funds, often at any price. Further, if this reallocation is long-lived, the shortage of credit for these borrowers helps to explain the persistence of the downturn. As the disappearance of bank financing forces lower expenditure plans, aggregate demand declines, which again contributes to the downward deflationary spiral. For debt deflation to be operative, it is necessary to demonstrate that there was a substantial build-up of debt prior to the onset of the Depression and that the deflation of the 1930s was at least partially unanticipated at medium- and long-term horizons at the time that the debt was being incurred. Both of these conditions appear to have been in place (Fackler and Parker, 2001; Hamilton, 1992; Evans and Wachtel, 1993).

In addition, the financial panics which occurred hindered the credit allocation mechanism. Bernanke (1983) explains that the process of credit intermediation requires substantial information gathering and non-trivial market-making activities. The financial disruptions of 1930–33 are correctly viewed as substantial impediments to the performance of these services and thus impaired the efficient allocation of credit between lenders and borrowers. That is, financial panics and debtor and business bankruptcies resulted in a increase in the real cost of credit intermediation. As the cost of credit intermediation increased, sources of credit for many borrowers (especially households, farmers and small firms) became expensive or even unobtainable at any price. This tightening of credit put downward pressure on aggregate demand and helped turn the recession of 1929–30 into the Great Depression.

The empirical support for the validity of the nonmonetary/financial hypothesis during the Depression is substantial (Bernanke, 1983; Fackler and Parker, 1994, 2001; Hamilton, 1987, 1992), although support for the "credit view" for the transmission mechanism of monetary policy in post-World War II economic activity is substantially weaker. In combination, considering the preponderance of empirical results and historical simulations contained in the economic literature, the monetary hypothesis and the nonmonetary/financial hypothesis go a substantial distance toward accounting for the economic experiences of the United States during the Great Depression.

To this combination, the behavior of expectations should also be added. As explained by James Tobin in his interview for this book, there was another reason for a "change in the character of the contraction" in 1931. Although Friedman and Schwartz attribute this "change" to the bank panics that occurred, Tobin points out that change also took place because of the emergence of pessimistic expectations. If it was thought that the early stages of the Depression were symptomatic of a recession that was not different in kind from similar episodes in our economic history, and that recovery was a real possibility, the public need not have had pessimistic expectations. Instead the public may have anticipated things would get better. However, after the British left the gold standard, expectations changed in a very pessimistic way. The public may very well have believed that the business cycle downturn was not going to be reversed, but rather was going to get worse than it was. When households and business investors begin to make plans based on the economy getting worse instead of making plans based on anticipations of recovery, the depressing economic effects on consumption and investment of this switch in expectations are common knowledge in the modern macroeconomic literature. For the literature on the Great Depression, the empirical research conducted on the expectations hypothesis focuses almost exclusively on uncertainty (which is not the same thing as pessimistic/optimistic expectations) and its contribution to the onset of the Depression (Romer, 1990; Flacco and Parker, 1992). Although Keynes (1936) writes extensively about the state of expectations and their economic influence, the literature is silent regarding the empirical validity of the expectations hypothesis in 1931–33. Yet, in spite of this, the continued shocks that the United States' economy received demonstrated that the business cycle downturn of 1931–33 was of a different kind than had previously been known. Once the public believed this to be so and made their plans accordingly, the results had to have been economically devastating. There is no formal empirical confirmation and I have not segregated the expectations hypothesis as a separate hypothesis in the overview. However, the logic of the above argument compels me to be of the opinion that the expectations hypothesis provides an impressive addition to the monetary hypothesis and the nonmonetary/financial hypothesis in accounting for the economic experiences of the United States during the Great Depression.

The Gold Standard Hypothesis

Recent research on the operation of the interwar gold standard has deepened our understanding of the Depression and its international character. The way and manner in which the interwar gold standard was structured and operated provide a convincing explanation of the international transmission of deflation and depression that occurred in the 1930s.

The story has its beginning in the 1870–1914 period. During this time the gold standard functioned as a pegged exchange rate system where certain rules were observed. Namely, it was necessary for countries to permit their money supplies to be altered in response to gold flows in order for the price-specie flow mechanism to function properly. It operated successfully because countries that were gaining gold allowed their money supply to increase and raise the domestic price level to restore equilibrium and maintain the fixed exchange rate of their currency. Countries that were losing gold were obligated to permit their money supply to decrease and generate a decline in their domestic price level to restore equilibrium and maintain the fixed exchange rate of their currency. Eichengreen (1992) discusses and extensively documents that the gold standard of this period functioned as smoothly as it did because of the international commitment countries had to the gold standard and the level of international cooperation exhibited during this time. "What rendered the commitment to the gold standard credible, then, was that the commitment was international, not merely national. That commitment was activated through international cooperation" (Eichengreen, 1992).

The gold standard was suspended when the hostilities of World War I broke out. By the end of 1928, major countries such as the United States, the United Kingdom, France and Germany had re-established ties to a functioning fixed exchange rate gold standard. However, Eichengreen (1992) points out that the world in which the gold standard functioned before World War I was not the same world in which the gold standard was being re-established. A credible commitment to the gold standard, as Hamilton (1988) explains, required that a country maintain fiscal soundness and political objectives that insured the monetary authority could pursue a monetary policy consistent with long-run price stability and continuous convertibility of the currency. Successful operation required these conditions to be in place before re-establishment of the gold standard was operational. However, many governments during the interwar period went back on the gold standard in the opposite set of circumstances. They re-established ties to the gold standard because they were incapable, due to the political chaos generated after World War I, of fiscal soundness and did not have political objectives conducive to reforming monetary policy such that it could insure long-run price stability. "By this criterion, returning to the gold standard could not have come at a worse time or for poorer reasons" (Hamilton, 1988). Kindleberger (1973) stresses the fact that the pre-World War I gold standard functioned as well as it did because of the unquestioned leadership exercised by Great Britain. After World War I and the relative decline of Britain, the United States did not exhibit the same strength of leadership Britain had shown before. The upshot is that it was an unsuitable environment in which to re-establish the gold standard after World War I and the interwar gold standard was destined to drift in a state of malperformance as no one took responsibility for its proper functioning. However, the problems did not end there.

The interwar gold standard operated with four structural/technical flaws that almost certainly doomed it to failure (Eichengreen, 1986; Temin, 1989; Bernanke and James, 1991). The first, and most damaging, was an asymmetry in the response of gold-gaining countries and gold-losing countries that resulted in a deflationary bias that was to drag the world deeper into deflation and depression. If a country was losing gold reserves, it was required to decrease its money supply to maintain its commitment to the gold standard. Given that a minimum gold reserve had to be maintained and that countries became concerned when the gold reserve fell within 10 percent of this minimum, little gold could be lost before the necessity of monetary contraction, and thus deflation, became a reality. Moreover, with a fractional gold reserve ratio of 40 percent, the result was a decline in the domestic money supply equal to 2.5 times the gold outflow. On the other hand, there was no such constraint on countries that experienced gold inflows. Gold reserves were accumulated without the binding requirement that the domestic money supply be expanded. Thus the price–specie flow mechanism ceased to function and the equilibrating forces of the pre-World War I gold standard were absent during the interwar period. If a country attracting gold reserves were to embark on a contractionary path, the result would be the further extraction of gold reserves from other countries on the gold standard and the imposition of deflation on their economies as well, as they were forced to contract their money supplies. "As it happened, both of the two major gold surplus countries – France and the United States, who at the time together held close to 60 percent of the world's monetary gold – took deflationary paths in 1928–1929" (Bernanke and James, 1991).

Second, countries that did not have reserve currencies could hold their minimum reserves in the form of both gold and convertible foreign exchange reserves. If the threat of devaluation of a reserve currency appeared likely, a country holding foreign exchange reserves could divest itself of the foreign exchange, as holding it became a more risky proposition. Further, the convertible reserves were usually only fractionally backed by gold. Thus, if countries were to prefer gold holdings as opposed to foreign exchange reserves for whatever reason, the result would be a contraction in the world money supply as reserves were destroyed in the movement to gold. This effect can be thought of as equivalent to the effect on the domestic money supply in a fractional reserve banking system of a shift in the public's money holdings toward currency and away from bank deposits.

Third, the powers of many European central banks were restricted or excluded outright. In particular, as discussed by Eichengreen (1986), the Bank of France was prohibited from engaging in open market operations. Given that France was one of the countries amassing gold reserves, this restriction largely prevented them from adhering to the rules of the gold standard. The proper response would have been to expand their supply of money and inflate so as not to continue to attract gold reserves and impose deflation on the rest of the world. This was not done. France continued to accumulate gold until 1932 and did not leave the gold standard until 1936.

Lastly, the gold standard was re-established at parities that were unilaterally determined by each individual country. When France returned to the gold standard in 1926, it returned at a parity rate that is believed to have undervalued the franc. When Britain returned to the gold standard in 1925, it returned at a parity rate that is believed to have overvalued the pound. In this situation, the only sustainable equilibrium required the French to inflate their economy in response to the gold inflows. However, given their legacy of inflation during the 1921–26 period, France steadfastly resisted inflation (Eichengreen, 1986). The maintenance of the gold standard and the resistance to inflation were now inconsistent policy objectives. The Bank of France's inability to conduct open market operations only made matters worse. The accumulation of gold and the exporting of deflation to the world was the result.

Taken together, the flaws described above made the interwar gold standard dysfunctional and in the end unsustainable. Looking back, we observe that the record of departure from the gold standard and subsequent recovery was different for many different countries. For some countries recovery came sooner. For some it came later. It is in this timing of departure from the gold standard that recent research has produced a remarkable empirical finding. From the work of Choudri and Kochin (1980), Eichengreen and Sachs (1985), Temin (1989), and Bernanke and James (1991), we now know that the sooner a country abandoned the gold standard, the quicker recovery commenced. Spain, which never restored its participation in the gold standard, missed the ravages of the Depression altogether. Britain left the gold standard in September 1931, and started to recover. Sweden left the gold standard at the same time as Britain, and started to recover. The United States left in March 1933, and recovery commenced. France, Holland, and Poland continued to have their economies struggle after the United States' recovery began as they continued to adhere to the gold standard until 1936. Only after they left did recovery start; departure from the gold standard freed a country from the ravages of deflation.

Temin (1989) and Eichengreen (1992) argue that it was the unbending commitment to the gold standard that generated deflation and depression worldwide. They emphasize that the gold standard required fiscal and monetary authorities around the world to submit their economies to internal adjustment and economic instability in the face of international shocks. Given how the gold standard tied countries together, if the gold parity were to be defended and devaluation was not an option, unilateral monetary actions by any one country were pointless. The end result is that Temin (1989) and Eichengreen (1992) reject Friedman and Schwartz's (1963) claim that the Depression was caused by a series of policy failures on the part of the Federal Reserve. Actions taken in the United States, according to Temin (1989) and Eichengreen (1992), cannot be properly understood in isolation with respect to the rest of the world. If the commitment to the gold standard was to be maintained, monetary and fiscal authorities worldwide had little choice in responding to the crises of the Depression. Why did the Federal Reserve continue a policy of inaction during the banking panics? Because the commitment to the gold standard, what Temin (1989) has labeled "The Midas

Touch," gave them no choice but to let the banks fail. Monetary expansion and the injection of liquidity would lower interest rates, lead to a gold outflow, and potentially be contrary to the rules of the gold standard. Continued deflation due to gold outflows would begin to call into question the monetary authority's commitment to the gold standard. "Defending gold parity might require the authorities to sit idly by as the banking system crumbled, as the Federal Reserve did at the end of 1931 and again at the beginning of 1933" (Eichengreen, 1992). Thus, if the adherence to the gold standard were to be maintained, the money supply was endogenous with respect to the balance of payments and beyond the influence of the Federal Reserve.

Eichengreen (1992) concludes further, leaving out many of the details here, that what made the pre-World War I gold standard so successful was absent during the interwar period: credible commitment to the gold standard activated through international cooperation in its implementation and management. Had these important ingredients of the pre-World War I gold standard been present during the interwar period, twentieth-century economic history may have been very different.

RECOVERY AND THE NEW DEAL

March 1933 was the rock bottom of the Depression and the inauguration of Franklin D. Roosevelt represented a sharp break with the status quo. Upon taking office, a bank holiday was declared, the United States left the interwar gold standard the following month, and the government commenced with several measures designed to resurrect the financial system. These measures included: (i) the establishment of the Reconstruction Finance Corporation which set about funneling large sums of liquidity to banks and other intermediaries; (ii) the creation of deposit insurance which effectively stopped the runs on banks that were so prevalent before the bank holiday; (iii) the Securities Exchange Act of 1934 which established margin requirements for bank loans used to purchase stocks and bonds and increased information requirements to potential investors; and (iv) the Glass–Steagal Act which strictly separated commercial banking and investment banking. Although delivering some immediate relief to financial markets, lenders continued to be reluctant to extend credit after the events of 1929–33, and the recovery of financial markets was slow and incomplete. Bernanke (1983) estimates that the United States' financial system did not begin to shed the inefficiencies under which it was operating until the end of 1935.

Policies designed to promote different economic institutions were enacted as part of the New Deal. The National Industrial Recovery Act (NIRA) was passed on June 6, 1933 and was designed to raise prices and wages. In addition, the Act mandated the formation of planning boards in critical sectors of the economy. The boards were charged with setting output goals for their respective sector and the usual result was a *restriction* of production. In effect, the NIRA was a license for industries to form cartels and was struck down as unconstitutional in 1935. The Agricultural Adjustment Act of 1933 was similar legislation designed to *reduce* output and raise prices in the farming sector. It too was ruled unconstitutional in 1936.

Other policies intended to provide relief directly to people who were destitute and out of work were rapidly enacted. The Civilian Conservation Corps (CCC), the Tennessee Valley Authority (TVA), the Public Works Administration (PWA) and the Federal Emergency Relief Administration (FERA) were set up shortly after Roosevelt took office and provided jobs for the unemployed and grants to states for direct relief. The Civil Works Administration (CWA), created in 1933–34, and the Works Progress Administration (WPA), created in 1935, were also designed to provide work relief to the jobless. The Social Security Act and the National Labor Relations Act (also called the Wagner Act) were also passed in 1935. There surely are other programs with similar acronyms that have been left out, but the intent was the same. In the words of Roosevelt himself, addressing Congress in 1938:

> Government has a final responsibility for the well-being of its citizenship. If private co-operative endeavor fails to provide work for the willing hands and relief for the unfortunate, those suffering hardship from no fault of their own have a right to call upon the Government for aid; and a government worthy of its name must make fitting response. (Quoted from Polenberg, 2000)

The Depression had shown the inaccuracies of classifying the 1920s as a "new era." Rather, the "new era," as summarized by Roosevelt's words above and initiated in government's involvement in the economy, began in March 1933.

The NBER business cycle chronology shows continuous growth from March 1933 until May 1937, at which time a 13-month recession hit the economy. The business cycle rebounded in June 1938 and continued on its upward march to and through the beginning of the United States' involvement in World War II. The recovery that started in 1933 was impressive, with real GNP experiencing annual rates of the growth in the 10 percent range between 1933 and December 1941, excluding the recession of 1937–38 (Romer, 1993). However, as reported by Romer (1993), real GNP did not return to its pre-Depression level until 1937 and real GNP did not catch up to its pre-Depression secular trend until 1942. Indeed, the unemployment rate, peaking at 25 percent in March 1933, continued to dwell in the 15 percent range in late 1941. It is in this sense that all of the individuals interviewed, most to a greater extent, attribute the ending of the Depression to the onset of World War II.

The War brought complete recovery as the unemployment rate quickly plummeted after December 1941 to its nadir during the War of below 2 percent.

The question remains, however, that if the War completed the recovery, what initiated it and sustained it through the end of 1941? Should we point to the relief programs of the New Deal and the leadership of Roosevelt? Certainly, they had psychological/expectational effects on consumers and investors and helped to heal the suffering experienced during that time. However, as shown by Brown (1956), Peppers (1973), and Raynold, McMillin and Beard (1991), fiscal policy contributed little to the recovery, and certainly could have done much more.

Once again we return to the financial system for answers. The abandonment of the gold standard, the impact this had on the money supply, and the deliverance from the economic effects of deflation would have to be singled out as the most important contributor to the recovery. Romer (1993) stresses that Eichengreen and Sachs (1985) have it right; recovery did not come before the decision to abandon the old gold parity was made operational. Once this became reality, devaluation of the currency permitted expansion in the money supply and inflation which, rather than promoting a policy of beggar-thy-neighbor, allowed countries to escape the deflationary vortex of economic decline. As discussed in connection with the gold standard hypothesis, the simultaneity of leaving the gold standard and recovery is a robust empirical result that reflects more than simple temporal coincidence.

Romer (1993) reports an increase in the monetary base in the United States of 52 percent between April 1933 and April 1937. The M1 money supply virtually matched this increase in the monetary base, with 49 percent growth over the same period. The sources of this increase were two-fold. First, aside from the immediate monetary expansion permitted by devaluation, as Romer (1993) explains, monetary expansion continued into 1934 and beyond as gold flowed to the United States from Europe due to the increasing political unrest and heightened probability of hostilities that began the progression to World War II. Second, the increase in the money supply matched the increase in the monetary base and the Treasury chose not to sterilize the gold inflows. This is evidence that the monetary expansion resulted from policy decisions and not endogenous changes in the money multiplier. The new regime was freed from the constraints of the gold standard and the policy makers were intent on taking actions of a different nature than what had been done between 1929 and 1933.

The Depression had turned a corner and the economy was emerging from the abyss in 1933. However, it still had a long way to go to reach full recovery. Friedman and Schwartz (1963) comment that "the most notable feature of the revival after 1933 was not its rapidity but its incompleteness." They claim that monetary policy and the Federal Reserve were passive after 1933. The monetary authorities did nothing to stop the fall from 1929 to 1933 and did little to promote the recovery. The Federal Reserve made no effort to increase the stock of high-powered money through the use of either open market operations or rediscounting; Federal Reserve credit outstanding remained "almost perfectly constant from 1934 to mid-1940" (Friedman and Schwartz, 1963). As we have seen above, it was the Treasury that was generating increases in the monetary base at the time by issuing gold certificates equal to the amount of gold reserve inflow and depositing them at the Federal Reserve. When the government spent the money, the Treasury swapped the gold certificates for Federal Reserve notes and this expanded the monetary base (Romer, 1993). Monetary policy was thought to be powerless to promote recovery, and instead it was fiscal policy that became the implement of choice. The research shows that fiscal policy could have done much more to aid in recovery, but fiscal policy was the vehicle that was now the focus of attention. There is an easy explanation for why this is so.

THE EMERGENCE OF KEYNES

The economics profession as a whole was at a loss to provide cogent explanations for the events of 1929–33. In the words of Robert Gordon (1998), "economics had lost its intellectual moorings, and it was time for a new diagnosis." There were no convincing answers regarding why the earlier theories of macroeconomic behavior failed to explain the events that were occurring, and worse, there was no set of principles that established a guide for proper actions in the future. That changed in 1936 with the publication of Keynes's book *The General Theory of Employment, Interest and Money*. Perhaps there has been no other person and no other book in economics about which so much has been written. Many consider the arrival of Keynesian thought to have been a "revolution," although this too is hotly contested (see, for example, Laidler, 1999). The debates that *The General Theory* generated have been many and long-lasting. There is little that can be said here to add or subtract from the massive literature devoted to the ideas promoted by Keynes, whether they be viewed right or wrong. But, for our purposes, the influence over academic thought and economic policy that was generated by *The General Theory* is not in doubt.

The time was right for a set of ideas that not only explained the Depression's course of events, but also provided a prescription for remedies that would create better economic performance in the future. Keynes and *The General Theory*, at the time the events were unfolding, provided just such a package. When all is said and done, we can look back in hindsight and argue endlessly about what Keynes "really meant" or what the "true" contribution of Keynesianism has been to the world of economics. For the purposes of this book the point is, at the time the Depression happened, Keynes represented a new paradigm for young scholars to latch on to. The stage was set for the nurturing of macroeconomics for the remainder of the twentieth century.

REFLECTING ON THE GREAT DEPRESSION

This overview has provided the background necessary to put the interviews that follow into proper context. As stated earlier, if understanding the Great Depression is "the Holy Grail of macroeconomics," we have the opportunity to pose questions on these matters to some of the very first individuals who began the search for the Holy Grail and lived the events. I wanted to get a record of the reflections on the Great Depression of these individuals before I, and the profession, missed the chance. I wanted them to reflect on their lives and the impact the Depression had on them, both personally and professionally. I wanted to know what they really thought about so many issues regarding the Great Depression. What did these economists really think regarding the economics of the Depression and where did they stand on the remaining questions? Did the Depression have an impact in shaping them into the type of economist they ultimately became? Where did they stand when Keynes arrived? What did they think about Keynes and his "revolution?" What did they see as his impact at the time? Where do they see Keynes now? All of the individuals interviewed were in graduate school during the 1930s. How did they adjust to an apparent new set of economic principles and a changing orthodoxy? But I also wanted them to reflect on the research that they have conducted on the Depression and the other work that has been written subsequently. Have they changed their minds any? Is there anything that they would like to embellish? I wanted to know and decided to ask for myself. Here is our chance to find out.

Paul Samuelson

Paul Samuelson appropriately holds the title of "Father of Modern Economics." Having already published *A Note on the Pure Theory of Consumers' Behavior* and *Interactions Between the Multiplier Analysis and the Principle of Acceleration* at ages 23 and 24 respectively, Samuelson's dissertation *Foundations of Economic Analysis*, more than any other single work, was responsible for incorporating the use of mathematics and the principles of optimization that characterize the modern paradigm of economic analysis. Indeed, his textbook *Economics* has been used to instruct more undergraduate students worldwide in the principles of economics than any other textbook you care to name.

Professor Samuelson's writings have had important influence in virtually every aspect of economic inquiry from production theory to macroeconomics. The reader is referred to the massive five volume set entitled *The Collected Scientific Papers of Paul A. Samuelson* for a complete review of the scholarly output of this remarkable individual. Samuelson received the very first John Bates Clark award from the American Economic Association in 1947, was President of the American Economic Association in 1961, and won the Nobel Prize in Economics in 1970.

Professor Samuelson has written essays on the impact the Depression had on his thinking as an economist and it is these thoughts for which I had particular interest. Moreover, in May 1969 in a televised debate against Milton Friedman, Samuelson maintained that the origins of the Depression lie in a series of historical accidents, not in misplaced Federal Reserve policy. As we will see below, this debate was not settled in 1969.

Professor Samuelson had fallen and injured his knee just prior to our scheduled meeting, so our conversation took place in his room at the Massachusetts General Hospital in October 1997. When I arrived, one of his nurses was gently rebuking him that he should put down his pad of paper and pencil and concentrate on resting more. Ever the gracious gentleman that he is, he delayed this rest for the hour and a half he kindly spoke with me.

The italics used in Professor Samuelson's answers is the work of his editing and is used for emphasis.

You were born in 1915 in Gary, Indiana.
Right.

You were born as an economist January 2, 1932.
The day I walked into my very first lecture at the University of Chicago.

You have said in the past that you don't perceive that your value judgment ideology has changed systematically since the age of 25. Born in 1915 and doing the math, the Great Depression era stands squarely in this time frame. What impact did the Great Depression have in shaping your value judgment ideology? What was it before, and how did it change as a result of living through the Depression?
I think that my life experience before I became an economist already exposed me to macroeconomic fluctuations. I was born in Gary, Indiana. Gary was a new, company-created steel town. And when World War I broke out, orders poured into America from the belligerents. So, the steel mills which were in sight of where I lived, in my earliest memories were flaring day and night. My father had a drug store: it was the right place to be at the right time; the largely immigrant labor supply had twelve hours a day, seven days a week, work. As a result, any time they got sick, they came to the druggist as the doctor, because they couldn't afford to lose the pay. It was an extraordinary Keynesian boom. Multiplier spending, but I knew nothing of this fancy terminology then. There was a boom then and a boom in the whole countryside, the farm country. I lived part of my time between seventeen months and five years old on a farm in Porter county near Valparaiso, Indiana.

Yes Sir. I'm actually from the Chicagoland area.
You wouldn't know Wheeler, Indiana. That's a town of about a hundred. And farmers got good grain prices, they went into debt and so forth. Of course strong actions like that have reaction. After the War there was the very serious recession in 1920–21 which had an effect upon real estate values. My father bought some real estate in Gary, right downtown. This is all background. What I'm talking about is strictly *before* the Great Depression. I spent a time from when I was ten to eleven and eleven to twelve in Miami Beach, Florida where the first big Florida land boom was going on. At the age of ten, after summer camp, my brother and I went down to join our parents, taking the Pullman from Chicago to Miami. Literally when I got off the train, there were men in plus four knickerbockers on the streets buying and selling land. The bubbles that we now talk about were already there in the Florida land boom. I was a freshman in high school when the bull market of the 1920s was raging. And I remember discussing it with my math teacher; we would study the stock market pages. All this time I had no training in economics. I had no notion I was to become an economist. My Aunt Sophie bought Ford Motors of Canada Limited stock, just before the bubble burst. So I was very aware of the prelude to the Great Depression. But up until the end of 1930 it was just a normal

recession. Bigger than the two itsy-bitsy recessions that occurred in the mid-twenties. 1920–21 was an important recession. The two in 1924 and 1927 are ripples in the NBER dates. But we let it get out of hand. The turning point actually came not on Wall Street, but on Main Street. The National Bureau peak turning point is the summer of 1929.

August isn't it?
Something like that. But it was October that the crash came. People identified the stock market crash and the Great Depression. They were of course related but they weren't the same thing. It was because a period of Herbert Hoover inactivism was allowed to snowball that the banks began to fail in hundreds and in thousands. Now, bank failures were not a strange and unfamiliar phenomenon in my part of Indiana. The farms that were mortgaged up and fully equipped at the peak of the War prosperity were hard hit by the drop in grain prices. And so country banks failed. But it wasn't until I was in high school that the virus became endemic and epidemic. So it was in the middle west generally. I was living by that time in Chicago; I went to the University of Chicago from Chicago and not from Gary.

So you were living around Hyde Park?
I was living in South Shore.

OK.
Right. And this is important because there was a considerable contrast between what I was learning in my money and banking course from Lloyd Mints and from my theoretical economics teachers like Aaron Director and what was going on outside the classroom. And not too far outside the Chicago classroom because the South Chicago steel mills were not too far away.

Isn't it true you could see them at night if you looked out over the lake?
Yes, and you could smell them and the stock yards. By 1931–32 nothing was moving in real estate. There were thousands and millions of effective foreclosures, that is, defaults on mortgages. But the banks didn't even foreclose because what could they do with the property? And also there would be a lot of local bad feelings. My family by this time was only moderately prosperous and I had wanted to work summers to pay for my education. But in fact, in the whole four years of my college, counting the summer after I graduated, I had one day's employment! I spent the time on the beach. But I didn't have reason to have any guilty feelings because I had friends who would apply to 800 different companies and not get one nibble unless you knew somebody. So there was a dissonance between the very good neoclassical economics that I was being taught and the way the system seemed

to behave. Nonetheless I became a pretty good Chicago economist. Henry Simons was an important influence on me. Frank Knight was a big influence.

What about Viner?
Viner was definitely – in the scholarly field. But Viner was away in Washington, working for the Treasury Department during much of the time when I was an undergraduate, but when he came back I worked with him. As you may know, Chicago is somewhat proud that the leading economists there had a memorandum in favor of deficit spending. Are you aware of this in 1931–32?

I am not. I talked to Albert Hart about it but he did not bring that up.
Right, I was an undergraduate but I knew Al Hart. I knew Milton Friedman, I knew George Stigler, I knew Alan Wallis, I knew Homer Jones, all those people. As far as having a grip on what was going on in the Great Depression on that staff, I think that Viner and Charles Hardy were the only ones. Do you know that name; Hardy?

Yes, I've heard that name.
Viner and Hardy wrote a very important research project for the Federal Reserve Bank of Chicago on why banks don't lend. And it's a much more complicated story than the Friedman–Schwartz account that there is a stable demand for money and that the velocity would be pretty stable if only you let it alone. You really had aspects of Irving Fisher's debt–deflation theory of the business cycle then going on.

His 1933 Econometrica *article.*
Right. And what was different about the Great Depression was that it was universal, it was everywhere. It did not spare the middle class. Usually in ordinary National Bureau ups and downs the unskilled workers, the fringe workers, the workers in very volatile industries, blue collar workers bear the brunt of it. But this time your neighbor down the street, in a modestly prosperous suburb, lost his Chevrolet dealership. The shutdown of the banks was extremely important; there was no banking insurance of course. And when a bank went bust usually you lost 90 percent, 95 percent, sometimes you hardly got a penny on the dollar. It isn't remotely like the rescue operations that we've had recently. The Bank of New England failed here in Boston. No depositor lost any money. There was no interference with the flow of mainstream income, from the event, because effectively it went on the tab of the US government. That wasn't the way it was then during the Depression. So I already was toying in my mind the puzzle of what paradigms could explain what was going on around me.

When Keynes's *General Theory* came out in 1936, we at Harvard by accident were among the first in America to know because there was a fellow named Robert Bryce, of Canada (later to become the principal top civil servant of Canada) who had been in Keynes's classes at Cambridge and had come to Harvard for further graduate work. Bryce arranged for us to get copies hot off the press. I did not take to it at once, I resisted it. It wasn't compatible with equilibrium economics. How could a market-clearing equilibrium have mass involuntary unemployment? Some price moves so as to clear the market, and then there's equality. There is a buyer for every seller, an employer for every employee. Well, that wasn't remotely what the situation was. If identical twins were equally skilled, equally trained, and one lost the job, and the other held on to the job, the one who lost the job would have been happy, deliriously happy, to have worked for 20 percent less. But there was no mechanism whereby you could go to the Ford factory or GM, lock yourself to the gate and say, "I'm not leaving until you hire me, and you can name your price and I will take it." Now that can't happen in an equilibrium market.

So what finally convinced me was *not* that I could find really sound microeconomic foundations for *The General Theory* from good neoclassical economics. If you had rigid prices and wages, then you could have a mismatch. The money wage and the real wage, although it had some "give" to it, the deeper and longer the Depression, the more "give" took place. But it still wasn't remotely adequate to restore full employment or even to lower unemployment. In a lot of towns in New England not very far from here, only one in three people were working. There also were no relief programs: the states were broke. That follows from the flexibility of the state's tax revenues; teachers didn't get paid. They got paid in the script, often. Instances like this happened, not before my eyes, but very near to me.

Not too far south of the University of Chicago was the black belt. Now it engulfs the University and has gone beyond it. An Armour Meat Packing truck would come into a block and suddenly out of nowhere twenty people would appear and knock it over. And ten minutes later it was stripped bare of all the meat it had. Crime went up of course.

I lived in South Shore in a middle class neighborhood. I can remember a knock on the door in the evening when we were at dinner. There would be a person or even a child with a note, "We are starving, can you give us a potato or ten cents?" Of course there were hobos on the street; we didn't yet know the phenomenon of homeless people but we knew about the hobos. And there were a lot of people who were known as good touches, word of mouth would spread. We had in my later small town of Belmont, Massachusetts, where I came to live, a wealthy woman who passed away in her nineties. I learned afterward that she had a standing order that she didn't want anybody in Belmont to be hungry. Social Services people could charge meals to her account. But that of course is the droplet of later private charity, private charity couldn't meet recessions. Well, what did I learn was the cause of all of this in my classes? I think at one time I naively believed that if we hadn't had all those tariffs, this wouldn't have occurred. How naive. Actually these are contraction processes which, once they slide, feed on each other. There are always fixed IOU commitments that entail a domino effect. We even perversely *raised* tax rates in Hoover's time.

How about that.

Of course by 1930 Hoover didn't have a Republican Congress anymore. You had to live through the period to see the figure of the starched collar Hoover, telling us that we needed to be even more financially orthodox. Now, Hoover had been, in the 1920s, the best Secretary of Commerce we ever had. He was the engineer who had fed people in World War I, and he had tried to have a shelf of flexible public works projects. So he was not a "ninny," he just was a person with the wrong values and wrong understandings. I don't think my basic value judgments were altered by the Great Depression. I came from a family where my father voted in 1924 for "Old Bob" LaFollette, of the Independent Progressive Party. He was Republican in Wisconsin, but a *progressive* Republican. But, generally speaking, coming from immigrant forebears, my parents had a bias against inequality and a willingness to use the public democracy to do some rectification of the inevitable inequalities that will occur under a competitive market mechanism.

Although I would stand by that quotation that you read, that since the age of 25 my value judgment ideology has not substantially changed, my inferences as to what the political market will bear and what is feasible have changed quite a lot and changed in what a radical would consider a conservative direction. I don't have a lot of sympathy with romantic, impractical programs that won't get passed, and won't work out in the perfect way that the "good intenders" want. I suppose that is left over from the Chicago education in part. On the other hand, I don't go to the other side where anything that the government does is ipso facto going to be inefficient, non-responsive to true human needs, and motivated by empire building by the civil servants, and so forth. The upshot, prior to Keynes's 1936 book and subsequent to Keynes's book, was that the Great Depression was a period of *mass poverty in the midst of potential affluence*. It was unnecessary, it was an aberration, it was not an efficient (a "Pareto efficient") market operating.

You were terribly uncomfortable with what you were being taught and what you were observing?
Right, but also the people who were teaching me were not as bad as what I was required to answer to get a good grade. (*Chuckling*) Because they departed themselves from orthodoxy. For example Henry Simons became rather skeptical about open market operations. He didn't know then the concept of a liquidity trap. But when the government takes in a very low yielding bond, that is a *close money substitute*: people didn't even cash in at the end of 90 days their 90-day Treasury bills. I once asked someone at the Treasury, "How can you explain this?" He said, "Do you know a better way to hold a million dollars?" You only gained, so to speak, 37 cents to turn it in and get a new one. How could you believe that the potency of an increment of M (*the money supply*) on $P \times Q$ could be the same under that situation? Much the same holds in Japan today. The discussion in my textbook, now a joint textbook, of liquidity traps got shorter and shorter. I don't know if it ever quite reached zero. But present day Japan has brought it back. So, I really find monetarists' analysis of the Great Depression over-simple. Of course the Fed could early on have done more about it.

Do you still think it's an injustice to blame Fed policy for the Depression?
No, did I ever say that?

Yes, you said that the monetary base not only didn't go down, but it's unrealistic and hindsight to say that they should have increased the money supply by whatever amount was necessary to avert the Depression, when nobody was even talking about it.
Well, it wasn't on the agenda of discussion. I stand by that. Given the attitudes that were prevalent within the profession and in the democracy, you could not have expected anyone to have been listened to. If somebody had said "just spend money until $P \times Q$ is what it used to be," it would have taken an entirely different amount of M-zero (*the monetary base*) when the banking system is collapsing around you. And remember the good banks were in trouble, when around them the less good banks were failing.

They were scrambling for liquidity.
Yes, but also reputation. People were going to the Postal Saving Service with their bank savings. By the way in those days Milton Friedman was not primarily a macroeconomist. Just a really smart guy ready to be into anything. His teachers, who were macroeconomists, began to fasten on 100 percent money.

That's my next question. You said that the people of the day were struggling with what policies to pursue. At one point 100 percent reserve money was talked about. Given the history of financial panics that we had before, and a successful suspension of the deposit convertibility in 1907, why do you think people were so confused about knowing what to do?

Well, ... the people tried to reduce all this to its simple formulas. You know I'm not against mathematics in economics, (*chuckling*) it has been my stock in trade. The *M*-zero base was actually increased in 1930–32. Books by Lauchlin Currie show that every kind of money, small or large bank money, had different reserve ratios. And that meant any spontaneous shift in relative weight among small banks and big banks would change the effective reserve ratio for the system. So, 100 percent money was to be the panacea: there couldn't then be any change, 100 percent can't move up and can't move down. Even Irving Fisher came out for 100 percent money.

Oh my.

He liked gimmicks. Didn't Al Hart talk about 100 percent money?

He did not.

But anyway, I believed in 100 percent money and I couldn't understand why Viner wouldn't sign up. Frank Knight did too, Aaron Director and all the usual suspects. But it's a ridiculous panacea for banishing depressions and inflations. You can't have 100 percent money. You haven't heard Milton Friedman talk about 100 percent money for a long time. Gary Becker I think converted him out of it. He said they'll just grow up a system of credit *outside* the banking system and out of control of the government, and it will have anything but 100 percent money. It's not as if you have to go to a place that bears some official seal of the US government to have depositories and promissory loans and so forth. And in the last recession, with the real estate blow-out and the savings and loans and so forth, the non-bank credit suppliers became much more important. I think of the Great Depression as a concatenation of a multiplicity of factors. This is a lousy theory. But it's more important to describe the facts correctly than to have a simple elegant theory which misses the facts. A concatenation of a lot of quasi-independent forces that all worked in the same lethal direction.

Does this go back to your debate in 1969 with Friedman? That you said the Depression was the result of a series of unfortunate accidents?

Right, and of course Freudians would say a fellow who this month breaks his leg or knee cap and tomorrow night is in an auto accident, he's accident prone.

But it need not have happened that way. If there hadn't been Herbert Hoover ... if the thing had not gotten out of hand. I believe that the Federal Reserve was not activistic enough. How much more activistic could it have been within the framework of the gold standard? You know even in 1931 before the British were forced off, Keynes did not advocate leaving the gold standard. It would have helped a lot if you had some kind of international order where many major countries, in an orderly way, found a way of expanding without creating adverse balance of payments for all of them or necessarily for any of them.

The Kindleberger hypothesis in other words, what Charles Kindleberger has said that you needed leadership to coordinate international forces.
Yes, right. But it's a little different because he's thinking of a particular leader. And in Victorian times it was London and the Bank of England. That might be good you know, to have a benevolent single dictator who doesn't behave despotically, does not behave sporadically, irrationally ... great! But, when England went off the gold standard, that was considered by most economists whom I knew, as in effect a beggar-my-neighbor policy. England was forced into doing something which enabled them to get business from the rest. In fact the Sterling Bloc was freed from certain constraints and was able to expand simultaneously. And when they expanded simultaneously they became *better* neighbors.

So that devaluation permitted them to expand a little bit?
Yes, a lot. And you can see it in the comparative recovery data of Scandinavia, which went off with Britain.

And Spain that never went on it in the first place. They averted a lot of the Depression, they were never on the gold standard.
Is that so? There is also a big contrast in 1936 between Belgium and France. Belgium went off gold to its advantage. Most economists thought it was terrible of Franklin Roosevelt to scuttle the 1933 International Monetary Conference and take us off gold. It was not a well thought out maneuver but it did free us up. People say that throwing money at a problem is not a solution. Of course it is a solution to a lot of problems, like to get more chocolate bars. If you throw money at a depression, that is a big expansion in spending.

Didn't getting off the gold standard free us from the deflationary vortex we were in?

Yes, but because of the impending World War II, reserves were coming here, investment money. So, I'm not sure we would have been short of reserves. I don't know if you have ever seen the book by Graham and Whittlesey, *The Golden Avalanche.*

No, I'm sure I have not.
This is a book, sort of a complaint, about the torrent of gold that came into this country with Hitler's rattling sword. It certainly liberated things. We used some of that money just recently in Mexico. That was where the $40 billion rescue dollars came from.

Came from where?
From the old gold stabilization fund. It did not require Congressional action.

Do you think Keynes's objective was to try and save capitalism from itself?
Yes. You must realize how bad, temporarily, capitalism had become in public opinion. I remember seeing a poll of small town attitudes in local newspapers. They asked questions like "should we nationalize the banking system?" More than half of those editors, about the most conservative group in the world, were in favor of nationalizing the banking system. Father Coughlin, the Detroit demagogue who turned anti-Semitic, complained about "fountain pen money, the perpetrators of great wealth, the money changers in the temple." It was kind of a crude expansionism. Huey Long and "every man a millionaire," or whatever it was. So I would say that Keynes thought of himself as saving the system. And lots of the New Dealers – original New Dealers, Veblenites, technocrats – did not like Keynesian economics. They said "that is using palliatives, it's not getting rid of the wicked capitalistic ethos." Keynes told Roosevelt when he came here in 1933 that he needed to spend so much more per month in deficit spending. He gave very precise figures with great self-confidence. Nobody is entitled to that degree of precision and that amount of confidence about it. I would say that the valuable part was that it was OK and salutary to increase the total depression budget deficit. I presume that you've read in the *AER* way back, the article by E.C. Brown?

Yes sir.
Trying to appraise what was spent and whether it was disappointing in its effects.

I know it real well. That is where the concept of the full employment surplus

was developed, I think.
In that article?

I think Brown developed that idea.
Right, and people have forgotten for example, once we were down so low, and once the recovery was pushed by this unorthodox spending, the annual increases in GDP in real terms and in the money supply, were colossal. I remember they were like 17 percent per year. A program in which you decided to reform, be sober, and have a 5 percent annual increase in the money supply because this system can grow at 3 percent with 2 percent inflation would have killed and nipped that recovery in the bud. Of course the reason it could have grown only so fast was because it had fallen so far.

What ended the Great Depression?
What ended the Great Depression? If you talk about the rest of the world, in Germany, it was the preparation for World War II. In economic terms that is fiscal policy. Not pump priming, because the pump priming notion is defective. When I put water in a country pump with a dry valve, a small amount of water is large enough to wet that valve so as to permit me to get any amount of water following it. The Keynesian multiplier says you have to put something in and you have to *continually* put something in. By the way, my disillusionment with straight monetary policy, orthodox policy like what Clark Warburton wrote about and what Friedman *later* came to write about, came when we had this "golden avalanche." We had this tremendous increase in central bank reserves. We were able to have, by this time I was at Harvard, interest rates which were really at bottom, often zero at times. And that did not operate with an infinitely elastic marginal efficiency of capital. So at that time you had to use the other macro tool of deficit fiscal policy.

Do you think that we were definitely in a liquidity trap in the latter part of the 1930s?
Yes. And we were in a *confidence crisis* so that the people who had really safe investment projects could get only a limited amount of money from banks. Anyone with anything that was on the margin of doubt, and almost all investment in its inception is a chancy thing, *could not get anything*. In this country, there is no question, that it was the New Deal which contrived recovery from the Depression. You could see it by 1933–34 when I was a sophomore at the University of Chicago. The week after the Inauguration and the banks closing and opening up, from that moment it was the billions of dollars being spent by Harry Hopkins and the billion or two being spent by

Harold Ickes that did the trick. They were competing to see who could get the most money out. But Ickes was so honest that he could not get as much money out. One was the PWA (*Public Works Administration*) and the other was the WPA (*Works Progress Administration*). Marriner Eccles got brought into the Federal Reserve as an unorthodox banker from Utah. Now there were a lot of things, like the NRA (*National Recovery Administration*) which only helped *momentary* psychology. But if the Supreme Court had not struck it down, it would have been a bad micro thing for the country. In the case of large parts of Europe, it was the relief that came from the 1931 involuntary devaluation from the gold standard of the pound. Now, you never got the unemployment out of Wales, and those structural/regional problems up to World War II itself. I'm not sure whether you still have in West Virginia and some places. What is true is we had memos in the files of the New York Federal Reserve bank warning about "Don't be too active because we will be back into a stock market boom." Or, "We will reactivate it and then be worrying about the next inflation." So, while the whole country was burning and going to hell, those people were worrying about the *next* recession! I think that the bull market and its 1929 collapse was an unfortunate event for Main Street. But it was a minor factor compared to other things. Main Street developed *its own* debt–deflation syndrome.

Does the memory of the Depression stay with you and still have an impact on your thinking today?
In minor ways. For example, one of my six children might, let's say, quit a job before he has a new job. We would never have thought of doing that. But, I had to consciously free myself from the influence of the Great Depression. What was most helpful there, was the famous, essentially wrong, prognosis at the end of World War II in which most of my generation were excessively projecting short-run increments in savings to come. If you needed to compensate for the loss of the heavy war-time spending, which became almost half of GDP by the end of the War, it was thought you would need an investment boom of unrealistic proportions. During the War I had written about the kinds of things that became the permanent income hypothesis. But I did not have it in the right degree, as I recognized by three, four, five months after the War. The build-up of wants, because we long had done without durables and luxuries, and the build-up of liquidity because there was no way you could spend your money during war – these cushioned the conversion-to-peace shock and meant that there was going to be a strong demand. So, the War permitted us to get away from the kind of economy which strongly deviates from Say's Law, and put Say back into the history books. And once

that happens, a capitalistic system does not need all that amount of fine tuning. It is not by itself going to be perfect, but it is going to be manageable through macro monetary and (occasionally) fiscal policies.

At age 70, you said you felt like you were 39. Holding your leg constant, how old do you feel today?
(*Chuckling*) When I said that to my doctor, I didn't say I felt like 39, I said "I can't believe I'm 70." He thought for a moment and said "You *are* 70. So who's kidding whom?"

OK, do you feel 82 today?
I've been very lucky. At my age I really don't know much about this hospital stuff. Not surprisingly, I have a little catch-up time from accidents and so forth.

Could it happen again? Could we have another Great Depression?
I don't think we could have a Great Depression similar to the one we had. Now, you could have a political chaos and disorganization and something that wouldn't be exactly like a macroeconomic depression, but could be as troublesome in human welfare. If it is *just shortage of purchasing power*, our mores have changed, our knowledge has changed, and money would be printed and borrowings would take place ...

And the lender of last resort would truly get used this time? Maybe?
Yes. What you could have would be a period of supply shocks. What's very hard to prescribe good simple policy for is when you get bubbles, up and down bubbles. It is tough then to know what to do. Stagflation related to supply shocks. You also could have a bad labor force. Why did Latin America do so badly after 1945? People like me would have predicted in 1945 that of any of the places that would grow most rapidly in the world, it would be the southern part of Latin America. There was no native population/heterogeneity left because of a cruel past. There were people from European backgrounds, Germany, Italy, and Spain in Argentina and Chile. And that proved all wrong because you had populist democracy, Peronism, and you had a lot of inequality from the market system. And then a lot of attempts to fix that by wrong-minded militant trade unionism. The government might raise wages in an election year by 40 percent. But of course you don't raise real wages by 40 percent, you primarily create an inflation. It is not untrue to say that inflation or hyperinflation is always and everywhere a monetary phenomenon. But that's an extremely misleading aphorism. Because, when you get the pathology

which isn't monetary, but has to do with the institutions in your labor market, that causes the hyperinflation to get started. To no longer permit the money growth then precipitates austerity and crisis. So it is not that the central bankers lost their senses on those occasions, they were sensible up to that time. But it is very difficult politically in a democracy not to overstimulate; but when you do it you front load the little bit of relief that you get, but you back load the effects of inflation. So in business cycle theory, I would even before we got such good substitutes for money, never believe in the constancy of the velocity of circulation. Once, as in the 1970s, I was earning 18 percent per annum on my checkable Fidelity money market fund. There's no reason why I should have a normal velocity. So if that kind of money doesn't burn a hole in your pocket, then that is portfolio money. And you go from that harmless truism, if taken literally, to quite wrong consequences. "If only you follow my simple formula about money, the business cycle would not disappear, but all that could ever be made to disappear of our business cycle would be achieved." Now that last part is wrong.

Robert Lucas has said that the Friedman–Phelps rational expectations school just had plain dumb luck that the 1970s came along when it did because, "most samples cannot tell you which of the stories about the Phillips curve is the best one." What is your reaction to that?
I'm not sure that I know that quotation. Friedman was not an original rational expectationist.

No, but the Friedman–Phelps hypothesis about the shifting Phillips curve.
You mean about NAIRU (*non-accélerating inflation rate of unemployment*)?

Yes sir.
Well I guess I'd say there is some truth to that. But there is also truth to the earlier Phillips curve. It had good luck that things just fit. If you look at the original 1961 Samuelson–Solow article, a lot of the provisions and qualifications to the Phillips curve are there. But there isn't an empirically valid invariant Phillips curve argument. I reject the naive kind of Friedman positivism ... "how steady are your regressions ... we don't need to have any theory, good steady regressions are all that count." There is not any doubt that all the fits changed – and in both directions. Once that's so, there are no strong rational reasons for believing that policy is *impotent* on all *real* variables or that only surprises can have any effects. What killed the complacency among the Keynesians, following Camelot (*the early and mid-1960s*), was not that an alternative paradigm, such as lagged money supply, gave a better description

of the past. There were only a few lucky years when M gave a "not bad" description. Reality sort of drifted in to fit the Friedman pattern for a few years, like a drunken sailor. And like a drunken sailor, it walked out. I remember Citibank had a monetarist economics department. They were getting more and more deviant predictions from the model. So they were adding epicycles to it, putting trends into the velocity factors and so forth. Finally in the end, Walter Wriston, the head of the bank, just shut up the whole operation. Can you imagine, the largest bank in the country just wound the whole thing up. So it was not a Kuhnian case where new aberrant facts arose and the old paradigm, funeral by funeral, got displaced with the new paradigm. A lot of the Lucas critiques were the sort of thing that some of us used in debunking Friedman's positivism on the stable money supply. I thought that Lucas's Nobel Prize was richly deserved and even overdue. But it was not because of the boldness and the correctness of the New Classical theory and rational expectations (that there is some kind of expected value that a group mind gets as a result, and which is in some sense "correct"). I don't believe in *macro* efficiency of securities markets. I believe in their *micro* efficiency. Convertibles are priced about right. Black–Scholes derivatives are priced about right, because you can make a lot of money in correcting any deviation. You can't make money in a bubble, by fighting the bubble. You will lose your shirt. That means the bubble can go on, and bubbles go in both directions. Usually maybe they do not last as long in the downward direction because the correction is more severe.

In fact, the supply shocks of the 1970s which made either fiscal or central policy very difficult to administer, gave poor performance to the macro system. And since the Keynesians had implicitly been boastful about the good performance, if you take credit for the sun you got to expect to be blamed for the rain. And not only was that puncturing the reputation of Keynesianism, but it was puncturing the *self*-esteem of economists and of Keynesian economists in particular. Because we always are looking in the mirror of the public to form *our* impression of how important we are.

Is the Phillips curve dead?
The Phillips curve is like the acceleration principle. In my lifetime a score of times somebody has killed off the acceleration principle. But a relationship between the productive use of a stock and the size of the stock is going to reassert itself. NAIRU is also not going to be dead. It is not as if by going to one higher derivative, to the rate of change of inflation, you're going to get forever afterwards a nice stable Phillips curve. That too is going to be very fluctuating. A good economist has to be an *opportunistic* economist. But not

so opportunistic that you, only *after* every fact, repeat the fact to your listener and give that as if it was an explanation. It is much more important to keep up with the true facts as they are than to wait for an elegant theory or use an elegant theory that does not fit the relevant facts.

You said about purchasing power parity that "every generation must rekill its phoenixes."
Right, I guess the other side of the coin is every generation must breed its phoenix or it would not be there to be rekilled (*laughter*).

Is the short-run Phillips curve a phoenix that needs to be rekilled or not?
I believe that pushing the labor market to lower and lower unemployment will generate bad inflationary wage behavior and that will transmit into a price level–inflation problem. And that is why, even though I'm a liberal and all that, I have been telling the Federal Reserve since mid-1996 that they should be *gently* raising interest rates. Now we risk getting into a pickle. Maybe we would not dare do it because we might cause a stock market crash for which we the Federal Reserve would be blamed. That is a bad situation to get yourself into.

I'm so happy to hear you say that because I'm not sure that the short-run Phillips curve, even if it exists, is worth taking a trip up anymore.
Yes. The Phillips curve is a discouraging curve, if were true, to a romantic economist – because it means that there are limits on what you can do. So, the thought that it is just some way-out Keynesians trying to substitute lousy economics for good sound economics is not quite the correct diagnosis of what is right or what is wrong about it.

That's it. Thank you so much Professor.

Milton Friedman

To the economics profession, and indeed the world over, Milton Friedman is probably the best known, and in some circles most objectionable, economist of the twentieth century. I asked his secretary for a complete bibliography of Professor Friedman's research, hoping to present an extensive summation for this biographical sketch. It is 41 pages long. Perhaps some of the many highlights will be adequate.

Markets and the efficiency of competitive capitalism have no more effective voice than Milton Friedman. His 1962 book *Capitalism and Freedom* remains a *tour de force* and has been translated into 18 different languages. Friedman's theoretical and methodological contributions, *Income of Independent Professional Practice* (with Simon Kuznets), *Essays in Positive Economics*, *Studies in the Quantity Theory of Money*, *A Theory of the Consumption Function*, and his 1968 Presidential Address to the American Economic Association "The Role of Monetary Policy," are but a few of his many great intellectual achievements. He was awarded the John Bates Clark Medal of the American Economic Association in 1951 and the Nobel Prize in Economics in 1976. Readers are referred to the book *The Essence of Friedman* for a masterful summary of his remarkable career.

Beyond all doubt, his book with Anna Schwartz, *A Monetary History of the United States, 1867–1960*, is one of the most important and most enduring contributions to the literature on the Great Depression. No other work regarding the failures of Federal Reserve policy and the economic effects of the catastrophic decline in the money supply in propagating the Great Depression stands above chapter 7 entitled "The Great Contraction." However, this monetary theory of the Great Depression was not established without decades of controversy. Many scholars in the past, rightly or wrongly, assailed the Friedman–Schwartz hypothesis, attempting to demonstrate its lack of explanatory relevance for the economic events of 1929–33. It is all part of building consensus I suppose. I continue to wonder, however, why it took so long and in many cases seemed so hostile to these particular ideas. Whatever the case, in my judgment, the Friedman–Schwartz hypothesis has stood the test of time. We spoke at his home in Sea Ranch, California in April 1998.

Professor Friedman, born in 1912 and doing the math, you were in graduate school at the University of Chicago during the worst part of the Depression.

What role did the Depression play in shaping your thinking and molding you into the economist that you are and have been through your career?
I guess the major role the Depression played in that respect was in leading me to become an economist. I graduated from Rutgers in 1932. While an undergraduate at Rutgers I had been studying both mathematics and economics. When I graduated from Rutgers I was lucky enough to be offered two tuition scholarships. One from Chicago in economics and one from Brown in applied mathematics. There's no doubt that the reason why I chose to go to Chicago was because it was clear in the middle of a major depression that economics was more urgent and important than applied mathematics. I believe that's the major effect which the Depression had on me as a person. Beyond that, of course, what was going on in the Depression was reacted to by all the members of the faculty of the University of Chicago. It was something we considered in class and we talked about, a major subject of discussion. I'm sure that various ideas I ultimately developed in respect to monetary policy, the role of government and things like that, reflected the experiences of the Depression.

Why do you think so many of your contemporaries got their credentials as New Dealers and were vulnerable to the "heresies of Keynes," as Paul Samuelson has said, but yet you turned out so differently?
There are two very different questions involved in that one question. Everybody was in a certain sense a New Dealer. The distinction you're making was not one that was relevant in 1934–35–36 when you had the initial emergency measures of the New Deal. The New Deal measures were of two very different kinds. There were measures of relief in the form of the Works Progress Administration, the Civilian Conservation Corp, and so on. I doubt that there was any division among economists on the urgent necessity of doing something along those lines. On the other hand there were measures that affected the institutional arrangements: the National Recovery Administration, the Agricultural Adjustment Administration, and so on. With respect to these, some economists tended to object. But again with respect to those issues, the distinction was not the one you're implying. The distinction was not a Keynesian versus a non-Keynesian one. You could perfectly well be an extreme Keynesian and still believe that the Agricultural Adjustment Administration and the attempt to fix the prices of agricultural products was a bad idea. Or that trying through the National Recovery Administration to cartelize industry was a bad idea. So, I believe in the early years 1933–34–35, the kind of distinction you're talking about was not of any importance at all. I think that distinction arose and became more important later on. Remember Keynes's book was not published until 1936. So it couldn't have had any influence in those days. Keynes had published *A Treatise on Money* earlier

which I as a graduate student studied at Chicago, but that didn't have the same kind of implications. So I don't believe that the Keynesian/non-Keynesian distinction becomes meaningful until the late 1930s. More important, but a different point, the New Deal was a God-send for economists. It provided us with jobs. I did graduate work at Chicago in 1932–33, at Columbia in 1933–34, and was back at Chicago as a research assistant to Henry Schultz in 1934–35. Then I got through in 1935. Where was I going to get a job? There were very few jobs in the Academy. Some of my fellow students did manage to find jobs. George Stigler did get a job at Iowa State. But there were very few such jobs available. The real saving thing for all of us was that Washington opened up and the New Deal was a potent source of jobs. It's something of a paradox which has affected the discipline of economics all along. Economics tends to teach that markets work. Economics in that sense tends to make people in favor of a limited role for government. And yet the government is the major employer of economists. And the more government intervention there is, the more nice cushy jobs there are for economists. You look at where economists are employed today. The Federal Reserve System employs a very large number. The International Monetary Fund employs a very large number, and you go down the line. So that in a way, economics has a conflict of interest. Its intellectual content is in some ways antithetical to its material self-interest.

But if you go on to the later 1930s, I believe that the difference between those who were susceptible to the Keynesian bug and those who were not, and I have written this in a number of places, predominately had to do with where they did their graduate work. There were those economists who essentially adopted what I will call for the moment the Austrian interpretation of the Depression, the Hayek/von Mises interpretation. That interpretation was that the Depression was a result of a prior inflation, an excessive supply of money during the 1920s. Although the excessive supply of money was not reflected in excessive price inflation, it prevented a price deflation that would have occurred and was responsible for the Depression. That led, in their view, to a lack of appropriateness in the structure of production between long-lived goods and short-lived goods. They believed that the only way you can correct that is by working it through. Let companies fail. You shouldn't step in, you shouldn't try to stop it. Let it cure itself as it were.

Purge the rottenness from the system. Wasn't that the phrase at the time?
Well I don't believe Hayek or Lionel Robbins would have used that phrase. They would have said you simply have to use up the excessive long-lived goods and get back to an appropriate relation between capital goods and consumer goods. That was the doctrine that was taught, for example, at the London School of Economics, very definitely. It was also the doctrine that was

taught to a considerable extent at Harvard. The one place it was not taught at all was the University of Chicago.

The professors at the University of Chicago took a very different position. They took the position that the Depression was not an inevitable result of prior mistakes, it was not something that had to be worked through, but had been produced and worsened by governmental mismanagement. More important, they believed that there were policies that the government could follow that would tend to offset the Depression. Throughout the years of the deep decline 1930–31–32, there were a whole series of memoranda that the professors at Chicago sent to Congress, and the Federal Reserve and so on, in which they urged first, monetary expansion and second, government deficit spending as a way to increase the money supply. A view which was very popular was that it might not be possible to increase the money supply effectively by open market operations because the banks would not use additional reserves to expand loans. However, you could unquestionably increase the money supply effectively by having a government deficit and financing the deficit by printing money. That was essentially the policy line that they took. Jacob Viner, Frank Knight, Henry Simons, Paul Douglas, Lloyd Mints, Aaron Director, all of them signed manifestos presenting that position.

So for students like us at Chicago, the situation was very different from what it was for students, let's say, at the London School. I made this contrast first when trying to explain the difference between Abba Lerner and myself. Abba Lerner was an Englishman who studied at the London School of Economics and who became probably the intellectually most effective promoter of the Keynesian view. Yet he and I agreed on many things, our objectives were the same. We had a very different opinion on this. And I attributed the difference to the fact that I had been schooled at Chicago, he had been schooled at London. He had been given a picture of incredible darkness. I had been given a picture that we had things we could do. Keynes had a real message to bring to him, he had no message to bring to me in that same sense. I believe you will find that the division you are drawing between the Keynesians and the others comes close to being a division between those who studied at places where their mentors were holding one view of the Depression and those who studied at places where their mentors were holding a very different view.

Actually my second question was going to be about that memorandum in favor of deficit spending, so I'm glad that you went on to that. When you wrote the chapter on "The Great Contraction" with Anna Schwartz, what was your reaction when you had the money supply series and saw what was going on? I don't want to be melodramatic, but you were on the verge of discovery here knowing that you really had something. So what was going on?

Well that is a little exaggeration because (*chuckling*) it wasn't an overnight revelation. Lots of people had been talking about the problem, in particular Clark Warburton had written a number of articles about it. So that we were somewhat surprised to find out how large the contraction was. But that there had been a contraction did not come as a sort of revelation (*Friedman chuckles again*). Somehow or another the kind of picture you're drawing is not a picture that is realistic. Attitudes and ideas develop gradually over time and they very seldom, I think, come as dramatic revelations at a moment in time. You don't just sit down and say "Oh my God, I saw these numbers." No, that doesn't happen.

Why do you suppose it took the profession so long to not view it in a hostile manner?
That's a very good question. And I'm not sure I have a good answer to it. Part of the answer is that the Keynesian revolution, beginning in 1936 and thereafter, was a very attractive revolution for a lot of people. It was very attractive to economists, especially the young economists, because they were faced, indeed everybody was faced, with a kind of a paradox, a real intellectual problem. How is it that a society could go on for years with people who needed houses, who needed clothes, who needed food while other people who were capable of producing houses, producing clothes, producing food, were idle and yet the two of them couldn't get together? They could not coordinate their activities in such a way as to have a reasonably fully employed economy which was using the resources to provide what people wanted. Unfulfilled needs and available productive power to fill them and yet the two couldn't come together. What was producing that paradox and what could you do about it? So far as economists were concerned, Keynes seemed to offer a hypothesis which explained that paradox. Moreover, it was a very attractive hypothesis, particularly, as various people have pointed out, because it enabled younger economists to have something that their elders didn't have. It was attractive in part because it was really basically simple, but dressed up in complicated form. It was mathematics, equations, technical terms, marginal propensity to consume, marginal efficiency of investment, liquidity preference. Old ideas in new clothes. The language was different and it was expressed, as I say, in technical ways. Moreover, it opened up a wide field for research. You had consumption functions you could compute, investment functions you could compute, you had the national income, which sort of came along at the same time. It was not a result of Keynes because the estimation of the national income had started years before and had been promoted mostly at the National Bureau of Economic Research by Wesley Mitchell and his associates. But the two fitted together very well. The Keynesian approach was an approach via analyzing national income accounts and thus the computation of national

income accounts fitted right into it. So here you had a development which was very attractive to economists by providing them with an interpretation of what had been puzzling facts. It also provided them with a new discipline, a new set of terms and relations and so on which would satisfy their desire for professional advancement, professional activity, and provided them with research topics.

It was also a very attractive development for politicians. Here an eminent, well-respected, world famous economist, was saying to them what they always wanted to hear. The way they could make everybody rich was by spending more money without raising taxes. Now, (*chuckling*) it's hard to think of a more attractive message to politicians. And of course it didn't really affect the public at large. So, the Keynesian doctrine was very attractive to professional economists, politicians, and government employees. Once you get any such revolution going, it tends to dominate the whole intellectual environment. There was not much of a counter movement. To begin with, the older ones resisted. But when Alvin Hansen, who was himself one of the older economists, came into the picture, he became a very effective promoter. Gradually Keynesianism became the dominant doctrine. Insofar as there was an alternative doctrine, it did not come so much from the Academy as it came from a few banks, from a few business groups and so on. I am thinking of people like the National City Bank, sort of the defenders of the old order, who were going back to a very traditional quantity theory approach.

People were latching on to 100 percent money back then weren't they?
When you say people?

All the usual suspects that you've talked about.
The only people who were latching on to 100 percent money were a group at Chicago, and, in addition, and very important, Irving Fisher. Irving Fisher did not regard the Depression as a cleansing episode, something that had to be gone through. Irving Fisher was all along in favor of more vigorous monetary expansion. He latched on to the 100 percent reserve system and indeed wrote a book about it. Irving Fisher is without question the greatest economist the United States has so far produced. He was a remarkable man in many ways, but particularly so as far as economics is concerned. His contributions not only through his monetary work and theory, but on real versus nominal interest rates or on index numbers, whatever you touch, his doctoral dissertation, they all were notable achievements.

Is there anything from chapter 7, "The Great Contraction" or from A Monetary History *that you would want to change or embellish?*
Yes, quite a lot. The one thing I will emphasize, where I believe that we didn't

give the right emphasis, is the relative roles of the US and other countries in producing the Great Depression. I have been very much impressed by an English translation of the memoirs of the head of the French Central Bank, Emile Moreau. I had read his memoirs in French before we wrote *A Monetary History*. But when you read something in a language that's not your own, you don't really get the finer points. Some years ago Moreau's memoirs were translated into English. Re-reading those memoirs in English, I got more out of it, and was persuaded that we had given too much credit, if you want to call it credit, or blame if you want to call it blame, to the US in promoting the international catastrophe and not enough to the role that France had played. That does not mean the US was blameless by any manner of means. But it does mean that if I were rewriting that now, I would paint a slightly different picture, one which made the great contraction and worldwide depression a consequence of the joint actions of both France and the US.

James Hamilton has said that the resumption of the gold standard could not have come at a worse time or for poorer reasons. Would you not say that in your mind, the resumption of the gold standard was doomed to failure from the very start?

The resumption of the gold standard was not doomed to failure. Everything depended on how it was resumed. And I believe it's a much more subtle story. Britain resumed in 1925. They resumed an exchange rate, which in retrospect seems too high. If they had resumed at a 10 percent lower exchange rate, you might not have had the same results. Moreover, France resumed two or three years later at an undervalued exchange rate. If France had resumed at a different exchange rate, even though Britain resumed at the rate it did, all might have gone well. So I don't believe the resumption of the gold standard was inevitably destined to fail. But given the way in which the resumption occurred, it could not last. Moreover, the US didn't help. If the US was going to uphold the resumption of the gold standard, it had to act in accordance with the rules of the gold standard. And it clearly did not. Because throughout the 1920s the US accumulated gold. Under gold standard rules, the US would have had to expand the money supply more than it did. Let me distinguish two things. I'm not saying it was desirable to resume the gold standard. I don't think it was. I think it was a bad idea. But nonetheless, I think that the gold standard could have been resumed and might have been successful if it had been done in a different way than it was done.

Do you think it was the adherence to the principles of financial orthodoxy that the gold standard required that drove the world's economy into the ground? Or said differently, that as long as the Federal Reserve was maintaining a gold standard it had no choice but to let the banks fail anyway?

The last statement is wrong. Gold was never a restriction on what the Federal Reserve did. In fact, the monetary gold stock of the United States was higher at the end of 1932 than at the end of 1929. In our analysis of the alleged problem of free gold in our book we dispose of that completely. A different question is whether the gold standard in the rest of the world had an effect. That's where France comes in. France insisted on maintaining the gold standard and at the same time avoiding price inflation when they returned to gold at a price that undervalued the franc. The only way to correct that would have been by inflation, but they were trying to achieve two inconsistent objectives. That led to their putting tremendous pressure on all of the countries of central Europe who tended to be in the French monetary zone. As a result, they drained those countries of gold and drove them into difficulties. The French situation plays a considerable role in explaining what happened in Austria with the Kredit-anstalt. The net result is that the attempt to maintain the gold standard played a very important role in making the Depression as severe as it was and as extensive as it was. Britain left the gold standard in September 1931 and it started to recover; it got out of the Depression at that point. If France had left the gold standard in 1931, it too would have gotten out and the world would have been far better off. But so far as the United States is concerned, I do not accept the view that it was the pressure of the gold standard that drove the Fed to follow the deflationary policies it did.

I don't mean to belabor a point, but Paul Samuelson has said that it is unfair to place the blame on the doorstep of the Fed for not increasing the monetary base by whatever was necessary to avert the Depression because he says it was hindsight, beyond contemplation at the time, and it wasn't on the agenda of discussion.

That's wrong. There's no doubt that it was on the agenda of discussion. That statement simply flies in the face of reality because the Federal Reserve Bank of New York, which is after all part of the Federal Reserve System, was from 1929 on, consistently in favor of a more expansive monetary policy. The President of the Federal Reserve Bank of New York repeatedly tried to get the Fed in Washington and the other banks and the open market committee to approve of more expansive monetary policy. This particular argument we meet explicitly in our book *A Monetary History of the United States*. We list the names of people who argued the other way. So, I believe that is not a correct statement. I don't believe it's hindsight at all. Moreover, let me go back to the case you were mentioning before. Was it hindsight when the people at Chicago were sending their petitions in? Was it hindsight when Jacob Viner gave a series of lectures in which he argued for monetary expansion? I don't think so. That took place in 1931–32–33. And I'm surprised that Paul made that statement. I wouldn't expect him to make it. Where did he make it?

He made that in an article entitled "Succumbing to Keynesianism" in 1985.
It's in his collection of scientific papers, volume 5.
I'm surprised that he made the statement.

Other than money are there any other theories of the Depression that you find
contribute satisfactorily to explaining its depth and projected length?
Some addenda have been made to our interpretation in *A Monetary History* but
they have to do mostly with other channels whereby the monetary collapse
played a role.

Transmission mechanisms.
Yes. Bernanke at Princeton, who has emphasized the effect of unavailability
of credit to particularly small enterprises. I think that those interpretations
have added a good deal of depth to the interpretation of what went on, but they
tend to center around the monetary nexus.

Correct.
The only other major argument that has been made was an autonomous
collapse in consumption, which was an argument that was made by Temin and
that's been looked at by Mayer (*1978*) and a number of other people. It has
very little substance to it, there's no strong support for it. So I believe we're
left with the fact that the monetary developments were the major explanation
for the depth and the length of the contraction. As I've said over and over
again, I'm not saying that that caused the initial recession.

Right.
And I don't doubt for a moment that the collapse of the stock market in 1929
played a role in the initial recession. But the conversion of that recession into
such a deep and lasting depression is a different thing. And I find it hard to see
anything other than money and the various ways it operated that accounts for
that.

Most everything that's been written since A Monetary History, *in my view, has*
been complimentary to it, like Bernanke's work.
Absolutely.

What ended the Great Depression?
That depends on how you define the Great Depression. We did not speak in
our book of the Great Depression. We talked of the great contraction. There's
no doubt that what ended the great contraction was the series of monetary
measures that Roosevelt took, including the bank holiday, the going off gold,
the program to purchase gold, the silver purchase program. Those things ended

the great contraction. I have never been happy about lumping the period from 1929 to 1933 with the period from 1933 to 1941. You had an expansion beginning in 1933, and that expansion went pretty well until 1937. It was hampered I believe by the NRA to a considerable extent, but then in 1937 you had another major monetary episode which was the doubling of the reserve requirements. If you look at the money supply, the money supply again went down and you had a contraction from 1937 to 1938. The argument that people make is that as of 1937 you still hadn't gotten back to 1929 in terms of the levels of production and output, and unemployment was still very high. There have been some questions about the figures on unemployment because of the problem of how people were counted who were employed in the PWA, WPA, civil conservation jobs and so on. If you include them as employed, you get much lower estimates of unemployment. But nonetheless you certainly were not in a situation of full prosperity by any manner of means until well after World War II. The standard answer to the question "What ended the Great Depression?" is World War II and government spending for armament. There is a sense in which that's right because that government spending for armament was financed by printing money. Indeed in a way you can say that what ended the Great Depression, if you want to call it that, was the application of the Simons/Knight/Viner/Douglas proposal for running a deficit and financing it by printing money (*laughter*).

What are some of the lessons of the Great Depression that seem to be forgotten today or have to be continually relearned?
I'm going to answer that in a little different way. The major lesson of the Great Depression that has affected our lives is the wrong lesson, a misinterpretation of the Great Depression. There is no doubt that the major lesson that was in fact learned from the Great Depression, whether it should have been or not, was the lesson that you could not count on the private enterprise system to maintain prosperity and that you had to rely heavily on government to play a major role. If you take the period before 1929, so far as public opinion in general is concerned, government was regarded as a necessary evil. I think there was widespread support for the kind of views that Jefferson had expressed a century and a half earlier on the virtues of a small government and of limiting the role of government. The Great Depression changed that because the lesson that the public at large learned from the Great Depression was that it was the result of a failure of business, a failure of capitalism, that big business had let them down, and that in order to be safe in the future they would have to rely much more heavily on government. That was the lesson that was in fact learned from the Depression. As you know, in my opinion, the lesson that should have been learned, the right lesson, was that government let them down. That it was mismanagement of the monetary

system that produced it and not a failure of the market system. But there is no doubt what the actual lesson learned was. So when you ask the question "What lesson should be learned from the Great Depression?" the question you should ask is "What lesson should be unlearned from the Great Depression?"

Did the Great Depression provide the whole foundation for post-war demand management policies?

To get some context, let's go back a bit. If you go way back, Adam Smith with *The Wealth of Nations* introduced the basic idea of laissez-faire, of the invisible hand and that dominated intellectual thought in Britain in the nineteenth century and in the United States in the nineteenth century and the early twentieth century. Toward the end of the nineteenth century in Britain there was a reaction against this thought in the form of socialism. You had first Marxism with *Das Kapital* in 1848. Then you had Fabian socialism with the Fabian Society developing when was it, 1880, something like that. You had a movement in the intellectual community away from the idea of the invisible hand and of laissez-faire and toward the idea of socialism. As my wife Rose and I have pointed out in our book *Free to Choose*, every economic plank of the 1929 socialist platform in the United States has been enacted in large measure. I have argued that the most influential political party of the twentieth century was the Socialist Party of the United States. It didn't win any elections. It didn't occupy any offices, but it dominated thought. So in large measure, the Great Depression and the loss of confidence in the market system, the increased confidence in government, reinforced an intellectual movement that was already underway. And that intellectual movement was further reinforced by the glorification of the Soviet Union, the belief that the Soviet Union had demonstrated that through central planning you could achieve greater equality and greater prosperity. Those all played a role in the expansion of the state from 1933 to now. During World War II of course, government activity was mostly military. After World War II you had a great decline in that role of government. But now you're back to a government that is as large or larger than it was during the height of World War II.

Not a good trend in my book.

No, it's not a good trend. Again, I'm an optimist. The movement that Adam Smith started took 20–30–40 years before it really got underway. The movement that the Fabian Society started took 20–30–40 years before it got underway. There's been a counter movement started by Hayek and von Mises. However misguided they were about the problem of the Great Depression, they were on the right track so far as the general principles of the role of government and the problems in a socialist economy. That movement I date back to Hayek's *Road to Serfdom* as being the most important stimulus. It takes 20–30–40 years before that's accepted. But I think we're beginning to see the fruits of it. Government is now bigger than it has been at any time since the middle of World War II, but it's stuck. Government spending as a fraction of income has stopped going up. In the last few years, it has gone down a trifle. So that I think we are beginning to see the effect of the change in public opinion. There is no longer the kind of universal support for government as a solution to every problem that there was 20–30 years ago. So, don't be too pessimistic.

Does the memory of the Depression stay with you and still have an impact on your thinking?
Absolutely. You're now talking about me as a person not necessarily as an economist?

Yes sir.
Then there is no doubt that there were habits ingrained during the Depression. Our children spend money the way we don't.

What's the biggest threat to capitalism?
The biggest threat to capitalism is excessive government. Not necessarily socialism, simply bureaucratic, managerial, regulatory government and egalitarianism.

Do you think that capitalism has to keep proving itself that it can be economically efficient without being destructive of reasonable equality as Robert Solow has said?
I don't think that capitalism can prove itself in that sense. I don't think it needs to. I think it is only because capitalism has proved so enormously more efficient than alternative methods that is has survived at all. The real thing that impresses me is that we have a situation in which roughly half of the resources of the country are disposed of by government edict either directly or indirectly including regulation and the other requirements that are imposed on people by the government. And yet, as it were, with one hand tied behind our back, we are producing a standard of life that is higher than anybody has ever enjoyed in history anywhere for a larger and larger number of people. It's an extraordinary tribute to the productivity and virtues of capitalism and it's only because it's so much better. What has saved us from becoming a completely centralized state is inefficiency. People complain about waste and inefficiency. I don't. I think if you're doing a wrong thing I'd rather have it done inefficiently. That's a more complicated statement than it sounds. There are some wrong things which are made even worse if they are done inefficiently. So, you can't really make a general statement. I'm not sure capitalism is the

right word. There is a sense in which every society is capitalist. The Soviet Union was capitalist, but it was state capitalism. Latin American societies in the past have been capitalist, but it has been oligarchic capitalism. So what we really need to talk about is not capitalism but free market or competitive capitalism which is the system that we would like to have adopted, not just capitalism.

Can poverty and the distribution of income be correctly viewed as separate?
Yes, they are very separate. So far as the United States is concerned, the major problems of poverty are in our inner cities, and those problems have been created by government. They've been created first of all by government welfare programs, second of all by the attempt to prohibit drugs, and third of all by the monopoly exercised over schools. Those have been the three main sources. But now I want to comment from a different point of view. It seems to me there is all the difference in the world between a situation in which 90 percent of the public taxes themselves to provide a minimum standard of living for the other 10 percent and in which 80 percent of the people impose taxes on the upper 10 percent of the people in order to benefit themselves and the lower 10 percent. That is, in order to redistribute income. So poverty can be associated with a relatively equal distribution of income for the other members of society, it can be associated with a very widely divergent distribution of income. I think they are very separate problems.

Do you think Keynes's objective was to try to save capitalism?
No. Keynes's objective was the right objective and like my objective is not to save capitalism. His objective like my objective was to contribute to the well being of society. I am a great admirer of Keynes. I think he was a great human being and a great economist. I don't agree with the particular hypothesis he offered about the Depression, but advances in every science come from people offering hypotheses that turn out to be wrong. No, I think Keynes's objective was to promote the well being of his countrymen, of his fellow citizens and of the rest of the world.

The current economy that we have right now, can we attribute this good time to price stability?
I believe that the greater stability of our economy is attributable to a high degree of monetary and price stability. This is by all odds the period of the best performance of the Federal Reserve System throughout its history. You had a period of pretty good performance from about 1923 to 1928–29. You had another period of pretty good performance in the post-war period in the 1950s, early 1960s maybe. But this period since about 1983 is the best long-term experience. For about 15 years, you've had a highly stable rate of

monetary growth. You've had inflation coming down and getting very stable, and I think that is a major reason why you've had a stabler economy.

Is money stock targeting dead?
Money stock targeting may be dead, but attention to what happens to the money supply is by no means dead.

That's what Paul Samuelson wanted to know. Whether or not you still say let the money supply grow at a constant rate.
That's a different question. You're not asking whether it is dead but whether it should be dead, and I think that if over the past 20 years we had had a steady rate of growth in the money supply we'd be in as good a position as we are now or in a better one. So, I am by no means willing to say that money targeting is a bad idea, but as a matter of practice it is dead. It is not going to be adopted. You will instead have the mantra of inflation targeting. We are living to some extent right now in something of a fool's paradise because I believe there is developing a greater confidence in the ability of central banks to maintain highly stable prices than the central banks will be able to live up to. So you're going to have some disappointments.

But the velocity of money hasn't behaved very well lately has it?
That depends on which money you speak about?

Right. OK.
In 1980, when important changes were made in regulations controlling the banking system, in particular when interest could be paid on demand deposits, velocity of M1 went completely haywire. Velocity of M2 did not go haywire. It stayed relatively stable until the 1990s and then it too went haywire. M2 velocity increased sharply and the M2 money supply grew very slowly. In the last four or five years, M2 velocity has stabilized around a higher level. It's easy to overstate the significance of those changes. If you had had a steady rate of monetary growth, income would have grown more rapidly during some of these years and would've grown less rapidly during others of these years. But it is by no means clear that the fluctuations in income would have been any greater than they were. They would've been different.

Ben Bernanke has said that business cycle models should explain both the post-war and the interwar eras and that we shouldn't have two sets of models to explain them both.
I agree with that, but I go further. I don't believe there is such a thing as a business cycle. I believe there are economic fluctuations.

Oh, the plucking model, OK.
That's right. That is a single model which fits both the interwar and post-war.

Victor Zarnowitz, I talked to him. As you know, he knows a lot about business cycles.
Oh, sure.

He says "I've come back to the plucking model."
Right now we haven't had for some years a serious shock, we haven't had any plucks and that's why I say I think people are living in a fool's paradise. Because there will be some plucks, and we'll react to it.

Last question. Everybody always wants to know, could it happen again?
Yes, but not likely. In 1954, I gave a talk in Sweden entitled, "Why the American Economy is Depression-Proof." And I stick by what I said then. Another depression like that will not happen until we first have a great inflation. We're always fighting the last war. And we are still fighting the war of the Great Depression. And as I say I gave that talk in 1954.

We're still fighting the war today of the Great Depression?
Yes, we're still fighting the war of the Great Depression in a sense. The major thing everybody's still afraid of is that you'll get into another Great Depression. Moreover people do learn from history, though from what's happening in Japan today (*laughter*) that seems a little dubious. But every central banker in the world knows that you must not let the money supply go down sharply. Everyone has learned the lesson of the Great Depression or the great contraction, that it was made far worse than it otherwise would have been by a sharp decline in the money supply. No central bank is going to let that happen and as long as that does not happen you will not have another Great Depression or great contraction. But if you once have a great inflation, then all bets are off and anything might happen.

OK, that's the official end of everything I had to say or ask you. Thanks so much Professor.

Moses Abramovitz

When the discussion turns to the pioneers of the literature on post-war economic growth, three names come immediately to mind: Simon Kuznets, Robert Solow, and Moses Abramovitz. Professor Abramovitz's contributions to this literature are substantive and include recent articles such as "Convergence and Deferred Catch Up" (1996), "The Search for the Sources of Growth: Areas of Ignorance, Old and New" (1993), "Catching Up, Forging Ahead and Falling Behind" (1986), and the book *Thinking About Growth and Other Essays in Economic Growth and Welfare* (1989).

Abramovitz's contributions to the literature on the Great Depression focused on the hypothesis that downturns and depressions were a natural consequence of long swings in economic activity. Moreover, given the international nature of the Depression and the commitment to the gold standard, the Federal Reserve was virtually powerless to prevent the slide in the money stock that took place during this time. His two papers on this topic "Determinants of Nominal-Income and Money-Stock Growth and the Level of the Balance of Payments: Two-Country Models under a Specie Standard" and "The Monetary Side of Long Swings in U.S. Economic Growth" were never published. I was aware of them and rather than let them fade away forever, I wanted Professor Abramovitz to talk about his ideas contained in these papers, among other topics.

Professor Abramovitz received his A.B. from Harvard in 1932 and his Ph.D. from Columbia in 1939. He was a lecturer at Harvard in the mid-1930s and worked at the National Bureau of Economic Research from 1938 to 1946. During World War II he served in the Office of Strategic Services (OSS), was President of the American Economic Association in 1980, was managing editor of *The Journal of Economic Literature* from 1980 to 1985, and was Coe Professor Emeritus of American Economic History at Stanford University. We spoke in his office in April 1998. He passed away December 1, 2000.

Professor Abramovitz, you wrote two papers on the Great Depression, "Determinants of Nominal-Income and Money-Stock Growth and the Level of the Balance of Payments: Two-Country Models under a Specie Standard"

and "The Monetary Side of Long Swings in U.S. Economic Growth."
I never published those papers because after I had finished them I became aware of the fact that Harry Johnson had some articles on the subject of the relation between general economic growth and money supply which took the view that it was growth that determined the money supply. It was demand for money created by the fact that we had economic growth.

So money was endogenous?
Money was endogenous, well it's endogenous in my papers too. But, the line of connection between money and economic growth runs from money to economic growth. The determinants of money as I saw them were the growth rate of capital exports plus capital imports. So, in my view, if you start from that international development then you got back to the money supply and from the money supply to economic growth. At that point I joined forces with Friedman, but the exogenous element in his theory was always the decisions of the central bank, in this case the mistaken decisions of the central bank. Whereas the moral of my story was that the central bank had very little latitude given the fact that we were trying to maintain a gold standard, given what was happening to our exports and capital imports. So that was my line, and that was Milton's line on the other side. Where we joined forces was at the point at which the money supply is affected by something. On the other side was Harry Johnson and his view that it was the demand for money determined by economic growth which determined the supply of money. And I could never figure out which way the causal chain went. While I puzzled over that and how to bring it to a head, I got drawn off to other stuff and abandoned my papers.

Let me just pull a quote from Schwartz's 1981 paper "Understanding 1929–1933" and see if you agree with it. "Abramovitz believes efforts by the Federal Reserve to sustain the growth of the US money supply in 1930–31, unaccompanied by the similar actions by leading European countries, would not have been adequate to prevent the massive decline in income that in fact occurred."
Well that is the end result of what I'm saying, yes.

"He regards the great decline of nominal income as inevitable, short of implausibly drastic accelerations in the creation of Federal Reserve credit or in the high-powered money multiplier sufficiently large to offset the declines in the sum of merchandise exports and capital movements."
Yes, that's right – given our commitment to maintain the gold standard at the

old rate of dollar–gold exchange.

That's the essence of it. But you joined forces with Friedman in realizing it was something that was exogenous.
Yes, it was exogenous so long as one is not capable, and certainly I was not, of putting together the theory which encompassed the rest of the world (*laughter*).

OK, that's refreshingly truthful.
Yes.

Well, let me ask you one more thing that maybe you could talk a little more about that's related to this, and I am quoting you now: "The experience with long swings suggests that our liability to severe depression may be a normal part of a swing in the rate of growth which may itself be due, in part, to recurrent causes."
That is right.

Can you please amplify and elaborate on that because there hasn't been a lot done lately with ...
Long swings, no there hasn't.

Rather than just let that die forever, I want you to talk about it now.
Alright, I'll have to approach this from several directions.

Please do.
A hint about the nature of one direction you'll find in a wonderful book by a man named Hoyt called *One Hundred Years of Land Values in Chicago* which traced the fluctuations in the prices of real estate in Chicago for 100 years, from the 1830s into the 1930s.

I am aware of that book.
Well if you're aware of it, then you'll remember that he described the fluctuations in the following terms. We were living in an expanding economy in the US in the first place, and Chicago in particular in this period of urbanization. So if you entered a period in which the supply of developed land was not able to meet the demand and the price of real estate began to rise, then you had an expansion in the rate at which settlement proceeded. I don't know if settlement is the right word when talking about a city. At any rate, the borders of the town expanded and the usage of land within the old town

became more intense. Given the rising price of those assets, banks became more and more willing to lend money. Mortgages became easier to float. Everything was getting bailed out by the rising price of real estate. This went on for a number of years and optimism about development would always increase, not only through the people involved in developing real estate, but in people who were financing the development of real estate and the banks got crammed with more and more of this paper. And you had an interacting and self-feeding process. We became, after a number of years of such expansion, what you see in the newspapers every morning nowadays, a bubble economy. And sooner or later something pricked that bubble. I connected that in my stuff with a greater difficulty in increasing our exports and in getting capital imports. That may have happened in part because the UK, let's say, had better uses for its money too. At any rate, it became more difficult to continue to finance ever larger expansion and the supply caught up with the demand and the bubble burst. When the bubble burst, the banks found they were full of illiquid assets and a banking panic developed with the kind of effects on real growth that Friedman and Schwartz have spoken about and so well described. This can be generalized. It wasn't Chicago alone which ended these periods of expansion. Chicago was only one of many cities in which such things were happening.

Florida too?
And eventually Florida, yes. This shows up then, in aggregate figures on money supply and the growth of national income. OK, so that's one direction. If you assume that it takes more than one business cycle expansion for a sufficient degree of optimism to generate a bubble economy, then you have a long swing. And it ends uniformly in a serious and protracted depression or period of stagnation. And that's one of the opening characteristics of long swings in everything that I've written. You asked for it so I'm talking about my stuff a little more than I normally would.

That's why I'm here. I want you to give me the long form.
That's what distinguishes what I have to say about long swings from Kuznets. He always treated long swings as a phenomenon in which there is no change in the intensity of use of resources. After he has measured his long swings in a fashion which in one way or another eliminates ordinary business cycles, he thinks he has an economy with a constant ratio of output to resource use and he develops a theory which is consonant with that. Serious depressions have no part in his theory of long swings. I began with the observation that a serious depression is the culminating event in each of these episodes and I developed

a theory which is consonant with that fact. If you go back to that article of mine in *Economic Development and Cultural Change* in 1961, my contribution to the special issue of that journal which was in celebration of Simon Kuznets's 65th birthday, was an appreciative article on Simon's work on long swings and an outline of what I have to say.

Now, if you start from the deep depression, and you look at measures of labor productivity in the course of the ensuing long-swing expansion, by that I mean you measure everything in averages of five years or in averages over business cycles. Suppose you measured growth rates between similar phases of business cycles. Then you discover that the growth rate of productivity comes to a peak very early in these expansions. The growth rate of output per worker or per unit of capital goes up very rapidly at the beginning and then tapers off but continues to rise for quite a while. I attribute that to the fact that the opening phases are a phase of re-employment. After that it's a question of longer-term growth. But with the ratio between the supply of a factor and its employment always going up, becoming more intense, reaching capacity, as the intensity of use goes up, of course, profits rise and the incentive to invest increases. So it increases, but of course at a declining rate of increase. So you have a long period during which investment is growing, but growing at a declining rate. And again you'll reach a plateau and then the other aspect of the matter comes in. The period of continuously rising profits and investments subject only to a period of minor recessions. What I'm trying to say is it becomes more and more based upon continuing optimism, by the long happy period, so that there is a decline in the quality of credit if you like. You can see how my views on the monetary side of long swings fit into this picture. I regard the long swing from the end of World War I, or if you'd like to start at the bottom of the recession of 1920–21 and going on up to 1929, then you have this collapse and a long period of recovery when indeed things are getting better at a very, very slow rate. I regard that as consistent in general with this longer view of history that I hold.

So that's where your long-swing theory fits into explaining the Great Depression?
That's right.

Just for the record can you tell me where you were born?
Brooklyn, NY. I spent the first 16 years of my life there. I was educated in a local elementary school and in what was then a very good high school, Erasmus Hall. I was a good boy and did my homework, and was able to go to Harvard.

Born in 1912 and doing the math, you were in graduate school during the worst part of the Depression.
I graduated from college at the bottom.

Then again in 1939 from Columbia right?
I completed my thesis in 1939, but I was essentially finished with Columbia in 1935.

What role did the Depression play in shaping your thinking and molding you into the economist you are and have been throughout your career?
The most direct and general effect of the Depression on me was that it, so to speak, prepared me to receive Keynes sympathetically. You can't imagine how the professors who taught me in graduate school and those whom I had known at Harvard and knew again from 1936 for a couple of years when I taught there, how they were floundering, caught as they were in neoclassical theory and believing that supply creates its own demand and literally that the Great Depression was caused by the fact that we were keeping wages too high. So when I first read the *Treatise on Money*, not yet *The General Theory*, which was in 1931 while I was still an undergraduate, I immediately felt illuminated because, for the first time, I got some appreciation of the influence of demand on output. And then when *The General Theory* came along in 1936, I was ready for it. I have one small personal reminiscence.

Please share it.
Well, I have this much to say about how I got into economics. I thought when I entered the university that I was probably going to be a lawyer. I never heard of anybody who became an economist. I was utterly and completely disappointed by the courses in literature and history that I took as a freshman at Harvard. I thought they were very superficial. Meanwhile I was taking a very good course in elementary economics from a very good instructor who gave us a piece of supplementary reading, a little book by H.D. Henderson in the old Cambridge economics series. This was a wonderful series of little elementary books put out by Cambridge people and this one was put out, as I say, by H.D. Henderson. It was called simply *Supply and Demand*. It presented neoclassical theory of value and distribution so compactly and so eloquently, I was absolutely entranced by it.

Anyhow, when I came back in the fall of 1929 to enter my sophomore year, I elected to announce a concentration in economics. I was assigned to Ed Mason to be my tutor. I walked into Mason's office at the end of September and I said to him "Well Professor, when is the stock market going to break?"

And he said without blinking an eye, "Almost immediately!" I went away and came back two weeks later and it had happened. So I thought this was sort of remarkable. I said to him again, like the brash fellow I must have been, "Well professor, you must have made a mint of money." Then I learned something about academics in those years. He said "Are you crazy, I never owned a share of stock in my life."

Well, Ed Mason was a really great man. Apart from the fact that he was a very talented economist, he was a man of wisdom, and force, and gravity. I mean he carried weight. That became more and more appreciated as he got older. I then worked for him during the War in the OSS. But he brought me back to Harvard after I'd done three years at Columbia graduate school and I was an instructor and tutor. One more story and then we will get back to business.

Between my first year as an instructor at Harvard and my second year, I got married. So when I got back to Cambridge in the fall of 1936, the chairman called me in and said "We're raising your salary $200." I said "Thank you very much, that's very nice." He then carefully explained to me this was not because as a married man my expenses were higher. Rather it was because as a married man he could now assign me Radcliffe girls to tutor (*laughter*).

Hooray for the windfall, huh?
Well, the point is just that when I tell this to a company of women, today they are really impressed. They think how strange, how fantastically old fashioned it was to think it would be improper for an unmarried instructor to meet separately with Radcliffe girls. But I was married.

Well that made a difference then.
Yes.

That's delightful.
Where were we?

The Depression and what effect it had on your thinking.
So I described one direction. The other important thing was that when I defended my dissertation, Wesley Mitchell then came and offered me a job at the National Bureau. That would have been sometime in the winter of 1936–37, something like that. I thought things over and decided that working for Wesley Mitchell on business cycles, which is what he wanted me for, would be an interesting thing to do. So my new wife and I moved down to

New York and I then began working at the National Bureau, and working on business cycles under Mitchell and Arthur Burns. Arthur by that time had become far more a leader of this enterprise than Mitchell was. And he then, in a sense, taught me the rudiments of actual empirical research. The line of development was the Depression, the inevitable interest that developed in business cycles, and the chance to work on business cycles at the National Bureau. Now, that has nothing to do with my outlook.

But it certainly gave you a career path.
Yes it gave me a career path and it affected the way I have worked ever since. I don't get as far from empirical observation as is so common now. I never have. That's the important thing the Bureau imposed on me.

Were you comfortable with what you were learning in your classes in graduate school and what at Columbia you saw observing the empirical world?
I was uncomfortable. The only course which dealt, even peripherally, with business cycles was Jimmy Angell's course on money and banking. The ideas never added up to a persuasive understanding of business cycles. Now, there were people there who could do better. One of them was J.M. Clark. But he didn't teach business cycles and I never knew about the work he was capable of doing. He wrote a small book, later, which I think is a little masterpiece called *Strategic Factors in Business Cycles.* The qualification I want to put in is that Wesley Mitchell was giving a course called "business cycles." I naturally signed up for it. When I got there, what he was doing actually was taking us through every observable element in the economy and introducing us to a time series and explaining to us how that series moved after you had deseasonalized it. What were the dates of the reference cycles, the specific cycles of the given series that denote the timing of the troughs and peaks, the amplitude and so on. It was aridly descriptive, and divorced from any general notion of what was going on. But after a month, I went up to him with a petition to drop his course with my signature on it and he signed it and I dropped out of the course. So that was my introduction to Mitchell. However Mitchell never seemed to hold it against me.

Then he hired you later on.
Then he hired me later on.

I think there is a lot more meaning to that. So there was a dissonance between what you were learning and what you were observing in the real world?

Well it wasn't a well worked-out dissonance. I just knew that what I was listening to was not, in itself, very illuminating.

Very well said. Did the sheer magnitude of the Great Depression have an impact on you?
It surely did. That was the whole point. Had it been the recession of 1923–24 or 1926–27 it wouldn't have had any impact on me whatever.

Those were mild recessions.
Of course. Look, I don't have to tell you this. There were sights to be seen on the streets of Manhattan which were very, very disturbing, to say the least. The apple sellers, unemployed men trying to pick up a few pennies to help support themselves and their families by buying a little carton of apples, putting it on a folding chair on a street corner, polishing them up and offering them for sale. They were being bought not because people wanted an apple. It was a way of providing some charity for this guy. There was relief, but it was miserable and disorganized. Unemployment insurance didn't come in for several years after 1932, never mind 1929–32. It was 1935 or 1936 before an organized unemployment insurance scheme was in force. Labor exchanges only began to be organized because the administration of unemployment insurance went through the states and it was they who had to dole out the dough and you had to register for employment in order to pick up your unemployment insurance. So it's the beginning of some exchange of information and obviously there was no Social Security to help maintain the incomes of elderly people and the general income at the same time. People were delighted by a heavy snowfall because it was a chance to put people to work clearing the snow. These were developments unprecedented even by serious depressions in the past. This was the worst thing that had happened to us and it kept on happening for a long time. As you well know, the rate of unemployment as late as 1939 was 14 percent, from the 25 percent at the bottom at a time when agriculture was far more important than it is today. Far, far, more important than it is today. It was the 25 percent multiplied by the inverse of the fraction of the non-agricultural sectors of our economy. It was higher than 25 percent.

I remember my father died in 1932. He died leaving my poor older brother with a contract to try to use a German firm's help to manufacture zippers. He set up a little shop in Stamford, Connecticut. I worked there one summer with him. We were paying machine tenders 40 cents per hour. It provided ludicrous and dreadful levels of income, even for so-called employed workers. It's upsetting to think about it, even now.

You were vulnerable then to the heretical analysis of Keynes as Paul Samuelson has said, that so many of your contemporaries were.
Right.

So the Depression set you up to be a ...
Keynesian. Right. I was still teaching at Harvard in 1936 when my friend and later colleague here at Stanford, Lorie Tarshis, came back from Cambridge where he had been attending Keynes's seminars, bearing with him the galley proofs of the American edition of *The General Theory* which were duly duplicated and distributed to all the young instructors and graduate students who thereupon then proceeded to make life miserable for their professors. It was we who converted Alvin Hansen. He, as you know, was a critic of Keynes to start with, beginning with the *Treatise on Money* which he didn't like. But, under the pressure of the boys in his seminar, he was converted. But that was one of the very few conversions. The Harvard professors of that day, a few of them put together a little book on the causes of the Depression. That still simply started from Say's Law, the axiom that supply creates its own demand. So unduly high and inflexible prices and wages were the cause of the Depression.

Yes, I've always found, on that one, that you have to suspend your disbelief there. "If prices would have fallen 50 percent instead of 30 percent we would have been OK." That's a real whopper.
Yes (*chuckling*).

Did you also have the feeling at the time that after 1933 there's no going back? Did you have this feeling that many of your contemporaries did that there was no going back to the previous orthodoxies? There will be no more status quo ante. Something has to take the place of what we've known before.
Yes. I never expressed it that way, but that certainly was the view of us young people. Not only did we need a different answer, we had it (*laughter*)!

Keynes coming in and having this new orthodoxy, Roosevelt and so on, you have written before that Mancur Olson has said "Defeat in war, and the accompanying political convulsion is a radical ground clearing experience opening the way for new men, new organizations and new modes of operations and trade better fitted to technological potential." Can we view the Great Depression as analogous to this?
I really don't know how to answer that one in its application to the Depression. What you sensed was a gradual change in the attitude of business

executives towards the incursion of the federal government into the regulation of the economy. The gradual change from the sort of opposition which expressed itself in the simple view that federal government regulation was tantamount to the beginnings of socialism and had to be opposed root and branch. Well, that gradually shifted and more and more people in the upper ranks of business accepted the fact that we live in an economy in which the government has to act as a make-weight in many spheres of the economy. And that view then held sway until relatively recent years when of course there's been a swing in the opposite direction.

That's a long swing too, huh?
A very long swing.

Paul Samuelson has said it's unfair to place the blame at the doorstep of the Federal Reserve since to have asked the Fed to increase the monetary base by whatever amount was necessary to avert the Depression is hindsight and it was beyond contemplation and discussion at the time, it wasn't ever talked about. Do you agree with that?
In those quantitative terms it certainly was not talked about. Nobody supposed that the Fed either should or could use, let's say, its open market operations to increase the supply of money by huge amounts. That was grounded on a simple fear of inflation. Never mind that we had 25 percent unemployment. Such a huge increase in the money supply equals inflation. So it wasn't talked about. And of course, in my view, it was not a possible Federal Reserve action so long as we were going to remain on a gold standard. And remaining on a gold standard was, for very long, the rock bottom policy. So Samuelson is right. I don't know whether he would have said it in those terms or not. But I think he came out in the right place.

For people like me, the Great Depression was a broadening of horizons in other ways as well. The New Deal was very much in our thoughts.

That was going to be one of my questions. What impact did the New Deal have on you?
Me personally, it simply broadened my horizons, it's about what a young man could do with himself. As a young economist, you didn't have to think of teaching as your only career line. You could think of a career in government, and we could see one scholar after another going for a longer or shorter period of time to Washington, being engaged in serious and weighty affairs. That appealed to anybody who wanted to have some influence on economic welfare.

*Did it personally invigorate you like the slogan "We will roll up our sleeves
and remake America"? Did it energize you like that?*
No, I can't say that it did. No, I never came to think that I had to devote myself
either directly to work in Washington or to writing articles with a direct policy
influence. I was caught up first in graduate work and second in research. I
thought research is how I contribute something. So I wasn't rolling up my
sleeves to go out and do battle with the dragon. Plenty of young men were, let
me tell you. The New Dealers, the brain-trusters, they were very public
spirited people at the time.

*But did you view the New Deal economically as at least a refreshing change
from what we had?*
Oh absolutely, there is no question about it. All of us youngsters were New
Deal supporters. We were all New Deal supporters in the sense that we could
see that something had to be done to increase demand. We wanted to increase
incomes, and so demand for goods, and so employment, and so on around.
And the structure of Social Security, the fact that benefits were divorced from
previous contributions, was part and parcel of the business of supporting
demand. We didn't want a Social Security system where everybody paid an
employment tax and didn't get immediate benefits from it. We wanted
something that paid immediate benefits. Later on the employment tax would
help pay for those benefits. But we didn't want to increase saving through
unemployment premiums.

You wanted to get disposable income in people's hands.
Right, exactly. I can't remember that there was any opposition to that at the
time. Look, I mean we were all strong economists enough not to like the NRA.
And for the same reason, we didn't much care for the Agricultural Adjustment
Administration either. We would have preferred an honest subsidy to farmers
to raise their incomes without the business of plowing in whatever it is they
were plowing in. We didn't want to raise prices, we wanted to lower prices.

*James Hamilton has said the resumption of the gold standard could not have
come at a worse time or for poorer reasons, back when it was resumed in the
1920s. What's your angle on the gold standard and its role in the Great
Depression?*
Well in a sense I've already told you. It meant that the money supply was, at
bottom, governed by our ability to attract international reserves through
exporting goods and importing capital. So, I trace both the initial decline in the
money supply and its subsequent drop to what was going on on the

international front. Now, never mind that I have in the back of my mind the fact that maybe the line of causation runs the opposite way. I put it away in the files (*laughter*).

Didn't many economists at the time consider it a mistake for Roosevelt to scuttle the gold standard?
Yes. Sure, many did, but not the young people.

They thought perhaps it was an international betrayal.
Well, it was worse than that, it was breaking our contract with everybody who invested his money, especially in government securities. We were no longer going to pay them off in gold dollars.

Wasn't there anybody that thought ...
I had a professor of finance who taught a course at Columbia, it must have been my first year there, that was academic year 1932–33. His name was H. Parker Willis. He must have at that time been approaching 60 or something like that. We came into his class on the morning when Roosevelt closed the banks. He was utterly livid. He literally was purple with rage over what he regarded as the cowardice of Roosevelt. "That's not how you deal with a run on the banks" (*laughter*).

That's how they did it traditionally though.
I know, the banks closed.

Wasn't there anybody who thought the British had set a good example in 1931?
Sure. Certainly, Roosevelt and his friends did.

Touché.
The fact that they chose to do it by bidding up the price of gold, because of the theories of Cornell Professor George Warren. So Warren and Roosevelt or Warren and Morgenthau met every day and decided how much to bid up the price of gold. Sure, so they went off the gold standard and that was a certain release on the economy.

What ended the Great Depression?
The War ended the Great Depression. As it turned out, presumably, the Great Depression would have ended sometime by other channels. But what actually ended it was the War and the defense program that we set in motion even

before we entered the War. That was the beginning. Then, of course, after Pearl Harbor there was no lack of demand.

What are some of the lessons of the Great Depression that seem to be forgotten today or have to be continuously relearned?
Well, I'd say beware of a bubble economy. Now, I think it's an immensely healthy thing that this notion that you have to beware of a bubble economy has percolated so broadly, however much people are increasing their commitment to the stock market and to real estate, they all do so uneasily because they realize this doesn't have to last. That's something which was absent toward the end of the 1920s. There, the notion became dominant, a notion that is not absent today, that we're living in a new era in which the old problems of economic fluctuations are behind us, and we have a new type of economic expansion. What they then called "profitless prosperity."

That makes me scared to hear people talk like that.
Yes. A good little treatment of that, as seen by a young man at the time, is Eli Ginzberg's 1939 book entitled *The Illusion of Economic Stability.*

Did the Depression have any effect on the 1946–73 growth record?
I think so, I can't demonstrate it. I think so. The American, so to speak, starvation for durable goods started in the Great Depression and was aggravated by the restrictions on output of automobiles and the scarcity of other kinds of consumer durables during the War. So, when the War ended and people had in the bank, so to speak, or in other liquid forms, the incomes they couldn't spend during the War, there was a backlog of demand which certainly had its influence for quite a number of years on the expansion of the American economy. Now, this applied also to civilian investment which was very low during the Great Depression and restricted during the War. And again there was a backlog, so to speak, of technology which hadn't been exploited for darn near two decades. And I believe this constituted a backlog of demand which stood us in good stead during the 1950s. I offer that as an opinion, but that's my opinion.

Do you think Keynes was trying to save capitalism, or to save capitalism from itself?
Oh sure. Yes. I can't quote you chapter and verse but I think he said so himself many times. So that's quite apart from the fact as the old communists used to say, "the objective material consequence of Keynesian theory was to help save capitalism."

What's the biggest threat to capitalism?
No, I don't have a ready answer. I have always had a sympathy for Schumpeter's *Capitalism, Socialism and Democracy.* I think it's worth another look, if you have not looked at it recently.

Does the memory of the Depression stay with you at all? Or have an impact on your thinking?
Oh boy, it sure does. If I had had the courage of my convictions, I wouldn't have had a dollar in the stock market for many years. But I didn't fortunately. Yes, the markets scare me. Now obviously, many, many things have changed. We're really not the same economy as we were in the 1920s and the early 1930s. There has been a substantial divorce of income from employment, so to speak, the circular flow does not comprehend the whole of the national income anymore. Much of it is divorced from employment. We have insurance of bank deposits, widely criticized because it's supposed to remove the risks of banking, change the risks so much that people make unwise credit decisions, and possibly that's so. But we don't have to think any longer about endless bank failures reducing the supply of money. Consumers really don't have to worry about their deposits in the banks anymore. And the Fed, we're not hooked to the gold standard the way we were, and the Fed has learned its business better. So I think we're different. But yes, does the memory of the Depression linger and affect me today? It scares me stiff.

That's a very sobering answer. Yes, my dad lived through the Depression and he still talks about it. Does contemporary France have the "social capability" to be a high growth, low unemployment country, to use the phrase that you've used in the past?
Do they have the social capability? Well, if they exist as a high unemployment country long enough, things will change in France. It has already taken a surprisingly long time. I think you can see many signs that things are changing in France, as they are in Germany, as they have in Sweden. The things that make it so expensive to employ anybody are getting shifted. So, maybe, we'll see. It's a highly civilized kind of country that they have tried to erect, but it turned out to have its difficulties. The wages and labor costs in general have become inflexible in France, to a degree that we never knew in this country. Never mind what my professors were talking about in 1929–30.

What are your comments on the explosion of the research on growth and the endogenous growth literature recently?
Well, to center the notion on the important question "Is technological progress

endogenous?", I'd say yes, but in a more limited way than the modern growth theorists assume. My colleague Nate Rosenburg, remembering Shakespeare, once put it neatly when he said "You can call up spirits from the vasty deep, but will they answer when you call?" You can have all sorts of conditions that favor technological progress, but if the state of technology and its underlying science is unfavorable to further progress at the same rate, it ain't going to occur. There can be dry periods without a change in all those circumstances which are supposed to control technological progress endogenously. That's my belief.

Could another Great Depression happen again?
My own sense of the matter is that the severity and length of the Great Depression of the 1930s could not happen again in the economy we know today. But serious reversals, lesser in magnitude, more transient than the Great Depression, I certainly think are possible. And who can forecast how the underlying features of the economy will change over time? It may make us more vulnerable to great disasters we can't envision now.

That made me nervous, what you said about some people, the profitless expansion, we can't have any more collapses. When people start talking like that it is a source of great anxiety.
This always makes me think of 1928.

Thanks so much Professor.

Albert Hart

Albert Hart was one of the first people interviewed for this book that came of age as an economist in the midst of the Depression. After finishing his Ph.D. at the University of Chicago in 1936, Hart immediately went to work on the influential book *Debts and Recovery 1929 to 1937*, which painstakingly documented and analyzed changes in the structure of the internal debts of all the sub-sections of the US economy. Although trained at the University of Chicago, Hart's career took a different path in that he was sympathetic to the Keynesian perspective and advocated active government involvement in economic affairs. Perhaps his best known book was *Money, Debt and Economic Activity* published in 1948.

I spoke with Professor Hart in August 1997 at his home in Sherman, Connecticut. When I arrived, he was at his computer, analyzing the National Bureau of Economic Research business cycle turning points since 1945. His house was neatly kept, but every table had stacks of open books and piles of papers, all of which had clear evidence of being examined recently. Hart had a wit and an intellect that was sharp as a tack, he had many stories to tell, and he was ready to tell them. As revealed in the interview, Hart had both a serious and a playful side. He let both of them shine. It was a delightful afternoon that I spent with him. I'm sure it was the last time he had a substantive discussion with someone about economics as he passed away the following month.

What year was your father born?
1851. He graduated from the Dearborn Theological Seminary. Did I tell you the difficulty with this Seminary?

No you did not.
He had a $400 fellowship which was supposed to take care of his fees and all of his living expenses, which was a quite different animal in those days. But it turned out that in order to qualify for this fellowship he had to swear that he believed unbaptized infants were damned and he was damned if he thought so (*laughter*). So he didn't get the fellowship.

You were born in 1909.
Yes.

Where at?
Oakpark, IL.

What year did you attend Harvard?
I was in the class of 1930.

You graduated in 1930 with your undergraduate degree?
Yes. I was the first fellow to graduate summa cum laude in economics from Harvard.

Son of a gun.
I studied with Frank Taussig who was a wonderful, wonderful man and a great teacher. He had a great habit of refusing to take a position on things and would get the students to argue. Emile Despres, Paul Davis and I were in his class together and got a great deal of joy out of it. There was one occasion when he came in and took a firm position on something at the beginning of the hour. So, he then asked whether this was an acceptable view and was there anybody against it? Well the three of us were against it and everybody else was for it. He said let that be a lesson to us. He came in and he had just finished a telephone call and he had some words stuck in his head from that conversation. He said something that he didn't mean at all, but he was trying to see if he could ride it out.

OK, take us from there. What happened to you during the Great Depression?
Well, I was in luck two ways. One was that I survived the Depression by getting first this traveling fellowship and then they...

Who was the traveling fellowship from?
From Harvard, it was called a Sheldon's traveling fellowship.

Alright, you traveled in Europe for a time.
Yes and this, well it was quite illuminating about the economic process, because I was right on the fringes of the first stage of the great financial catastrophe of the Depression.

Which was?
The Kredit-anstalt.

The Kredit-anstalt, yes.
At the moment, they had sent an installment of my fellowship, father's secretary in New York organized it, and it took the form of remit as a deposit to my account in the Kredit-anstalt.

Oh no, you don't mean it.
Yes, but I was just going to leave Austria so that I converted it at the moment I heard I had it into American Express checks.

Oh boy.
I was just going down into Italy. I spent some time in Palermo and Sicily and then I spent a fair amount of time in France and arrived in England just in time for the British devaluation in 1931. The British economy had been depressed during the 1920s but it had gotten them out of that depression.

Exactly, that was the first step in the right direction. OK, we'll come back to that. So you left Europe and went back for your graduate studies when?
I arrived in Chicago in 1931. In the spring of 1931, I stopped briefly at the London School of Economics where I was thick with the Hicks family. Ursula Webb, who was an Irish Quaker, well she involved me in two things of which one was a wonderful crowd which sang music. She also wanted me to go across for a skiing holiday with her in Norway which I balked at because I could see that she was fixing to marry me and I really wanted to have children and she was too old to have children.

OK, I see.
So I ducked that one (*laughter*). This had a very fortunate consequence because John Hicks, who was one of the very best economists in my age group, was so incredibly shy that he had great difficulty projecting himself. And since it didn't seem very important for him to have children, he married Ursula. And they were both very pleased that we hadn't gotten involved with each other.

So you hooked up Professor Hicks then?
Yes.

That's a juicy little story there that I like. OK, so you started your graduate studies in Chicago in 1931?
Yes, when I was in London, here was a notice on the bulletin board for Albert Hart. They had a message for me and this message was to the effect that I had been given a teaching assistantship at the University of Chicago. So I went back and connected myself with the University of Chicago which turned out very well for me. We had a wonderful collaborative seminar which was in those days a gathering at which the professor and his doctoral candidates met to hear boringsome papers by the doctoral candidates. We did them because we had this collaborative seminar which was run by the students themselves. The only faculty member that we had involved was Frank Knight. He and I

had offices next to each other on the sixth floor of Harper library at the University of Chicago.

Well then, you were in pretty good company there, huh?
Yes, and he was great fun. There was a social science tea where people got together later in the afternoon. I think it was three days a week. And he was always there, and was very forthcoming with students.

Well, that made their time easier then, I'm sure. When did you graduate from Chicago?
1936.

OK, and then from there you professionally developed in which direction? What was your first job, and how did you wind up at Columbia?
I think it was from Chicago that they placed me at Iowa State College.

Well, wait a minute, if you graduated in 1936, you must have started to write Debts and Recovery *right away then. Because that was published in 1938 wasn't it?*
Yes, we have a copy of it around here somewhere.

Oh, I've got it right here in my briefcase. So you must have started writing that immediately.
Yes, and of course, the great thing was getting it reprinted after almost 50 years.

So, how did the Twentieth Century Fund find you out? Rather, let me ask the question more directly. How did you get involved in writing Debts and Recovery*?*
There's a list of the members of the committee there somewhere, and it sticks in my head that Jacob Viner was among those. Viner was great on finding roles for his students. So, I think that he pushed me into this position.

So Viner got you on to this project.
Yes, and Viner also got me into the Treasury at the time of the War. There was a Division of Tax Research, which had several subgroups, and I constituted one subgroup all by myself.

OK, so you graduated, you wrote Debts and Recovery, *and you went on to work in the Treasury? Is that the order of your professional progression?*
Yes.

OK, what happened after the War then?
Right at the end of the War, there were quite a lot of jobs going and there were one or two at Johns Hopkins in which I was somewhat interested. But then came along the possibility of going to Columbia. And so, this appealed to me very much and I grabbed at that and found it very enjoyable. We had very good people to work with. The students at Columbia were of an odd mixture. Really good men students all went to Princeton or MIT. But people with financial interest, of course, tend to end up in New York on account of Wall Street. So they had very intelligent wives with similar interests, and they became graduate students at the university.

Well, there you go. So you had said that you went to Iowa State?
Iowa State College of Agriculture and Mechanic Arts.

But you didn't stay long.
Well, as I say Viner got me moved on to the Treasury in 1943 and, by the way, I was also mixed up with Beardsley Ruml. Ruml was Dean of Social Sciences at Chicago. He and Paul Douglas, who was a professor at Chicago, were mixed up in the business of putting taxes on a current collection basis. And Ruml did this with a great trap. He invented a giveaway program. If you would allow the 1942 taxes to go on a basis of collection at the time of your earnings, rather than with a lag, then your 1941 taxes were forgiven. Now your 1941 taxes didn't amount to a hill of beans (*laughter*), because the exemptions were very high and collections were very low. And this giveaway program had the consequence of putting taxes on a current collection basis, and this is the great secret for why the American economy has been so stable since World War II.

I think that was an entertaining summary of your professional experience. So, let me ask you then, we'll get into the meat and potatoes if you're ready.
Yes.

The first question I'd like to ask you is back during the interwar period what happened and when that made you think we were in real trouble? That the recession was going to turn to a depression and we've got real problems.
Well, I got this through my head in 1931; as I told you I had this account which I turned into express checks at the Kredit-anstalt and then from there I went down into Italy.

So, when the Kredit-anstalt failed, you knew that we had problems going on.
Well, yes, but as I say, I was rescued from these problems by having made this transfer of funds into express checks. Because at this point the dollar appreciated against other currencies quite a lot. My recollection is, and I don't

think that I'm fooling myself, that I realized that this could be a big move. In the US we had the budget balancing movement of 1931. Herbert Hoover was President with the advice of all the people who were regarded as wonderful economists in those days. They figured that the way to get out of the Depression was to balance the budget (*laughter*). So he came in and asked Congress for a 2 percent transaction tax. They balked at that but instead of having a transaction tax they gave him excise taxes and tariff duties which had the same magnitude and this took us of course into a very serious depression. It was a perfect "how not to do it." And I'm pretty sure I realized it at the time.

So that was another thing that led you to believe that we were really going down the wrong path and fast?
Yes.

OK, so those were the two things. What about Britain leaving the gold standard?
Well, of course. I realized that the British example set a different course. But France, the Netherlands, Belgium, and the US all hung on and all got themselves in hellish situations.

Did you see that coming too? That if England would be the only one to split that there might be problems for others?
Well, I don't suppose everyone could have gone along successfully but any one of the others might have and that would include the United States. The United States' economy was always so big relative to the rest it might have overstretched things if we tried it.

OK, so that's what you might have been thinking back at that time?
Well, I was very much impressed with what the British did and was kind of hoping maybe it would be us too.

So 1931 was really the watershed year where you said we have problems coming?
Yes.

What parallels, if any, do you see between the recession of 1921 and the Great Depression? In other words, let me ask you differently. Do you think that policy makers at the time figured that since we successfully deflated after World War I, that's what's going on now in 1929 and 1930? The economy grew wonderfully after the deflation of 1921, it's going to be the same thing here, we're on the right path. Do you think that they saw this as a repeat of the early events of 1921, so we need not vigorously fight the Depression here

because as soon as we liquidate, which was a big school of thought back then as you know, the economy is going to grow right back like it did in 1921?
Yes, I think that was the feeling. You have to remember that the 1920s were really a very pleasant period. There was the 1923 peak, the 1924 slump which was very mild, the 1926 peak, 1927 slump which was very mild, then in 1928 and 1929 it went on up and at the beginning of 1930, yes we had a setback, but it had very much the feel of the setback we had in 1927. Then things really started to slide.

But 1929–30 certainly was not historically unprecedented.
No, as I say, if it hadn't been for the tax increase movement started in 1931 this might very well have turned out to be the correct view. But we couldn't carry that.

People didn't think this was a recession out of the ordinary. Would that be fair?
Yes. And if it hadn't been for this "boner" in 1931 who knows what would have happened?

Next question. What are your views on monetary and fiscal policies during the mid and late 1920s? For example, even though they repeatedly said that they were not the arbiters of the security prices, the Federal Reserve in January of 1928 proceeded to do exactly that. They proceeded to be the arbiter of security prices. So do you agree that the Fed should act as the arbiter of security prices? And was this contraction justified?
Now did I mention Tinbergen's rule?

You did not.
Now Tinbergen's rule is quite important. Namely if you have a policy target and instrumentalities, you can't expect one instrumentality to serve two targets. You need at least as many instrumentalities as you have targets, preferably more. The consequence was that the Federal Reserve's capacity to steer the economy was overrated. There was a feeling, which of course was justified by hindsight, that the stock exchange had lost its head and gone wild. And that there surely was a latent slump and the only question was when would it bite and how deep would it go?

But do you think that the Federal Reserve should be in the business of arbitrating security prices like they did in the late 1920s?
Well, I think that the Federal Reserve has always overrated its capacity to manage things. But as I said they don't have enough instrumentalities, there is no way that the Federal Reserve can manage several things at once.

Certainly this is not enough to manage the economy with.

What was your instinct, at the time, regarding what was driving the stock market, and were you correct?
Well, it sticks in my head that the dividend yield on stocks was going very low, and I think I was one of the numerous people who regarded this as ominous.

People were worried about it back then?
Yes. I think that the widely held view that stock market booms have their own dynamic makes pretty good sense.

Alright, that's fair enough. Did you think back then that it had its own dynamic and was just running on its own?
Such is my unreliable recollection.

What explanations do you find most compelling and think do the best job of accounting for the Great Depression? That is, what in your judgment was the initial impetus and what accounts for the protracted depth to which the economy plunged?
This blunder of 1931 was sufficient to explain why a serious recession turned into a horror. When the New Deal got organized, I think the expression really was quite apt, that they really felt that we were making a fresh start on policy and that the breakdown of 1931–33 had really discredited our standards as to how the economy should be run. It would not have been possible to start operating along the old lines again.

No matter how they might be resurrected?
The public would not have gone for it and I think they just had to find something which would strike the public as fresh and promising and the onus of novelty was of crucial importance. If we hadn't had those we would have slipped right back in the soup.

So just that one tax package by itself you keep mentioning, it was that substantial in your judgment?
Well yes. You see in an economy with the potential of $100 billion per annum which was running at about 80 percent capacity, along came this beasty thing. And $2 billion was a big downward jolt. Two billion out of 80 billion was by no means chicken feed. There really weren't economists with alternatives to propose until we started again with the New Deal when there was a whole fresh crop of influential economists.

Is it this commitment to a balanced budget that you see as the culprit? Did the people understand that raising taxes in a depression was the wrong thing to do?

No, I don't think they did. I flatter myself that I was on to this and I may not have been. But the public as a whole certainly wasn't. I think it's quite possible that if we'd avoided this tax boner in 1931 we had alternative futures which were much more cheerful.

Did the Depression change the psychology of the country?

Yes, it seems to me that this was what the New Deal was about. It was the intense depression of 1931–33 that was regarded as demonstrating we just couldn't go on the way we had been going, and that we would have to find new patterns since the old patterns had ceased to work for us.

Did anybody have a good idea what they wanted those new patterns to be? Or did they just know that they had to be something different?

Who was it that used the expression "We will roll up our sleeves to make America over?"

Sounds like a general New Deal slogan.

This, in a way, was the creed of the New Deal.

Was that the whole psychology behind the New Deal, to make America over?

Well, Roosevelt, by the way he was a budget balancer in the election of 1932.

Isn't that something?

Well, he got it through his head that this was not a workable strategy and the New Deal was certainly very congenial to him. Of course, Roosevelt had an electoral shoe-in, Hoover really didn't have a prayer.

But he knew that he had to do something different, correct?

Yes, though as I said in his campaign he was a budget balancer. When he was there things were quite different. He did have this band of advisors and I think he probably found them very convincing.

How did the Great Depression shape your life professionally?

Well, again you see, thanks to Viner I went from one secure position to another, and I was never personally scared that I remember.

But did it change your thinking professionally at all?

When Roosevelt said one-third of the nation was left stranded, he had his orders of magnitude right. A lot of economists were trying not to believe that, but I felt I had to.

Was the Depression the biggest single event that shaped you professionally or has something else occurred in our history since then that had a bigger impact?
Yes, I'm inclined to think that this was a real difference in kind. I really was brought up in a much more conservative school, but I really did have to go along with the New Dealers.

And that's the biggest thing that shaped your life professionally?
I don't think anything else was bigger. I think the basic shock to my views came in 1931, reinforced in 1933.

By the events of just how poorly the economy was performing?
Well the fact that one tended to assume in Stigler/Friedman style that the market mechanism would naturally work if we gave it a chance. And it seemed to me that the market mechanism was inadequate to solve our problems.

Did you have a faith in the ability of markets to work and that demonstrated how wrong you were?
I found that view plausible and I no longer found it plausible (*laughter*).

Can you point to one particular contribution in economics, one book, person or article that did the most in shaping you as an economist?
Well, I'm inclined to think of this joint effort of what I called the cooperative seminar in Chicago, that was the thing which gave shape, and this you see contained a lot of the key figures of that period. Kenneth Boulding was there, Stigler and Friedman were there but found themselves in the minority on most questions.

Right. What is it that you came away with from those seminars that has done so much to shape who you are and how you think? Was it the vigor with which you pursued economic research there?
Well, I think it was that I caught on to the importance of externalities. And on this I tend to be still somewhat the minority. The effects of externalities are quite unpredictable and this means that effects of policies and policy steps are quite unpredictable.

What role of government did you feel was appropriate in the midst of the Great Depression?
It seems to me that I went along with the New Dealers and had the impression that we could make a fresh start along their line and that it was really the only

thing to do because if we tried to go back to where we were, we would be trying to operate a discredited system that public opinion would not believe in.

What did you think was effective in ending the Great Depression at the time?
Well, of course I think you have to say it took World War II to lift us out of the Great Depression and you are wondering whether I take that view, well yes I do.

But something started us on an upward path though. Instead of a continual downward path, something started us in the other direction. World War II, I share the opinion, got us out of the Depression. That ended it. But what do you think was the impetus that swung us in a downward direction in 1931–32–33 to an upward direction in 1933–34–35 and 1936?
Well, but that upward move didn't get us much of anywhere.

But it stopped us from continuing the fall.
Well, yes, but that was pretty poor consolation for the fact that it left us in a serious depression (*laughter*).

True enough. OK, so then you would want to say that it wasn't until World War II that we made any substantial progress.
Right.

Do you place any of the responsibility of the New Deal on reversing the downward trend?
Well, yes, should we say it converted the downward recession into a stagnation (*laughter*).

Do you think that monetary policy had any role in creating the stagnation or ending the Depression?
It's hard to say because we developed finance companies and things like the General Motors Acceptance Corporation got to be the most important source of new credits.

So that's not explicit monetary policy per se then.
And besides this we also had a change in that savings and loan associations and savings banks, they were allowed to give the customers checkbooks and this made a difference in the payment pattern and it meant that the previous concept of money supply no longer applied. It became open ended. And it is extremely hard these days to say what you mean by money supply. The M1 money supply is of no use, and the M2 is of very doubtful use.

So you see more financial-oriented policies rather than explicit monetary policy. Do you say these are the types of things that were positive instead of explicit monetary policy?
Again, if we were not going to have a guarantee of bank deposits, then we would be wide open for panic at any moment.

But you see that type of government intervention, rather than monetary policy per se, that contributed to creating the stagnation after March of 1933?
Well, again it was a stagnation instead of a series of downward bumps (*laughter*).

But, you see that rather than monetary policy as being something that contributed to that.
Well, yes.

What are some of the lessons of the Great Depression that seem to be forgotten today or that have to be continually relearned?
Well, first you have to remember, the world is a lot bigger than the United States, and for instance, the question of whether the Russian economy can be managed is very much involved in these things. There's a tendency there to rest the integrity of the monetary system on a government guarantee rather than on making reasonably sure that credits make sense. Certainly a lot of the things that command loans in Russia are junk. It lends itself beautifully to corruption. And then we have had permissiveness in our pattern of bank regulation. I don't think that is at all a promising strategy.

Does the Depression and the memory of the Depression stay with you and have an impact on your thinking?
Well, shall we say, I don't regard serious depressions as impossible.

Yes, but does it stay with you psychologically, and the impact it had on you? And does it still shape the way you think?
It must, and to a considerable extent a good deal of this must be below the conscious rationalization level (*laughter*).

What are your views on our capitalist system? Is it the best going or is there a better alternative? Do you think as Robert Solow said, "Capitalism still has to keep proving that it can be economically efficient without being destructive of reasonable equality?"
To put it mildly, there certainly is room for tax policies that affect the distribution of income.

You don't think that tax policies currently have that distribution of income in mind?
Well, I don't think we're doing terribly badly, we have these personal exemptions and allowances for dependents. There is a marked tendency to build meaningless complications into these and someone who has a smart tax lawyer comes out a lot better than someone else who doesn't. I can remember when the tax regulations were a document about like that (*Hart points to a small group of papers*), whereas these days it's about a five foot shelf. The complications are mostly built in order to enable somebody to get off with something. Of course this is also true at the state and local level. There is a marked tendency to build in favoritism.

So then this doesn't have anything to do with the allocation of resources, it has to do with political corruption.
Well, but political corruption is the allocation of resources too (*laughter*).

Touché! What about capitalism in general? Do you have any mixed feelings about it at all, or relative to any alternative?
Well, who's really got an alternative? There was a time when it was possible for people to persuade themselves that communism of the Russian model was an alternative. But I think this has evaporated. Hindsight tells us that communism was a corrupt system inherently, even more than capitalism (*laughter*). And with less possibilities of getting correctives introduced.

Does the distribution of income ever bother you? Is it troubling to you?
Well, shall we say, I find it rather easy to favor measures which would get the people above my income level (*laughter*).

What are your views on the role of the gold standard and the international transmission of the Depression? Do you think that the gold standard was the wrong institution, as James Hamilton has said, and couldn't have been adopted at a worse time or for poorer reasons? Or as Peter Temin has said, it was the adherence to the principles of financial orthodoxy that the gold standard required that drove the world's economy into the ground?
This last view it seems to me makes very good sense.

What was the sentiment back then, as best as you can remember, about going back to the gold standard in the 1920s?
I think a lot of people had the sense that before World War I it was a better world. And that there was a presumption in favor of reverting to pre-war practices. Winston Churchill made a famous speech in Fulton, Missouri (*the famous "Iron Curtain" speech*) in which I think he walked out of that. One of

my earliest recollections of Columbia University is when I was in high school, there was a meeting of the Inter-Scholastic Press Association which took place there. I walked on to the Columbia campus and to the library. And there was Winston Churchill stumping up those steps to receive an honorary degree.

After Britain went off gold in 1931 was there a sentiment here in the US to do the same? Did people think that was going to happen?
I think the Americans felt the British had set a bad example.

OK, last question and I think you probably know what it's going to be. Everyone always wants to know "could it ever happen again?"
No.

Why not?
(*Hart pauses*) Obviously my quick answer was rash or I would have been able to come up with substantiation by now.

Have we just learned so much about how the economy functions that it couldn't happen? Or we have this one under our belt and are not likely to make the same mistakes?
Well, to a considerable degree this last remark makes sense and yet the extent to which individuals make the same mistakes in their own lives is so considerable (*laughter*) that to make mistakes about other people's lives does not seem all that incredible.

So then maybe we can say instead of a flat "no" it's unlikely. Are you comfortable with that?
Well, I feel that it's unlikely but I can't quite sort my wishes and judgments from each other.

So how do you want to leave it then? Is it "no?" Is it "unlikely?" I want you to phrase it actually.
It seems unlikely to me. That is a very tricky answer ... and so intended (*roaring laughter*).

Charles Kindleberger

Charles Kindleberger was one of the first economists to emphasize the international nature of the origins of the Great Depression. Moreover, his influential book *The World in Depression 1929–1939* provided some of the most ardent resistance to the validity of the Friedman–Schwartz hypothesis. Focusing on the impact of the stock market crash in 1929, the international transmission of deflation through falling commodity prices and the subsequent debt deflation that these events precipitated, Kindleberger rejects the notion that the worldwide Depression was largely started in the US and propagated through failures of policy. Instead, what was bad was rendered far worse by the lack of international leadership in promoting any adequate remedy to the ravages of debt deflation.

Professor Kindleberger had a rich career which focused on international economics in general and European economic history in particular. He was responsible for helping to train some of the best international economists of the last quarter of the twentieth century, such as Jagdish Bhagwati, Ronald Jones and the late Carlos F. Díaz-Alejandro. His many experiences during World War II put him at the forefront of the strategic decisions made during this time, as we shall see. I spoke with him at his home in Lexington, Massachusetts in August 1997.

Professor, if you would, please state what you were doing during the Depression, and where you were born, where you got your Ph.D. and where you spent your career.
I was born in New York City, as one of five children, four daughters and one son. My father was a lawyer. He was ambitious to be a judge, but with five children in the apartment we had to move out of the city to Flushing, Long Island which was a very attractive suburb as it no longer is. We moved there in 1919.

What year were you born?
I was born in 1910. I grew up for nine years in the city. My father was successful in the 1920s. His peak income was $17,000 and that was big money in 1927. He got down as low as $4,000 in 1932 and this is the kind of thing that happened in the Depression. I went away to a boarding school from 1924 to 1928, then went to the University of Pennsylvania for four years where I got

my Bachelor's degree, then to Columbia after an interregnum from 1934 to 1936. I got my Ph.D. in 1937 writing on international matters. My family was really middle class, not rich, but certainly not poor. I'm not like so many good economists who made their way against odds. I had all the luck. I got a job through nepotism, during summers, sailing on ships. In fact I wrote a book called *Mariners and Markets*. The interesting thing is my uncle got me the job because he was Vice-President of a shipping company. Ten years later I met a guy at MIT who got a job working during the summer on ships. He got the job through his uncle who was a trade union executive. That tells you quite a lot about what happened in those years. In 1931, I got a fellowship for the summer in Geneva, Switzerland, and sailing on ships for two summers and going to Geneva one summer got me involved with international economics. I spent my early career in international economics and moved slowly into international economic history, mostly on Europe, not the United States. When I came to write the book *The World in Depression*, I got involved in the United States.

When you graduated with your Ph.D., you went to where after that?
Before that I left Columbia in the spring of 1936 with everything completed but my dissertation. I went to Washington for the summer of 1936 and I worked in the Treasury Department under Harry Dexter White. That gave me a lot of trouble later on because he got in trouble and anybody who was infected by him got into trouble too. The FBI listened to my phone calls and things I said in the course of my work at the State Department, and gave gossip and some misinterpretations to columnists like George Sokolsky. J. Edgar Hoover fed them such gossip.

So you were subjected to that?
Yes. I only worked for three months in the Treasury because I got a job at the Federal Reserve of New York and it was to start in the fall of 1936. I tell the story about Harry White, whom I dislike and most of my friends dislike intensely. One of my dear friends said he was the only economist he ever wanted to punch in the nose. I don't know how many economists you have wanted to punch in the nose, but most of us don't have many.

Well, none that I can think of. But I hope you don't want to punch me in the nose when this day is concluded.
Exactly, I'll buy that. OK to go on, in the summer of 1931 there were a great many attractive young women in the (Zimmern) Graduate School of International Relations in Geneva. I thought I was in love with one and when I got back in the fall of 1931, I looked at my record and saw that I could graduate in February rather than waiting for June, get a job, and get married,

which was silly of course. I got out and had six weeks of unemployment. My father happened to know the President of the Federal Reserve of New York, he gave me a letter to him, but I was a kid who didn't know anything. Finally I got a job, which was a terrible job I must say, with something called the Liberty League. The Liberty League was organized by Archibald Roosevelt, the son of Teddy Roosevelt, and it was a right-wing organization trying to balance the budget in the spring of 1932. I had not learned enough economics to know how stupid that was. I was an office boy and I did not like it much. I got another job through my shipping uncle at Johnson & Higgins, which was one of the two big insurance brokers. I was interested in marine insurance and he got me a job as an office boy there and I thought maybe I could work my way up. I was there until the fall of 1934, a year and a half. I was very, very lucky at that stage. Fellowships devoted to graduate work were very few and far between. I was a member of a fraternity that had a chapter at Columbia which was dying. Some of the rich alumni from the 1890s said, "Hey, if we could get some more people to go there and study we could build it up." They asked me if I wanted to go there and study law and I said no, but I'd be happy to study economics and they said OK. They paid my way for two years there. In the third year I got a fellowship in the business school, and that's how I got through. That's a little shameful, to do it all through these social contacts, but those were tough times.

It happened.

Yes, with my father's income dropping like a stone to one-fourth of what it had been, and his securities were all hocked, it was very hard for a man with five children, some in college and some going to private school, to cut his expenditures very rapidly. So he would go to the bank and borrow against his stocks and after a while he'd have to sell them, so he had a tough time. Life was tough for the middle class and poor people had it tougher selling apples and such. We did what we had to.

I started at Columbia in the spring of 1933 by taking the night course, which I paid for, under a man named Ralph Robey. Robey was in the School of Business, in banking, which I was interested in and he was also editor of the financial sections of *The New York Post*, which was quite a different newspaper then than it is now. It's a terrible rag now. He was running around all day chasing the bank holiday and he would come up two nights a week and tell us about what was going on. There were reporters besieging the Federal Reserve Bank. My friend Emile Despres, who was working for the bank then, was one of the people who slept in the infirmary along with some officers because they didn't want to go face the newspaper people. This was a very dramatic time.

Who was your major professor at Columbia?

I wrote my thesis with James W. Angell but I did a lot of work with H. Parker Willis. James Angell was a rather cool fish. He kept calling me Mr Kindleberger while I was doing my thesis with him. I didn't warm to him, he didn't warm to me. On the other hand, I admired him tremendously for the fact that when I was in Washington in the summer of 1936, and later at the Federal Reserve back in New York, I would mail him chapters of my thesis and he would write back single-spaced two and three page letters critiquing them. That was very impressive to me and I have tried to apply that to my own doctoral students. In fact when anyone writes me today and sends an article I comment on it. We disagreed about my thesis. I don't know if he minded or not but he didn't take action on it. My thesis was on international short-term capital movements. I suggested that the test of disequilibrium in the balance of payments was gold plus the net of short-term capital movements. In other words, if you were losing gold and also capital was flowing out you ought to net them. On the other hand, if you were losing gold and people were piling up big balances against you, you ought to add them. He was just for gold alone and I thought that was a mistake. But he tolerated that and one has to admit that is a broad point of view.

When did you move on to MIT?

I should say a word about that. I was at the Federal Reserve Bank of New York from October 1936 to May 1939. The reason I left was because the Bank of International Settlements (BIS) in Switzerland asked the Fed of New York to recommend somebody to hire. One of the people there asked if I was interested and I said I was. So I went to the BIS in July 1939. It was a terrible thing. I accepted before the Germans invaded Prague. I sent my furniture over and when I got there the work of the bank was turned off by the War. Professionally it was a disaster. After the fall of France in June 1940, I had been negotiating with my dear friend Emile Despres who had moved from the Federal Reserve in New York to the Board of Governors. I said "Get me the hell out of here." I had a three-year, not contract, but understanding with the BIS. On the other hand, my father, who was a lawyer as I said, claimed *force majeur* cancels contracts. In effect the War canceled the contract. Despres also sent telegrams to the BIS and got Marriner Eccles to sign them saying "Kindleberger must come home to save the country" and so on. That was good because my wife was 7½ months pregnant. We left July 3 from Geneva. We took a bus to Barcelona, took a sleeper train to Madrid, took another train, sitting up all night, to Lisbon and came home on the boat that they had sent to get people from Europe to home.

Then you weren't bothered going from Switzerland through France?

I didn't like it at all.

I don't suppose. The Germans didn't bother you?
No, we went through unoccupied France.

I see.
But there were a number of Jewish people on the bus and one tipped the bus driver or tour director $100 to see to it that if he saw any Germans to stop the bus and turn back. So you were conscious of it. We saw a lot of dispirited French soldiers and when we got to the border, I realized behind me on the bus was Ludwig von Mises. He was feeling very badly and his wife wanted to have the window beside me closed. I wanted, because of my wife being pregnant, to have it open. I didn't realize who he was until I got to the border going into Spain. He was not my favorite economist. It wouldn't have done me any good to know who he was, I wouldn't change my attitude about the window. We got back to the US and my son was born nine days later. I then worked at the Federal Reserve Board of Governors in Washington for two years. The Board really had nothing to do, a fleet in waiting ready to be allocated. Since the Board paid my way back from Europe and brought back my furniture, I had an obligation to them, so we stayed on. Meanwhile Emile Despres – nobody knows Despres, he didn't write much, but he was a terrific economist – went to the Office of Strategic Services (OSS). My take on the OSS is that while Bill Donovan was the head of it, hero of World War I, New York lawyer, he had the insight to know that the military services would leave a lot of things undone that had to be done. So they were slow to see where the gaps were. If you had someone to fill them, that would be good. The OSS had a research and analysis group of economists, historians, geographers, and so on. They also had secret operations and secret intelligence, which I knew nothing about. I was a research analyst. They had a Board of Analysts, the head of which was James Phinney Baxter, the President of Williams College and also William Langer, the Professor of History at Harvard, and Edward Mason. The United States decided that Canada was an important ally, and they established a Joint Economic Committee of Canada and the United States to solve all of our problems. Alvin Hansen was the chairman of the American side. On the committee were people like William Batt of SKF, the Swedish ball-bearing company, Harry Dexter White, Jacob Viner, I forget who else. Most of them didn't come, they sent proxies. We had the problem of the post-war dumped on us. Post-war planning, I happen to think, is a big waste of time because you never can predict what the conditions will be. I see that all the time as I read English memoirs. The British started to plan the post-war when they were losing the War badly! I am writing a piece on the 1948 German monetary reform and I read that Hitler, in 1942, forbade any post-war planning

because people were already beginning to think about losing the War.

Anyway, my big heros are Omar M. Bradley, my general during the War, William Clayton my superior in the State Department, and George Catlett Marshall and Allan Sproul, the President of the Federal Reserve of New York, under whom I worked. But there were people there with whom I worked closely who were also my heroes: Alvin Hansen is one. He was a wonderful guy and Ed Mason at OSS is another. He was also a Harvard professor. So I went over to OSS in July 1942 and they began to build slowly, and in building they had an economics division in research analysis. It amuses me now, but there was a certain amount of tension between the historians and the economists. Now, I'm more of a historian, I switched sides. I began to see historians had some valuable contributions.

Perhaps you were successful in bringing the two sides together?
Oh no, no (*laughter*). My group was in charge of armaments. After a while we found that the air force spent a long time perfecting their machinery but they didn't know what the hell to do with it, rather typical I think. So at an early stage in Washington we wrote a plan of what to bomb. Then Chandler Morse ran into a guy in London, a dandy fellow who is in my second tier of heros, Colonel Richard Hughes. He was in World War I as a lieutenant in the British army at the age of 18. After he survived that he spent ten years in the British army in India, met an attractive woman on a world cruise, married her and moved to St. Louis with $10,000 he saved up and started investing in airplanes. He lost it, but then he was a guy who would do anything. A good military man is not a man who is a specialist. He's a generalist. Hughes was clever. When he didn't know something, he tried to find somebody who did. So he knew when he was the head of air force planning in Europe, he better find someone who knew something about it. So he met Morse who told him "We'll supply you with economists who know how to take an economy apart. They don't know how to put it together yet, but no matter." So we started something called the Enemy Objectives Unit, and from the bureaucratic point of view, it was glorious. We were paid by the OSS, housed by the embassy, and worked for the air force. So, nobody could tell us what to do. It was wonderful. This was set up in London and the air force asked us to do a program for bombing for the invasion. We called our plan "interdiction." We got into a big fight with the British. They wanted to bomb railroad yards and we wanted to bomb railroad bridges. We thought of precision bombing and they thought of carpet bombing. We thought that if you took out 90 percent of the capacity of a railroad yard, the people who would suffer the most would be the French. Whereas, if you took out all the bridges, everybody would face the hardship. I was arguing with a fellow named Solly Zuckerman, who later turned out to be Lord Zuckerman. So often you run up against Kindleberger's

Law of Alternatives. When you have a big problem as to which to do, you do both. Then you can't tell which one is right. So we did both.

I switched over to go with General Bradley and the 12th Army Group and I was there from July 1944 to June 1945 and that was an interesting time, the attack on the Ardennes and other events. Then I came back ... here we have Despres again. I'd been away from my wife and two children a long time. I didn't like that much. I numbered the airmail letters I sent to my wife and got up to 172. So Despres said I can get you back if you're willing to work in the State Department. I said I'll do anything. So I left on June 5, got to the United States on June 12, then I said I'll take a month off and come to work with you. He said "one week," because he was going to Potsdam with Truman and Clayton to settle the economics of the Potsdam Agreement. I was his back-stop, dug up data, stuff like that. I finally said "I'm sick of Germany." So I went with Clayton to work on the British loan for a while in the fall of 1945. But then things got too tough. The German problems were worse and worse and worse and my friend Willard Thorp, a hero of the second level, a great guy, said "You have to come." I became head of the German and Austrian Economic Affairs division and worked on that until the Marshall Plan came along. I worked on the Marshall Plan until I got sick and lost weight, had an operation and recovered and went to MIT in the fall of 1948. I stayed there until 1981.

And then you were forced to retire when you were 69, is that the age?
I was first retired at 65 and went on half time until I was 70. Now I'm 87 so that was a hell of a long time ago.

You're still in great shape. I hope I make it to 87 and look half as good as you.
You can't look inside, I hope.

I want to ask you a series of questions about the Great Depression and given that resumé you're certainly qualified.
Let me add one more report.

By all means.
I had a friend at the Fed, Alexander Gerschenkron, who then came over to Harvard. At one point a man named Wolfram Fischer came to Gerschenkron and said he was planning a series of books on decades. Five decades beginning in 1890 and Fischer told Gerschenkron "Take any decade you want." But Gerschenkron was busy so he said "Ask Kindleberger." Fischer came to me and asked if I would like to pick a decade and I said "I'll take the Depression." That's how I came to write the book *The World in Depression*, thanks to Gerschenkron. Notice how much luck plays in this. My luck in

getting into graduate school, my luck in having Despres get me out of all the trouble I got myself into and then Gerschenkron. He was a fascinating guy. Russian born, raised in Vienna and he and his wife knew 16 languages together. I was having lunch with him the day before back then. I must have been on his mind.

If you can think back to the Depression and the events as they occurred, what happened at the time that made you think we were in real trouble? What happened to turn the recession of 1929–30 into the Great Depression? Is there one event back then that you can point to, or even now in hindsight, where you said "That's what started it and broke the camel's back?"

Well, I did not have much of an idea at the time. Using hindsight it was the stock market. I should tell you a word about the stock market. In the spring of 1928, the boarding school that I was in had an epidemic of pneumonia and three boys died. That is scary for a school of three hundred. So, they sent everybody home. I got home in March of 1928, and did not know for how long. All of my friends who went to regular school were away during the day and I asked my father "What am I going to do?" He said, "Let me get you a job with my stock broker." So I got a job as an office boy in the first 4 million-share days. I think as I look back on it, that was the start of the boom that led to the peak in September 1929. I was not conscious of that crash. My father was away on a trip to a conference with the Bar Association, somewhere like Chattanooga or Nashville. When he got back he found that the market had crashed and his securities were not in good shape. He mentioned to me what, in retrospect, has become a take on the stock market crash that no one else has. The market started to tighten in the spring of 1929. People like Rostow say it was automobiles, and Barber says it was housing, these markets were turning slightly negative. But interest rates were tightening because of brokers' loans. There was a lot of foreign money coming into brokers' loans, but the brokers' loans were hurt by the Hatry crisis in England in September. Clarence Hatry went broke in September, he was a big speculator, a bit of a swindler. When his companies collapsed, that tightened money in London and drew money out of New York. That started to put pressure on brokers' loans and led slowly, inevitably to the crash of October 24–29. What happened was that the brokers' loans mess was hideous and the banks had to sort that out. This took a lot of time and meanwhile they were not making loans. Take Bernanke's 1983 *AER* piece: very good work saying it wasn't the volume of money, it was the rationing of credit. But he didn't realize, or didn't seem to realize, it was who got rationed the most that had an impact. It was commodity brokers. At that time, international commodities were traded by shipping them on commission to New York and London. The buyers had to borrow in order to buy. If they got rationed, they couldn't buy. And if they couldn't buy, the prices of commodities would fall. Very few people think about the fall in the price level of internationally traded commodities between October and December of 1929 except me. That's my idea of what started the Depression and it follows the Irving Fisher debt–deflation model. The debt–deflation model says that if prices start to fall, people with loans get into trouble and it pyramids. By the way, that couldn't happen today because international commodities aren't traded that way at all. They are bought in the place of origin. If you look at commodities which were like that, sugar didn't fall as much as rubber, tin, and silk because sugar was purchased from plantations abroad. I never had a student, and I'm too old myself to do it, to really pursue this in great detail in the archives of the banks. It should be done. But I happen to feel this is much better than, say, Eichengreen's explanation in *Golden Fetters.*

What is your instinct into what was driving the market upward at that time?
You know me, I wrote the book on manias. It was manic, just like the market is today, crazy!

What do you think is driving the market now?
Mutual funds and the lemming instinct.

A herd mentality?
Yes. You know my book *Manias, Panics, and Crashes*? That grew out of these events easily.

What do you think explains the differences between 1929 and 1987?
I think you didn't have the squeeze. One important thing is the financial institutions are all different. Brokers' loans, that is margin requirements, today are 50 percent. So, the ordinary guy who would borrow from his bank to buy stocks can't get as manic. But commodity prices haven't been affected at all. I have a piece on asset price inflation in the Banca Nazionale del Lavoro *Quarterly Review* for March 1995, talking about the fact that most central bankers say what you want to watch is the price level. The price level of commodities, goods, and services. But I say you want to keep an eye on asset prices too. We know that in 1929, Paul Warburg said the stock market was too high, and they laughed. If you read Lester Chandler's book on Benjamin Strong, in 1925 and 1926 he got worried about the price of wheat going down but the price of stocks going up. That's a problem.

What about monetary policy in 1987 compared to 1929? Do you think that...
Much better. There was a fight in 1929 between the Board of Governors and the Federal Reserve of New York. George Harrison tried to inject liquidity into the system but he got bawled out by the Board. Whereas Greenspan did

a great job.

Do you see any parallels between the recession of 1921 and the Great Depression? That is, do you think policy makers of the time figured it would be a repeat of those events and so did not vigorously attempt to fight the Depression?
I have a hard time with that. I think in 1920–21, people thought the boom was transitory, it would be over soon and we'd go back to 1914. It's a question of what you had your eye on. I think people then had their eye on pre-World War I. They expected prices to come down and didn't get excited. Peter Temin says I'm wrong about prices going down causing credit rationing and depression because it didn't happen in 1921. My good friend Eichengreen says "Prices fell in London and they didn't have the stock market crash." My response to that is if a world price falls anywhere it falls everywhere. If New York drags down the price of tin, rubber, silk, copper and so on, the price in London has to follow. You can see in Eichengreen's book that he's a little skeptical about my view, but I think he didn't quite see the arbitrage aspect of it.

Do you think the Fed should act as an arbiter of security prices? Even though they said they weren't back in the 1920s, all the empirical evidence seems to suggest that they were. Do you think that's something that they should do?
I think it doesn't pay very much just to talk about it. But it's a very good idea to inch up interest rates. Greenspan got his lumps talking about "irrational exuberance."

I don't know why he said that.
A guy in *The New York Times* said it was the first time there is any record of securities prices in a Federal Open Market Committee meeting discussion.

Oh come on now.
He must have only been reading from 1951 (*laughter*). Maybe they discuss it and don't record it.

I think it would have been awfully hard to anticipate the Hatry crisis which I think was the precipitant. The Hatry crisis tightened interest rates dramatically. We really should have brokers' loans data by months or weeks, but we only have them quarterly from that time period. So that you can't tell exactly what happened.

What explanations do you find most compelling and think do the best job of accounting for the Great Depression?

I'm a debt–deflation man. I think the fall of international prices and the stock market crash put big pressure on banks. Friedman said the stock market had nothing to do with the Depression at all, I can't believe that. Banks got hit with bad municipal loans. The Bank of United States got hit by bad mortgages. I think you had falling prices and debt deflation and this was tough on banks. The fall in asset prices hurt firms. But the world depression strikes me as being a way to commodity prices. I should add that Friedman thinks that the Depression was all US. He's changed that a little bit. There is a book in French, the memoirs of the Governor of the Bank of France, Emile Moreau. I helped some people translate it, and I wrote an introduction as did Friedman. He said before this he had thought that the Depression was all made in the US. Now he thinks the French have something to do with it. This strikes me as wrong. The world got involved through prices. Canada had a 45 percent drop in GNP. Chile had a 50 percent drop in GNP. These had nothing to do with banking.

That's the gold standard if you like. Temin in his 1989 book has said that it's the adherence to the principles of financial orthodoxy, the intransigent sticking to the gold standard that drove the world economy into the ground.
I would have thought if Harrison had been allowed to pour liquidity into the New York market, the way Greenspan did in 1987, it would have been a lot different. Let me go on to say that I believe in the "lender of last resort." I think in 1931 when the Kredit-anstalt failed in May, the world behaved in a very stingy way.

If you had a lender of last resort the way that we poured money into England in 1964, or Mexico recently, it would have been different. We had a lot to learn and it took a long time before we finally did.

Do you think though that the gold standard was an institution at the time that was not capable of handling what was going on?
What you should have had was a lender of last resort. Don't think about the gold standard, think about lending, think about pouring liquidity into the system to float it up. What you hope to do is pull it out of a crisis and then later restore the gold standard.

James Hamilton has said that at the time the gold standard couldn't have been adopted at a worse time or for poorer reasons in the late 1920s. Countries re-adopted the gold standard after World War I because they wanted to impose fiscal discipline and monetary discipline on themselves, but proved themselves incapable of doing so.

The worst case is the Japanese who did it in January 1929. Bad timing. But the British didn't get a lot of help. The interesting impression is the British thought they could restore the gold standard after World War I the way they restored it after the Napoleonic wars. I think that comparison is a very interesting one. They went off gold in 1797 and they said they would restore the gold standard six months after the end of the War. Well in 1815 they didn't do it in six months, they kept postponing and postponing. Finally they decided to do it in 1819, and did it in 1821 and it worked. Any success like that, even though it's not quite the way it was planned, makes you think you can do it again. I think the discussions of Churchill and others were extremely interesting. A certain amount of it was pride. They wanted to look the dollar in the eye and restore the pound sterling to its proper place in the world. That was tough to do.

But if there was an international lender of last resort perhaps it could have worked?
Yes. By the way, the French and the Americans did lend to the British in 1931, but not on a big enough scale. One of the things about the lender of last resort function is don't be stingy. This idea was developed particularly by Walter Bagehot but also before him by Henry Thornton. What if people said, "I'm going to lend you $10 and no more." That does not help.

Eichengreen said that it was cooperation and commitment that mattered for the gold standard and that wasn't there during the interwar. You said what was needed was leadership. It seems to me that Golden Fetters *is a wonderful book and it rightly belongs among some of the best work on the Great Depression.*
He's good and so is Temin.

No doubt about it.
These guys are good. But I can't believe it was the gold standard rather than a series of bubbles. They go way up and something, I don't care what, pushes them down. In my case it was the Hatry crisis and interest rates. Then you had this spillover into commodity prices and debt deflation. That's not the same thing as the gold standard. But if Eichengreen wants to say that, that's fine.

It seems to me that cooperation and the lack thereof was pervasive throughout your book.
Here's an interesting thing about cooperation. Cooperation works best when somebody drives it.

That's exactly right. What's your view on the relationship between the Great Depression and World War II? Do you see 1914–45 as the second 30-year war as Churchill called it?

I know the historians said it's all part of the same thing. I doubt that. Kindleberger's Law of Alternatives also leads to Kindleberger's Law of Multiple Causation, and that is tough too. You have the post-World War I inflation, the Treaty of Versailles, reparations, the deflation and the unemployment after 1928 in Germany. Which ones brought on Hitler? All of them. Political scientists say it's not the middle class who brought on Hitler, it is not these particular men and it is not those other individuals. All of them together, were they all necessary conditions? Were they all sufficient conditions? I don't know and I don't think anybody knows. Multiple causation is very tough stuff to sort out.

So the post-World War I inflation and the Treaty of Versailles, Kindleberger's Law of Multiple Causation says that you wrap them all together and ...

And the unemployment from 1928 to 1931. There was a big debate in Germany between Knut Borchardt who said that the Prime Minister (*Brüning*) had no choices and he could not operate, and Carl-Ludwig Holtfrerich who said he could. Was there room for a policy to do better in 1931? It is a dandy question. There happened to be a meeting in the Reichsbank the day after the British went off the gold standard to discuss a memo by a man named Wilhelm Lautenbach. Lautenbach said to forget the gold standard, even though you'll violate the rules under the Dawes Treaty, you've got to do it. The other people said we have to follow the rules. That's a tough one, but a dandy topic. Do you follow rules or do you say, we got to do what we got to do? This is true of the French in the 1920s. The French had a ceiling on Bank of France debt owed by the government. And some smart kid said "You got to break it. Don't go to the Chamber of Deputies. Just tell them you are going to break it because this is an emergency, you've got to break it." The others said, "No we can't." I love that kind of history.

Did the Depression change the psychology of the country?

Oh yes. I mentioned earlier how my uncle got me a job on a ship because he was Vice-President of a company. Ten years later an uncle got a friend of mine a place on a ship because he was Vice-President of a union. That's a big change. I thought the rise of unions was important.

What role of government did you feel was appropriate then in the midst of the Great Depression?

Well I have to be a little more critical of Roosevelt than most people I guess. He was a man who was not encumbered by any ideology. He tried one play after another, throw the bomb, statue of liberty, go through the center, etc. Do anything to try it. But his attack on the World Economic Conference of 1933 struck me as an awkward economic analysis. A lot of people admired it. James Meade admired it, Keynes admired it. I also thought NRA was a mistake.

Do you think the Great Depression changed the psychology of the country in viewing what role government should play in the economy?
I guess. But Ronald Reagan comes along with another view of how the government should stop. Milton and Rose Friedman in their book *Free to Choose* are for cutting government down. I have the feeling that there's a cycle in these matters. When you're in trouble you need government. When you're not in trouble get rid of it. It just so happens that the people who excoriate bureaucrats have a small point. But if there's trouble, you attract bright people to government. If there's no trouble they leave and you are left with the slower thinkers. So it's harder to generalize. If you say all bureaucrats are always only interested in themselves, the way, say, Buchanan does, that's unfair. In the 1930s you had a lot of smart people as you did during the War. A lot of them couldn't get out afterwards when things calmed down.

So there is a cycle then?
Well the cycle is chaotic, it's not smooth. And the chaos comes from when do the crises appear and how?

How did the Great Depression shape your life professionally?
I guess I got into economic history in a different way. I got into economic history because when I left the State Department and went to MIT, I took a drop in salary from $9000 per year to $7500. I was married with three children and a fourth coming. I moonlighted a bit. I moonlighted a course at Columbia, on the economy of Europe. It was a two-term course. The second term was easy because I knew as much about Europe as anybody. But the first term, I didn't know the history. So I read history extensively for that period and came up with a paper on the fall of the price of wheat and what it did to European countries. Now, an economist would say there are two ways to react to a fall in price. Get out of the industry or put on a tariff. The British liquidated agriculture, the Germans and French put on tariffs. It doesn't take account of the Italians who put on a tariff very late but meanwhile they emigrated. In international trade theory you are not allowed to do that. In international trade theory we assume factors are fixed. And it doesn't take account of the Danish.

They stopped exporting wheat, they moved into dairy products and meat, and they imported grain to feed cows and pigs and so on. That's a dynamic response. That article called "Group Behavior in International Trade" came out in *The Journal of Political Economy* in 1951 and basically said don't believe the Stolper–Samuelson theorem. And recently I got a check for $80, it is being reproduced somewhere. That's 46 years ago. How wonderful.

Can you point to one particular contribution in economics, one book or article that did the most to shape your thinking as an economist?
How much time have I got (*laughter*)?

You're the one who dictates that.
I want to talk about people who shaped my thinking.

By all means.
Emile Despres was smart as hell. But he was a perfectionist. As a perfectionist he couldn't publish because he wanted to improve it still more. When he was in the Harvard Development Service in Pakistan, some said he was the most brilliant civil servant you ever thought about. I followed him to New York, I followed him to Washington, and to the OSS. He went to Williams College and I was offered a job at Williams. I said no, that's enough. I don't want him to be my Svengali. I learned enormous amounts from him. It was said back then, maybe by me, that an assistant professorship at Williams College was the best graduate school in the country talking to Despres. But yet he has no reputation at all.

Was the Depression the biggest single event that shaped you professionally? Or has something else occurred that had a bigger impact?
I think it was my work in the Enemy Objectives Unit in London, trying to pick targets to bomb in Germany and planning the targeting for the invasion of France. It was the biggest responsibility I've had and the biggest challenge. It was interesting and God, we worked our tails off. We would walk home through the blackout and spent nights there working. It was a very exciting time and very rewarding, except for the separation from my family.

What do you think was effective in ending the Great Depression?
The War.

We talked about this some but, the New Deal programs, you didn't see them as a positive force, correct?

Well, people like Currie and Eccles were pushing, pushing, pushing, but I don't think there was much Keynesianism around. Cary Brown's paper showed that. Of course, after the War, like Nixon said "We are all Keynesians now." Nowadays there are no Keynesians left, except me (*chuckling*).

Do you see any role then for fiscal policy in ending the Great Depression? Or monetary policy?
Fiscal policy could do it but it is a hard policy to play.

What about monetary policy? Any pluses or minuses at all?
I don't know, the short-term rate of interest got down to negative values, just like Japan today. That's a nice parallel. The Japanese have driven short-term rates very low. During the Depression, the nominal rates were negative because Henry Morgenthau did not understand finance at a deep enough level. He thought that anytime you had a big bid for a security, that was great. So he set the prices too low. Everyone would pile on and then the security would go up two points, people would sell and it was easy money. Then he said, "So many people want long-term bonds that we'll give a priority to those who turn in short-term bills." It turned out that people who exchanged short-term bills were given 1/2% when they did so. Thus the nominal rate was negative.

It's very hard for any type of interest rate transmission mechanism to work then.
Yes, it was very hard and you didn't get any spending boom or durable goods production and automobiles were coming back slowly.

What are some of the lessons of the Great Depression that seem to be forgotten today or that have to be continually relearned?
I think the lender of last resort function is an important one. On the other hand, I'm disturbed by the fact there is a lot of loose money around in the hands of speculators like George Soros and the extent of the high gearing of the futures market.

This means that the market can overwhelm the authorities. I think maybe something should be done about that. I would like to see, for example, margin requirements applied to futures.

One of the worst mistakes we've made in post-war times was made by the Federal Reserve Board. Arthur Burns, chairman in 1971, trying to lower interest rates in a political cycle to help Nixon get re-elected at a time when the Germans were trying to tighten interest rates. In my judgment, an attempt to lower interest rates in one country and raise them in another country when the two markets are joined is a recipe for disaster. I call it a crime of 1971, apropos of the crime of 1873 about one hundred years earlier. I think that Burns made a bad mistake. The eurodollar market was the intermediary between the German market and the American market, and it flooded the eurodollar market. In the first place, American companies who had borrowed in Germany paid off those loans with eurodollars that they borrowed. Then German companies did the same. The eurodollars were then sold to the Bundesbank who put them back into the eurodollar market. So you had the regular expansion of money with a monopoly bank and that was a serious thing for world inflation of the 1970s and 1980s leading up to the crash in 1987. That's not a lesson of the Depression but it is a lesson of economics. If you have one market, there can only be one price. But if you have two markets that are joined with a market in between, you only have one price. Try to make two prices and you get into trouble.

Does the memory of the Great Depression stay with you, or still have an impact on your thinking in any way?
I can't think so, no. *Manias, Panics and Crashes*, I think about that book. I have a book called *A Financial History of Western Europe*, which has much history of the Depression, and I think about that a lot. Now I'm working on the German monetary reform of 1948 which is very moving. So you can see these things are on my mind.

So the Depression doesn't pervade your thoughts.
No, what pervades my thoughts is what I'm working on.

Okay, let's ask a bit of a trite question. If you were a policy maker knowing what you know now, what would you have done to prevent the Great Depression from happening? What would you advise?
It was probably impossible to stop the stock market rise. We probably should've tightened interest rates earlier. We didn't have margin requirements on brokers' loans then, but it would have been a useful idea. One thing I say in the Banca Nazionale del Lavoro *Quarterly Review* paper about asset prices was if you have two targets, you need two policies. Tinbergen said it, but people before him did too saying "You can't kill two birds with one stone," unless you have a ricochet shot.

Those are tough to execute.
Yes, you are so right. So, I would have thought that if you try to handle asset prices as well as commodity prices, you really ought to work on margin

requirements and how much you allow people to borrow to buy assets. There is a very good book called *One Hundred Years of Land Values in Chicago* by Homer Hoyt. This book talks about the relationship between the stock market and the real estate market. That's interesting, it's the lemming/herd mentality principle. Everyone makes money in the stock market and people say "Hey come on, let's get going." Then you ordered one condominium to live in and bought five others and sold them for a profit. Should you regulate that? I have no idea. It's tricky. But the real estate market is different from the stock market because when it collapses, they collapse together. The stock market gets cleared up in six months. The real estate market takes years and you cannot see a better example of this than in Japan now. They're still trying to clean up the real estate mess from 1990.

And the stock market in Japan remains a bear market does it not?
Well, 19,000 on the Nikei index. The top was 39,000 and the bottom was 14,000 so it has been up and down. The stock market is OK and commodity prices are OK but real estate is still a terrible drag. They should've had more lender of last resort. It would've been better if they had been able to slow it down. This is the agony people had in the 1920s. The price of wheat was falling and the price of stocks was going up, what do we do? It's tricky. That's a big lesson I would think. On the other hand, I'm also scared of putting too many weapons into too many people's hands. You give a guy a gun to shoot a tiger and he may use it to shoot something else.

What are the big problems you see confronting us as we enter the next century? As you reflect back to your experience of Depression and your knowledge as an economist over the years, what do you see confronting us in the next century that are big problems in your mind?
You may remember the last chapter of *The World in Depression*, which says you need leadership, somebody who's prepared to take charge, to move in in a crisis. I believe that in a crisis, you need a benevolent despot. The problem is, I admit, it's very difficult to keep a despot benevolent. After a while he begins to think he's OK and he's not. So this is the problem I think. In serene times, less government. In turbulent times somebody take charge. I worry about the international world. The US seems to be losing its leadership. People want to cut aid, they want to cast off the United Nations and so on. That is more general than just international finance, but the same thing is true in finance. Luckily we have in Alan Greenspan a leader that strikes me as being smart and responsible. He's good, no doubt. But I'm a little afraid we may end up with nobody prepared to take responsibility for world peace or for stability.

In serene times you don't need it, the market will equilibrate. On the other hand, there are times that require it. That's my take, but don't believe it. I'm just an old man babbling on.

We'll let the readers make a judgment about that. Do you view our capitalist system as the best going or is there a better alternative?
I think I'm like Winston Churchill, it's a lousy system, but it is better than any alternative, like marriage. That's from a man who was married for 59 years and 10 months. For me it was wonderful.

That's an incredible accomplishment. What do you see as the biggest threat to capitalism?
Greed, I suppose. I'm quite unhappy about the way people now want money. The notion that the guy who dies with the most toys wins strikes me as being not very long viewed.

It's spiritually empty, too.
You better believe it. The head of my department said "Enough is as good as a feast." I think greed is a threat.

Are you bothered by the distribution of income and the trend in the distribution of income?
Yes, quite a lot. It is related to this question of greed. I don't know there is anything you can easily do about it.

Do you see the distribution of income trend as a threat to capitalism, or is that pushing it too far?
It's like the French Revolution. It's not a threat to capitalism, but a threat to society.

Are there any particular trends in economic research or schools of thought that you find disturbing?
I'm a little distressed as I look at the National Bureau reports. So many people are talking about such insignificant topics, and getting money for it. I suspect there's too much money around for research topics. I used to count my aphorisms by the decade and I can't remember which decade this belonged to, but I said "Foundations corrupt and the Ford foundation corrupts absolutely." Mind you, I've taken Ford foundation money too. But you see what I mean. If you look in the National Bureau or the *American Economic Review*, there are so many papers about trivial matters and tiny problems.

Could it happen again? Do you feel that another Great Depression could happen?
No, but I think another crash could happen. I think the lender of last resort function has been so well developed now that we're not going to get deflationary policies applied. If you do get trouble it will come another way, as Germany, Sweden and others have it now, from rising demands by labor. I'm not against that, but a high cost of labor makes it very tough to compete, particularly in world markets. That gives you 10 percent to 12 percent unemployment. That's troublesome, particularly for young people. There are problems around, but another Great Depression, I'd say no.

Excellent. Thanks so much Professor.
I've enjoyed this. It reminds me of a James M. Barrie play, "The old general counts his medals."

Anna Schwartz

In terms of written research, Anna Schwartz has been the point person deflecting criticism and defending the validity of the monetary hypothesis of the Depression. As co-author with Milton Friedman of *A Monetary History of the United States, 1867–1960*, Schwartz has steadfastly attempted to refute (some would say attack) any and all theories proposed to supplant the monetary hypothesis as the leading explanation of the Depression. In particular, Peter Temin's 1976 book *Did Monetary Forces Cause the Great Depression?* dismissed the role of money and instead claimed the Depression was caused by a decline in autonomous consumption. This set off an exchange between Temin and Schwartz with which any student of the literature on the Depression is well familiar. I had a few questions on this matter that I felt compelled to ask. Additionally, of all the interviews conducted, Anna Schwartz possessed the most extensive knowledge of the literature on the Great Depression and the questions I asked her in this regard are the most detailed and academically oriented. We spoke at her office at the National Bureau of Economic Research in New York in December 1997.

When and where were you born and what were you doing during the Great Depression?
I was born in New York. I was at Barnard College between 1931 and 1934. Before that I was in school. I guess I didn't really study the Great Depression until I got to graduate school at Columbia. But my views were transformed when I began working with Friedman, so I don't think I knew anything about the Great Depression until long after it happened.

What were your views prior to your work with Professor Friedman?
Well, I guess essentially I was exposed to the standard Keynesian explanation of how the economy worked. And certainly that big British study that I worked on with Walt Rostow and the late Arthur Gayer is definitely infected by the Keynesian view although there were some twists that were really Walt Rostow's view of the world. But I didn't really come to understand what I had missed in that British study until I started working on *A Monetary History* with Friedman.

What was the name of that British study?

The Growth and Fluctuation of the British Economy 1790–1850. So it was a historical study, it was an empirical study, we had whatever data we were able to collect and we analyzed it using the National Bureau business cycle technique. So that was the first really big historical study that I worked on. When a second publishing of the two volume work was issued in 1976, I had an opportunity to disavow parts of that study (*laughter*), whereas Rostow was firm in saying everything was just fine, he had no complaints at all, or any second thoughts about how the study had emerged. The world can see that I had learned something since I first ...

The best was yet to come, huh?
Well, that's the way I feel.

So you were in school during the Great Depression, and then subsequently went on to work with Rostow and so on. Were you with the NBER then?
No, because I was in New York and at Columbia, I was often at the NBER offices. Wesley Mitchell was extremely interested in this business study and encouraged us to go ahead with it. So I learned the National Bureau business cycle technique without being an employee of the Bureau simply because I was in the office there absorbing what it was that they were doing.

During your student days, the City College in New York was active in radical economic thought. Can you give me a synopsis of what they were saying back then?
(*Schwartz answers without hesitation*) I had nothing to do with it. I had no contact, except possibly what I read in the newspapers. But I wasn't really familiar with what was going on there.

So they didn't have any influence on you at all.
No influence at all.

OK, so you didn't react to it since you weren't aware what they were even necessarily talking about.
And I was never a rebel, I was never a communist, I never had any interest in unions or any activity of that kind.

Did you have any interaction with Burns and Mitchell when you were at Columbia?
Not at Columbia, but in relation to the British study, I did have contact with them. I never took a course at Columbia with either of them, so ...

What about what you were saying? That Mitchell, he encouraged you to ...

Yes, he was extremely, in fact, I think it was Mitchell whose support for the funding of the study made it possible for it to be pursued. The Columbia Social Science Research Council gave the grant that, in a sense, made it possible for the study to go on. So his interest in the study was important for its eventual completion.

How did the writing of A Monetary History *come about?*
Well, we started out with the intention of producing a money stock time series. That was the first aim and this is a typical National Bureau way of proceeding. You first collected the data, then you analyzed the fluctuations in the data according to the National Bureau technique of analyzing business cycles. And that essentially was the way we started out. But once we had the series and once the technique had revealed to us what this series was actually demonstrating, it seemed important to clothe the series with the actual events that it was reflecting. And that was the way we started out by saying, well, we would begin with a history. That was something that we had done in the British study too. Start with the history and then we would go on to the analysis of the economic meaning of this history. So we started with the history, we were going to do a separate cyclical study of the behavior of the money stock at some later date ... we never did. We did that initially, studying the cyclical movements as a conference paper. But that was the only work we actually did on cyclical fluctuations in the money stock.

Had you graduated from Columbia by then?
I had finished my graduate studies. The idea at that time was that I would use my contribution to the British study as my dissertation.

Who was your dissertation advisor?
Well, I didn't have an advisor in that sense, because I was working on this study when I proposed to Burns that I would use my part of the study. He said no, he wanted me to do something altogether separate. By that time I had begun working with Friedman. I wasn't going to start on another subject when I knew that I would have something that would emerge from my collaboration with Friedman. So I did nothing. But when we had finished *A Monetary History* and it had been published, Friedman said "Why don't you present *A Monetary History* as your dissertation?" Now this was irregular in the sense that Columbia didn't regularly give degrees for a published study, but there had been a precedent. Friedman's work with Kuznets on the income of professionals had been published. It was a joint work and he got his Ph.D. on the basis of that study. And I got my degree, many years after I'd finished graduate work after the publication of *A Monetary History*.

When you wrote that chapter on the Great Contraction, what was your reaction when you had that money supply series and you saw what was going on? I don't want to be melodramatic, but you were on the verge of discovery here, knowing that you really had something startling.
That's right.

What was your feeling? What was going through your mind?
We were excited about it. But the reaction of the profession after the book was published was negative. I mean we were some kind of nuts! Who believed that money had anything to do with the way the economy functioned? So as I say our excitement didn't mean that we were ready to believe that the world would accept our conclusions. It took a long time I think until the message of *A Monetary History* became convincing to a large part of the profession. And I'm sure that in the work that you're doing, asking people who lived through that time what their views are of the relation of money to the actual Depression, you may have already heard people who are dubious.

Oh indeed. My view is it took until 1987 with James Hamilton's Journal of Monetary Economics *paper "Monetary Factors in the Great Depression," before people even said, "Oh, money really was tight back then wasn't it?"*
Yes.

Anyhow, with that in mind and please understand that I'm not trying to be "cheeky" at all. But on that related thing, what's your angle on the debate with Peter Temin? Was it a miscommunication or were the positions just that fundamentally, diametrically opposed?
Well, my view is that he recanted when he wrote those three lectures ...

Lessons from the Great Depression *in 1989.*
Yes, but he insisted in his preface that he hadn't changed one iota from the positions he had taken in 1976. But in elevating the gold standard as the key element in the transmission of the Depression, I don't see how you can deny the central role of money. But that's not the way Peter Temin wants to be remembered. His attack on us in 1976 was first on the importance of the banking panics which he tended to dismiss, and then on the role of money in general. He was iconoclastic in many ways. The notion that the stock market crash was not responsible for this idiosyncratic behavior of consumption, but rather it was an unexplained decline in consumption in 1929–30. Well, I don't think any of his positions really have stood up under examination by later students.

Do you have any angle on why it became so contentious?

Well, people blamed me. I thought his tone in the book, was very ...

Acerbic perhaps?
Yes. So when I answered in the same way, I was attacked for not behaving the way scholars should.

In 1981, in the book The Great Depression Revisited*?*
Yes. But, I mean, I can talk to Temin now without any acrimony. If he resents it I don't know, I don't see it in his behavior. We were on a panel together last October, a Bureau conference on "Was the Great Depression a Watershed?" And he and I were both supposed to sum up what the conference was about. He said one thing and I said another thing but it was perfectly friendly. Not at all the tone that I think he had in 1976.

Well I think his moving toward the gold standard has elevated our understanding of the Great Depression a lot, and it's like you say, then how can you deny money?
Yes.

So let me go on to a related question then. What is your view of the role of the gold standard in the international transmission of the Depression?
Well, I think we had a couple of pages in *A Monetary History* making just that point. That if you're on the gold standard and the central country is deflating and reducing nominal income, wages, profits and prices, there's just no way that your trading partners aren't going to absorb the thing that you're emitting from the center. And any one of those countries that stayed on the gold standard grimly went through exactly the same kind of intense depression that the US did. And those that abandoned the gold standard as Britain did in 1931 had a much earlier recovery.

And Spain, for example, was never on it to begin with.
That's right, they escaped. So I don't think there's any denying that the transmission came through, to the world, came through the gold standard. And that's another point that Temin made that I thought couldn't be sustained. He argued that yes, the gold standard was important but you couldn't put your finger on the US as the one that was the central point.

That's false. You can put your finger on the United States and France both.
That's right. Because they really deformed the classical gold standard. And it was the fact that the countries that were gaining gold didn't expand their money supplies while the countries that were losing gold didn't have the therapeutic kind of behavior that under a fully functioning gold standard

would have relieved the situation that the losers were in, but it didn't happen. So, what you had was the countries gaining gold deflating and the countries losing gold deflating. And that's the way you got a worldwide depression.

Does my memory serve me correctly on Lessons from the Great Depression*? Temin said, it isn't money and it's not the Fed because these banking panics were going to happen as long as the Fed and the US stayed on the gold standard, they had no choice but to let it happen anyway.*
If you're the lender of last resort, which is a key feature of a functioning gold standard, you don't permit banks to fail. You do something either to sustain banks that have just suffered contagion from a bad bank and you shut down the bad bank and don't permit the rot to spread. And that it seems to me is not a lesson that had to be learned in 1929–33. Central banks had known that for years, for decades. So it was failure of policy at the Fed. It was not the gold standard which compelled them to behave in that way.

So then I would be correct in saying that Peter Temin thought that it was the gold standard and the intransigent adherence to the principles of financial orthodoxy that drove it right into the ground and you would say that's not true.
First of all, we now know what we may not have understood too well earlier. The commitment to the gold standard was not one that you couldn't break, that you couldn't temporarily suspend. And you did that, as Britain did, when there was an internal drain or an external drain. And when you suspended, the public knew very well that you intended to resume as soon as the underlying problem had been solved. So it could be a very brief suspension, or a longer one such as the US suspension after the Civil War. You wait until you are able to adjust your economy to go back to the parity that you had abandoned. There was no compelling reason for the US not to have suspended in 1931–33, to say we will not continue this deflation. When we have righted the economy we will go back again to the gold standard and the commitment we made in 1879. Apparently that conception had absolutely fled from the minds of the policy makers. Although as I say, I think it was one of the foundations of the way the gold standard actually operated. In time of war it was alright to give up the gold standard. In time of domestic drain, it was alright to relax the gold standard limits, and if there was ever an external drain. So the conditions for the Federal Reserve to have taken such action existed, but they resisted. I mean, their misconception basically reflected the belief that they had been profligate during the 1920s. Therefore the economy had to be submitted, subjected, to this kind of cleansing as it were, the word that has become popular nowadays, liquidationist, you have to ...

"Purge the rottenness from the system!"
That's right. And you couldn't do anything to relieve the obvious deflation in the economy because you would then be untrue to what the gold standard required of you. So with that kind of mind set you couldn't get an expansion going, although certainly from 1929–31 our gold stock was just way in excess of what our reserve requirements were. There was no reason why they could not have expanded, it would not have reduced the reserve ratio to some unsustainable level. But, these are all hindsight ideas that some people at the New York Fed were uttering at the time without convincing the system as a whole.

What about what James Hamilton has said in his 1988 gold standard paper "Role of the International Gold Standard in Propagating the Great Depression" in Contemporary Policy Issues *where he said that it couldn't have come at a worse time or for poorer reasons when it was reinstituted after World War I? Do you agree with that?*
I think so because when it was reinstituted it was a unilateral decision by each country at what parity it would return. So you had Britain returning at an overvalued pound. You had France returning at an undervalued franc. There was no joint decision, even though there was cooperation during those years; until the Great Depression it was very hard to run a gold standard that was healthy when you had one of the reserve currencies then under continual pressure. The US was trying somehow to help Britain by adjusting its discount rate so that it would relieve Britain. At the same time Britain was being hurt by the undervalued franc which affected gold flows out of Britain, and France was amassing gold. So the whole episode of the return to the gold standard after World War I was badly managed. One of the ideas I have had, when you say Britain returned in 1925. Well suppose it had had another few years to adjust. If it hadn't gone back at that point, when the general statement is it was 10 percent overvalued, if it had waited until its price level had adjusted further before actually committing themselves to the gold standard, maybe the six years that Britain suffered with the gold standard could have been ameliorated. I don't know, that's a thought I have had which is just not something we'll ever be able to test.

What about Eichengreen's Golden Fetters *book, have you read it?*
Yes. Well, my main objection to the Eichengreen book is that I don't believe that you cannot have a successful monetary regime unless there is cooperation. Countries cooperate when it is in their interest to do so. They don't cooperate when it's against what they regard as their interest. So I think you need a monetary regime that responds to the interests of the people of the countries that adhere to it. You don't start out with a kind of Boy Scout idea of what's

going to make this regime work. Everybody's got to cooperate. Everybody isn't going to cooperate if they don't think it is in their interest. The regime has to be something that makes sense to the individual country. That's the way he interprets the whole experience ... a failure of cooperation. I don't think it's a failure of cooperation. The regime didn't provide the individual countries with what they needed by their lights to conduct a successful economic experience.

Can you run a successful gold standard if you don't have that type of cooperation and coordination though? If national interests diverge?
If national interests diverge, I don't see how. Because the gold standard was automatic in the sense that gold flowed in and flowed out, or short-term capital flowed in or flowed out without anybody really saying we're going to do this, we're going to do that, it happened. But if countries are able to interfere with the way this system, this mechanism ...

So then the price–specie flow mechanism ain't what it used to be.
That's it. And that's what the interwar experience proved. If each of the countries was going to pursue a different tack, you were going to interfere with the way this mechanism was supposed to work. And then it broke down.

Cooperation is overrated, isn't it?
I don't think cooperation can be the fundamental principle. It emerges as a result of the fact that there is ...

Beneficial trade.
That's right. Yes.

What a concept, huh?
Yes (*laughter*).

Do you have any other criticisms of that literature?
Well another criticism of the Eichengreen book which is akin to the Temin notion is that if they had attempted to be expansionary, the US and the other countries had attempted to be expansionary, they would've suffered a drain of gold. It was illusory, you couldn't do it. Because if the US had tried to expand in 1929–31, the world would've thought, "Oh, they're getting ready to leave the gold standard. We better take out whatever dollar assets we have," and that in itself would have crippled the attempt to be expansionary. Therefore it didn't happen. They were helpless. Well, I don't believe so. I mean, the US had an enormous gold stock. No country in the world had ever amassed such hoards of gold.

Of free gold.
Of free gold – I mean from 1929 to 1931 how could you say that they could not have afforded to be expansionary? Even if they had lost some gold, we know that in February 1933 when there was both internal and external drain in the US, they lost about $250 million in gold. They had $4 billion at the end of that month. So what's the scare that you're trying to create that would make people say they're going to leave the gold standard? France removed whatever gold assets it had. It was doing this all along, it had nothing to do with fear that the US wouldn't be faithful to the gold standard. France just believed it should not hold foreign exchange, it should hold only gold and it was slowly repatriating whatever dollar assets it had. So, I think that this notion of Eichengreen's, which as I say is related to Temin's, that they couldn't have done anything, is just made up of whole cloth. It doesn't really fit the facts.

Didn't he also show himself (with Jeffrey Sachs) that if they would have devalued their currencies that it would have been inflationary and beneficial?
Yes, it would have helped and that's one of the conclusions that these people who want to emphasize the role of the gold standard and its transmission, that the only way you got out of that bind was by giving it up. So, I don't know. There's some confusion I think.

Another thing. I have never appreciated how much Eichengreen was indebted to that two volume study of the gold standard by W.A. Brown. I've recently been going through it. He got an awful lot of what he has in his study from the Brown study of the gold standard between 1914 and 1934. An amazing collection of information about individual countries, how they fared during the War, during the interwar period and that's what Eichengreen really drew on.

Another thing. The only one who gave Eichengreen a very unfavorable review was Moggridge in the *Economic Journal*. His point was how can Eichengreen compare his work with what W.A. Brown had done? I guess that study appeared in 1940. But I mean, Eichengreen is a very industrious guy, he writes well. I'm not sure he's the greatest economist.

Well that book is, I think, a very useful contribution for a number of reasons. But it is useful, if for no other reason, in that it makes us rethink these things again.
Right.

I promise you this is my last cheeky question. Kindleberger didn't mention this, but I read it in his book The Life of an Economist. *What did you mean when you told him "better luck next time?"*
(Chuckling) Which ...

You said it to Kindleberger, I think at a conference somewhere in Switzerland, he splashed you in the pool and then later commented that his book The World in Depression 1929–1939 *was not universally accepted and he sneered at you when he said it. When the conference broke up and people were saying goodbye you told him "better luck next time." What did you mean by that?*
I thought the first edition of Kindleberger's book downplayed money in a way that I thought was just unacceptable. I know in the second edition he modified it, but he hadn't done the second edition yet when I made that comment.

OK. Your views on the origins and driving forces of the Depression are well known. Is there anything you'd like to add or embellish or modify or subtract?
Well, I think there has been an enormous amount of work since *A Monetary History* and we've certainly modified some views that were presented in the study. I mean the big one had nothing to do with the Great Depression. For me it is the way we elevated the deposit insurance corporation to the greatest thing that had happened in the post-war world and I certainly don't think so now.

But at the time, though, it gave the financial markets instant rehabilitation though, didn't it?
Yes, no question. I mean, if you have a central bank that isn't operating as a lender of last resort, you better find something else. But given that, as I say, the Federal Reserve could've taken that role, the deposit insurance corporation becomes redundant and the great performance that it gave for the first – until the 1970s – I have subsequently attributed not to deposit insurance but to price stability. And once we got into this period of unstable prices, the banking system became unhinged and the deposit insurance system became unhinged.

Yes, that's an outstanding point.
I think that part of *A Monetary History* would have to be re-written if it were to be done again. But with respect to the Great Depression itself there have been so many studies either correcting us, disputing us, elaborating on us that you can't ignore all this work that has gone on since. I'm sure that we would have to take into account the subsequent research. I don't by any means play it down. I think it's important and I think people have done a great service by going further than we had. So I may criticize individual comments, individual points that others have made, but not the entire effort itself. I think it is praiseworthy. I've just reviewed Wicker's (*1996*) book on the banking panics where he is critical of us. He claims that the banking panics tended to be regional not national. I don't believe that at all. I mean just because the panics were concentrated in some particular area doesn't mean that it didn't have nationwide effects and we see that ...

Psychologically.
Yes. And on the deposit/currency ratio and the money stock. Anyhow, on the subject of transmission, of course we did very little on how what happened to the money supply got transmitted to the real economy. That's something that we didn't discuss at all. A lot of work has been done in that area.

And how do you view some of that work like Bernanke's hypothesis in the 1983 American Economic Review?
Well, the hypothesis that it was the collapse of financial intermediation, which was the non-monetary propagator of the Depression, I think is overblown. I mean we may never have made anything of the credit market. Brunner and Meltzer have elevated the credit market so that it is equal to the money market in its role in the Depression. But they say Bernanke's emphasis on financial intermediation as an independent variable is unacceptable. This is something that is subordinate to what's happening to the money stock, even though I don't deny that financial intermediation was important. Bernanke in general plays up financial crises rather than what's happening to the money stock as the transmitter. Well, I don't deny that financial crises produced the money stock changes. But I wouldn't for that reason say don't look at the money stock, look at financial crises.

Yes, and I'm not sure that he would say that either would he?
Well, that's pretty much what I get from recent work that he's done with James and with Carey.

Just for the record, I view Bernanke's work as much more complimentary to what you did. I mean he said, "We have Friedman and Schwartz, and that's the main story. Let's add to that now."
Yes, I agree with you, which is not the tack that Temin took. Temin was going to displace us. Bernanke was going to build on us. And I think my attitude to all the research of recent years is that it is building, and you understand more and that's fine.

Can't the real estate debacles that generated part of the savings and loan problems in the 1980s correctly be viewed as a redux of what happened during the Great Depression? Bought high ... made loans ... price deflation?
Yes, and that's the undoing of the bubble.

That's what you're talking about with price instability?
Yes, in that way.

Instability like that, then you have bank risk and so on.

Right.

How did the Depression shape your life professionally? Was it the biggest single event or did something else occur that had a bigger impact?
Well, the Depression shaped my life the way it shaped everybody. You got used to a level of compensation that was much lower than what you eventually earned. Well, that's part of the growth of income as you mature. I was never without a job, I didn't have that kind of experience in the Depression. Neither did anyone in my family. So in that sense, I was immune to the ravages of the Depression. But I'm sure it has shaped the way I live. I'm probably much more frugal than my children are. They grew up in a household where you can always find an extra dollar, which is different than the way it was when I was growing up.

Did it channel you into economics, though? The pain of that experience?
No. I became interested in economics when I was in high school. I had a course in economics then and I thought that this was the most interesting thing I would study. I always wanted to major in economics. It had nothing to do with the Great Depression. I just thought the questions that were asked were so stimulating and to be able to think of the answers, and as many answers that there were. So I majored in economics when I got to college, and I went on to graduate school. I never thought of pursing a different subject. So ...

So, the Depression certainly gave you a whole fruitful list of questions to work on then if nothing else.
Right (*laughter*). So the Depression was just one stage in my life, that's all. I went on to other stages.

Can you point to one particular contribution, book, article, or person that did the most shaping how you think as an economist?
Well, undoubtedly my contact with Friedman. He transformed my understanding of economics and it's because he is such a stimulating person to be with. You can't talk to him about anything without having a new idea as a result. And the fact that we had such a comfortable kind of intellectual experience together. He could tell me "No, that doesn't make sense," and I could tell him "No, I don't think that makes sense." And we would go on. There is just no question in my mind. Of course, I've been influenced by other people too, but if you ask me who is the one person, it's Friedman.

I have to say, I have never met him and am going to meet him for an interview for this book, but he has done the most to shape my thinking.
Yes, and I think that is true worldwide. I mean, why is it ... he is just a college

professor who has such an influence around the world. You can't think of many other professors who have this kind of name recognition. People may not think of him for the right things. Friedman, in some universities, wouldn't be honored with an honorary degree because they don't approve of what they think are his conservative views.

Now that's silly.
Yes, but that's what I'm saying.

You could take out his 1968 Presidential Address right now and it would be more enlightening than a lot of the, no, may I say most of the stabilization work that has been done in the last 30 years.
I agree with you.

Just that one article alone.
That's right.

Did the Depression change the psychology of the country?
Oh no question. It not only changed the psychology, it changed the art, the movies, the books, any kind of expression of how you think the world works. A depression is a picture of our economy. That's why there was this continual fear that we were going to relive the Depression after the War. In 1973–75, Franco Modigliani organized a session at the American Economic Association, the title of which was "Another Great Depression?" He asked me to chair that session and I did not know that he had given it that name in the directory. I objected violently. The idea that 1973–75 was another Great Depression just seemed to be absurd. Anyhow, the novels we've read, the movies we've seen all reflect that fear of the kind of experience that people all over the world endured.

I hate to have to say it, but what about the way in which government's involvement in the economy was then accepted?
Well, absolutely (*laughter*). I should have mentioned that first. This was the comment that I made at this NBER conference I mentioned earlier, in October 1996 on "Was the Great Depression a Watershed?" What Temin did was to summarize the different papers and I said that if it was a watershed, it was a watershed because of the role that government assumed has never been reduced since the Great Depression. And of course this was a conference of economic historians and I think I probably was the only one there who had this feeling about what change the Great Depression wrought. All of them are believers in government. I mean government does things that ...

Are goods in and of themselves.
That's right. Sitting with Lance E. Davis, he was saying to me "You know Anna, you really hadn't had an experience in the Great Depression." His father was out of a job. They had very hard times and moved in with his grandparents, that kind of thing. So when the government, when Roosevelt came along with the New Deal that was salvation! And he's never changed his mind.

Well, Temin was right in his book Lessons on the Great Depression. *That opened the door to socialism and it's stayed cracked ever since.*
Yes.

Was there anything that happened back then – that you didn't think was so big – that turned out to be pretty big? This is one of the tougher questions that may or may not be easily answered.
Happened then from 1929–33?

Or 1929–41.
1929–41.

Or even, no, let's go 1919–41. Let's take the whole interwar.
Well, I would say it's the emergence of the Keynesian view of the way the economy operates. You need government for investment, you need to cut back on saving, you need to stimulate consumption by tax policy. I mean the whole Keynesian ... what do I call it ...

Don't call it a Revolution.
No, I don't want to call it ...

Lucas doesn't like that term either.
Um, I want to give it some ...

Bill of goods?
Bill of goods is good for me, yes (*laughter*). Anyhow, that's really the thing that, as we said in the book on trends in income and prices in the US and the UK, Keynes put us on the wrong track.

Right, so that happened back then and you didn't see it necessarily happening?
No.

What are some of the lessons of the Depression that seem to be forgotten

today or have to be continually relearned?
Well, I think one of the lessons was that a central bank should not be involved in correcting the stock market, that ...

"An arbiter of security prices," huh?
Yes, that ...

So then you don't endorse chairman Greenspan saying things like "irrational exuberance?"
No, I think that's why I'm glad he backed off. And to learn what the Federal Reserve Bank of New York did after the 1929 crash was a lesson that, I think, Greenspan learned in 1987 when he announced that the discount window would be wide open, which was the right thing to say and we didn't have any kind of repercussions after the crash and ...

He said it that afternoon.
He said it that afternoon.

He was in a hotel in Dallas.
That's right, I remember that. So that was a lesson I think that you have to learn both ways. Keep your mouth shut about what's going on in the stock market. But if it happens, get in there quick and say we know what to do to contain this thing. I think that there is just no possibility that we would even see a replay of the US money stock declining by 33 percent in a period of four years. I think that really is something that every central bank has learned. Maybe the lesson had to be learned in the opposite direction when they began to inflate and became petrified at the idea that in order to cut the inflation off there would have to be a recession. And the fear of the recession kept the inflation going long after it should have been stopped. So there's a lesson in reverse. You don't let contraction of the money stock go on without halting it. You don't let an expansion of the money stock at a rate above the real growth rate of the economy go on because you are going to be in worse trouble by the time you finally have to take some action in order to curb it.

So, again, we come back to the central theme of A Monetary History, *that money, more than anything else, can be a source of instability if you let it get out of hand.*
If you let it get out of hand, that's right. And if you can produce a stable money supply, chances are you'll have a stable economy. I think that's what's going on right now.

Does the memory of the Depression stay with you or affect your thinking today at all?

Oh, sure! I think about it all the time because I'm reading all this research (*laughter*). How can I not think about it? It isn't a memory in the sense of re-living an experience, but re-living the intellectual understanding of the Depression.

That's fair enough. Was there anything that happened at the time, that made you think we were in real trouble – that this recession was going to become the Depression? Do you have a memory of anything at the time?

Well, I knew of people who had lost money in the Bank of United States. I knew of people who had lost jobs, in a sense of the times are bad. But in a sense of understanding how all of this fits together, no. When I was in college I didn't really understand it, it wasn't even something that we talked about in economics class. I mean we learned micro. And macro? When I got to graduate school we read Hawtrey and Keynes and so on, but not in a way that became part of me later on.

What about Fisher's 1933 Econometrica *debt–deflation paper?*

The debt–deflation paper I was aware of but it didn't really fit into some kind of context. But of course it's gotten a big replay in recent years with the work of all these people trying to see whether deflation was anticipated or unanticipated.

Cecchetti, Hamilton, and Nelson.

That's right and whether it's debt deflation that explains the transmission or whether it's real ex ante interest rates because the Depression was anticipated.

Where do you come down in that literature? Do you think that debt deflation holds any water?

First of all, I'm not impressed with Fisher's contribution as an intellectual contribution. I think he was just explaining his own life (*laughter*). I mean here's this guy who's a million dollars in debt to his sister-in-law because he had played the stock market and had expected the stock market ... I don't blame him for expecting that the stock market would just continue in the direction in which it had been moving because he didn't really know what the Federal Reserve was going to do. But then when he got stuck with this enormous debt that he couldn't repay his sister-in-law, I think this seemed to him the explanation of why the Depression had happened.

What was effective in ending the Great Depression?

I think when the banks were closed and Roosevelt started devaluing the dollar. I think there is no question that Roosevelt had a very tonic effect on the

American public. People really believed he was going to fix this economy. And I think that kind of belief was infectious in a way that didn't really translate into jobs and income. Not certainly in the first year of his Presidency. The actions that he took made people feel "He's really trying to do something," they were just paralyzed before and wouldn't do anything. Opening the banks I think, even though lots of banks were no longer there, I think all these positive sorts of steps, whether they had any kind of ultimate importance, certainly. Talk about changing the psychology of the country. And the readiness to believe that a great man can be your savior, that played a role.

So then do you see that the New Deal had any impact at all?
Well, the New Deal impact, I think, was negative in many respects. We know that the cartels, the price fixing, all these things were going to harm the economy, but the ...

Psychology?
Psychology was very important and once prices began to rise, once relief began to be extended, people began to be hopeful, began to buy. As I say, there wasn't much of a recovery in that first year, but ...

What ultimately got us out of the total malaise though? What got us back on a pre-1929 secular trend?
Well, it's clear that the money supply had started growing even though it was 1936 before output was at the same level as in 1929. It was the contraction from 1936 to 1937 that absolutely devastated people.

Here we go again!
That's right, for that period Roosevelt lost his magic. People said what kind of a magician is he? It could have pushed us right back down again.

Were we in a liquidity trap from 1934 on, with the interest rate down along its zero floor?
Well, certainly the real rate was down to the floor and nobody's ever been able to show that there was a liquidity trap. But, that was an idea that emerged throughout without anyone really having any belief that it was something that we could expect to see, but Keynes's followers act as if this was the ultimate explanation of why there was a Great Depression.

But isn't it hard for the interest rate transmission mechanism to work if the nominal rate is down around zero?
Well, the interest rate transmission mechanism can work even if you are just increasing your money supply. That's what the Japanese did when they had

interest rates at ½ percent but really started gunning the money supply. That's what's finally got them to move out of this prolonged ...

It made loanable funds more available and ...
Sure it did. Yes.

OK – so then you can do that even if you're in a liquidity trap.
Absolutely.

Is Keynes dead?
Well, you know that Solow is never going to lose his belief in Keynes, and I don't know where Samuelson comes out at this stage. I'm sure that he gives some role to money, but I don't think he ever abandoned Keynes. I think Keynes would have abandoned Keynesianism.

Do you see any parallels between the recession of 1921 and the Great Depression? That is, do you think the policy makers saw the Depression as a repeat of that deflation and we're just going to deflate again, like we did in 1921? So, why should we attempt to fight it vigorously? Do you think that holds any water?
What they couldn't understand was why that very sharp deflation was turned around and the economy seemed to be able to grow again. Whereas that didn't happen after 1929. And of course, there was a very sharp contraction of the money stock, but the explanation for the fall in prices and in wages in the earlier recession was never matched after 1929. Now after 1929, they thought the experience of 1920–21 taught them that you should not let wages decline. If you let wages decline you would kill purchasing power, therefore wages, nominal wages should be maintained. That's why the business community accepted that view. They saw the way their sales had declined in 1920–22 and they attributed it to the fact wages were low. I mean this was $4–$5 a day, because if workers didn't have enough compensation, how could they buy your product? This was a view that I think was very much uppermost in the minds of not only Hoover but businessmen. And in 1929–31, what you can't understand is why they just stuck to it so long when they saw that their sales were absolutely crashing, despite the fact that they were trying to maintain wages.

And even have rising real wages after 1933.
Yes, it is a big mystery.

Are there any particular trends or problems in our country or economy that you find disturbing today?

Well, I am critical of Mr Greenspan for leaping to bail out Mexico. Why he wanted to be involved in such a political decision, I don't know. The fact that they warehouse foreign exchange for the exchange stabilization fund. In January 1995 Greenspan got the Fed to expand the warehouse capability of the Fed to $20 billion because at that point it looked as if the exchange stabilization fund was going to make a loan of $20 billion to Mexico. In the end, Congress wouldn't approve and they created this $50 billion package. I don't know how much of it Mexico actually got, but I don't know why the Federal Reserve should be involved in such a political bailout. In the end, of course, it was the exchange stabilization fund more than the Fed that extended medium-term loans to Mexico and the Fed and the exchange stabilization gave short-term loans. I disapprove. I think the Fed should not be involved in bailing out foreign countries. This is not an above board way. If the Fed is prohibited from making direct loans to the Treasury it has no business making loans to the Treasury in order to be able to bail out a foreign country. I consider this a disturbing element in our economic life. I have been very critical of the Fed for extending discount window assistance to banks on the verge of failure from 1988 to 1991 until the law was changed limiting the amount of loans the Fed could make to banks that are in dire condition. The Fed is limited now, but who knows what it might do because it gets worried that the banking system is failing. "There will be global ...," I mean it's this kind of scare scenario that I think the Fed can be prone to. "The whole world is going to collapse if you don't save Mexico, if you don't save this institution ..."

So they should just take these banks over and close them down?
Close them down, if you can't find someone to merge with them, shut them. Don't tolerate it.

Also, the fact that we have made no dent at all in the thousands of programs that the federal government runs despite all the talk about trimming government, despite all the talk about balancing the budget, all this ...

Ah, it's hocus pocus.
Yes, hocus pocus is right.

Does the distribution of income bother you?
I don't know what we can do about the distribution of income. I really do believe that people are paid their marginal product. I mean improve education? Of course. But Mr Reich's idea of giving people whom he doesn't consider to be paid fairly some kind of handout is not my way of wanting to run the economy.

Why not $100 an hour?
That's right. They should be allowed a fair wage, that's the talk.

A living wage.
A living wage.

Does that mean to live on Park Avenue? What does that mean? Define that. The other thing that bothers me is this recent research by Card and Kruger (1995) and Neumark and Wascher (1995). Robert Barro wrote about it in the editorial page of The Wall Street Journal *where it shows that if you raise the minimum wage you get higher attaining high school students quitting and supplanting just the people you're trying to help. But I don't hear that talked about in Washington. I mean they supplant the lowest skilled people, by quitting high school.*
My son told me a story of a book that Stephan Thernstrom (*1973*), the guy who had just written a book with his wife about race relations, wrote a book about Newberry Port, Massachussetts, where people in straitened circumstances, living Spartan lives, save money in order to become property owners and build their wealth. And it seems to me that's the only way to do it.

Are there any trends in economic research or schools of thought that bother you?
I am bothered by fancy econometrics which isn't backed up by an effort to see whether the statistics you've created are matched in the real economy. I'm thinking especially of the econometrics that generate demand shocks and supply shocks. And the people who do this kind of research tell you that there were demand shocks in the Great Depression from 1929 to 1931 and then there were supply shocks. And when you say "Well can you tell me what were the demand shocks and what were the supply shocks," oh, they don't know! All they know is that this technique shows results. And I say "I'm not convinced." Unless you can identify what it is that the statistics give you reason to believe are shocks, I'm not interested. The numbers don't tell me anything. And it's this kind of arid econometrics that just leaves me cold. But so many of them do just that, and they're happy. I mean, they've got a result. And it seems to them a significant result, to me it's nothing, it's numbers. And somebody else will come along and say your technique is deficient or my technique is better and so forth.

And on it goes. Radical empiricism can even go into economics too.
Yes, right.

Other than money are there any other theories of the Depression that you find

contribute satisfactorily in explaining it? We talked about a lot of these.
I sure don't believe that the real business cycle explains the Depression.

What's your angle on current European unemployment?
Well, it's clear that the incentive to remain unemployed is very substantial.
And until they do something about the transfer payments they make to the
unemployed, and until they reduce the burdens on employers of employing
workers, there will still be high unemployment rates, high costs of hiring
somebody and high costs for letting somebody go.

So what we would wind up with is that nobody will hire a permanent worker.
No.

*It's rather like the 51st employee here in the US. Hire that marginal worker
and you get a whole new set of rules. It seems to me that in Europe their
economies are replete with those labor costs and those incentives for, what
was the old British term for it, vagrancy? That's what they called the
unemployed before that word "unemployment" came around. So it's really a
pretty simple answer then isn't it?*
That's right! You don't have to be an economic giant in order to understand
it. And the thing is, they understand it too, but they want it that way.

*What are your views on our capitalist system? Do you think as Solow said,
"capitalism still has to keep proving that it can be economically efficient
without being destructive of reasonable equality?" What is the biggest threat
to capitalism and from capitalism?*
Well, the biggest threat to capitalism is running an economy the way the
Europeans do. And if eventually there are unemployed who rebel, that will be
the downfall of that kind of society. At the present time, they will riot in
France if any attempt is made to reduce a benefit. This is an entitlement that
you cannot touch and governments are fearful and won't. But if a whole
generation of school leavers never has any kind of gainful employment, I don't
believe people will be willing to just continue in that condition. And I think at
some point the government may well find a backlash from the people who
have never had a job and have had the dole and keep on having the dole and
think this is no kind of life. But who knows when that kind of uprising might
actually happen? I think that's a big danger. I think if you have an economy
where people can look forward to employment and to improving their status,
capitalism is in good shape. And the fact that we have had an economy in
which there are continual technological improvements in which nobody wants
a 1950 refrigerator they're very happy with the current model, nobody wants
a 1950 car, they're very happy with the current model, tells you something

about the quality of life that people value. This is what capitalism gives us.

Is there a threat from capitalism?
If you don't understand what the system is about you might think it's a threat. I think you would have to educate our ... you can't educate people who already have mistaken views about capitalism, those who are imbued with socialism. But I think an effort should be made to imbue the youth of our country with an understanding of what it is that this system provides.

What role do you see for fiscal policy? I want to say back then during the Depression, but it seems to me that the E. Cary Brown paper just basically erased that completely. But I want to know about now. I've got this idea. It's not new and it's not novel, but fiscal policy belongs in the realm of economic growth, not in the realm of stabilization. What can we do to increase the long-run growth rate with tax reform and changing the tax codes, and encouraging indexing capital gains? Do you agree with that, it belongs in economic growth and not stabilization?
Absolutely. And we know that using fiscal policy for stabilization is a bust. It hasn't worked and it can't work.

Do you have any comment on monetary policy today? Is price stability the thing to focus on and like Ed Koch said, "How are we doing?"
Well, for the time being, Mr Greenspan seems to be doing very well and as I indicated before, I think maybe a stable money supply is the trick that will give you a stable economy. So he's got low unemployment, low inflation, we've got real growth at a very respectable level. But you know that nothing is forever, and one mistake can undo all this and Mr Greenspan will cease being a hero. For the time being he's a hero.

But isn't price stability the key?
Yes, price stability for my money is the key.

At long last now, we finally focus on it.
I think price stability is important for financial stability and I think it is important for growth. So, if we can get that settled, I think it will be an enormous improvement.

I was born in 1960. Would it not be fair to say that this is the first anticipatory Fed that we've had rather than reactionary Fed in my lifetime?
Yes.

Wouldn't you say that's true? I mean if you wait for inflation to show up in a

CPI, it's too late.
Yes, and Greenspan knows that.

And so for the first time in my lifetime we've had somebody that's actually executing it the right way.
The only thing that bothers me about Greenspan's presentation ... I don't believe that you can detect inflation by looking at real growth. I think you have to look at what is nominal demand. And if nominal demand is moderate and doesn't exceed what you expect the inflation rate to be plus what real growth can be, that explains why you have moderate inflation. But to say he has to see whether the employment rate is acceptable or whether growth has gone beyond 2.5 percent. Why doesn't he talk about nominal demand?

He says he looks at everything nowadays, but let's go back to that because there's something that intrigues me right now and I can't put my finger on it because he won't put his finger on it. He seems to be hinting in his speeches and in the paper that there's a breakdown in our historical relationships that the model that we have won't explain inflation and unemployment. They don't seem to be working anymore. Are you hearing that from him?
I really haven't paid that much attention. I haven't even read the Humphrey–Hawkins testimony. But when I hear "the old principles are breaking down" I think of Arthur Burns. Where "the old economic principles no longer work" which was nonsense.

When did he say that?
When, I think he was giving Humphrey–Hawkins testimony.

So that was in 1973 or so?
That's right. So I don't think any principles are breaking down. I think he should look at the thing that really matters which is how much demand is he creating by what he's doing at the Fed. And if that is not excessive, he will have the kind of economy that we have been having. But that makes me uncomfortable talking about how he's scrutinizing real growth to see whether there's inflation on the horizon.

You'd rather just worry about the price level then.
Yes, worry about the price level. So far he is on the right track. Let's hope he doesn't detrain at some point.

We're on the last question. Everybody always wants to know, could it happen again?
Unless we repeat the mistakes, and I cannot see that anybody that has any

understanding of the past would entertain the thought of making it happen again. You would have to make it happen again. It won't happen again by itself.

That's it. Thanks so much Professor.

James Tobin

When drawing up the list of the most influential economists of the twentieth century, James Tobin would be at the top. His many contributions on the economics of financial markets, the behavior of money demand, portfolio choice theory, and the transmission mechanism of monetary policy among many others, led to his being awarded the Nobel Prize in Economics in 1981. Moreover, Tobin came of age as a graduate student just at the time of the arrival of *The General Theory* and remains a staunch defender of Keynesian policies. He was also involved in a very long-standing debate with Milton Friedman regarding the relative efficacy of monetary versus fiscal policy.

Tobin has spent most of his career at Yale University, but did serve for 20 months on President Kennedy's Council of Economic Advisors together with Arthur Okun, Robert Solow, and Kenneth Arrow. Having written my dissertation on tax-adjusted Tobin's q, I was familiar with a great deal of the work Professor Tobin had published. I anxiously anticipated our meeting. We spoke at his home in New Haven, Connecticut on December 30, 1997.

Will you give us some brief biographical information about when and where you were born, and what you were doing during the Great Depression?
I was born in Champaign, Illinois in 1918. My father was a journalist and he was working as the publicity director for the University of Illinois athletic association. So I was a fan of the Fighting Illini and in those days with Bob Zuppke and Red Grange they were doing all right. I got to go to games with my father, all kinds of intercollegiate athletic contests. My mother was a social worker. She had grown up in Wisconsin and got a job in Champaign, met my father and after they were married she suspended her career. But she came back to it in 1932 when the state of Illinois decided that they would have to do something about the problem of all the unemployed and poor people, and people who had not been poor, but were getting that way.

Were those counties primarily Republican controlled back then?
Yes, almost all counties south of Cook county were Republican. And the welfare mechanism was in the hands of the county Board of Supervisors. Herbert Hoover would not set up any federal agencies on his principle that it was a matter of state responsibility. So there was not federal money until Roosevelt. They ran out of social workers for the state agency and so she was

called back to take over the management of Family Welfare. She took it over for six weeks and stayed in the job for 25 years. I got a lot of exposure, at least second hand, to the problems of people in the depths of the Depression in 1932, 1933, and 1934. Of course, at home we talked about it a lot.

I went to the University of Illinois high school. The School of Education ran that school as a place for training teachers, college students who were going to be teachers, so this school was a very good school because teachers were teaching both us and college students. It was not a very big school and it only cost $25 per term. But most did not take advantage of that opportunity. Of course, there were a lot of faculty children in the school. There were also others who came from villages around Champaign county and elsewhere in the state.

I remember when I was a sophomore in the election year of 1932 one of the teachers had a straw vote of the election in our class. There were 35 students – 33 voted for Hoover, I voted for Roosevelt and one girl from a faculty family voted for Norman Thomas. That is the way it was in down-state Illinois even among the faculty at the University of Illinois. So I certainly got into economics indirectly because of the Depression, I was so appalled by it. We personally were not in bad shape. My father was still employed by the university and my mother had a job, one that did not pay very much. Nevertheless, she was employed. So we did not have any problems except my father had inherited his parents' house in Danville, Illinois. The house was now in the downtown business district and my father, in an uncharacteristic entrepreneurial move, got talked into constructing an office building on that property. I guess it started in 1929. By the time it was built there was not demand for office or store space. He lost his shirt and most of his inheritance money in that investment. But in reality we were doing relatively well.

Have you not said in the past that when you looked at the Depression, you did not understand why you could not have your cake and eat it too? Is that what spurred you into economics?
Well, I guess I did not understand why people could work and produce things and earn money before and could not do it now, in those times.

And nobody could give you a satisfactory answer could they?
No, there were not any answers around. I did not get an answer satisfactory to me. I started off thinking I was going to be a lawyer, and always thought I was going to the University of Illinois until August of 1933. That's when they finally got around to informing me that I'd won admission to Harvard. When I first applied to Harvard, I did not even know where it was. It was in Cambridge or New Haven and I did not know which. At any rate, that was my father's alertness as he read about the availability of new scholarships tailored

for Midwest students. I was lucky enough to get one. I did not know really what economics was as a subject. Economic matters in American history courses did not contain any analytical economics. I do remember the controversy about the Smoot–Hawley tariff. That was a Republican move and not a good idea. When I went to Harvard, economics was thought to be a subject you did not take until you were a sophomore. So now we're into the New Deal. You were asking me about personal experiences during the Great Depression, so maybe we'll go back a bit.

Asking about the New Deal is one of my questions.
I'll go back a bit and tell you a little more about that. My grandfather, my mother's father, was a leading citizen of a little town of 5,000. It was about 30 miles from Milwaukee and 90 miles from Chicago. Those distances seemed long for most people in those days. It was a beautiful place with many lakes and was a desirable place for well-off people from Milwaukee and Chicago to put summer homes. My grandfather was President of The Bank of Oconomowoc, a bank that his father had been founder of. He also had been mayor. I stayed a lot with my grandparents before high school. His bank went bust, and he was very susceptible to farm real estate investments both with his own money and the bank's money.

He never borrowed another nickel after that did he?
He did not have another nickel after that. The bank went under and he was kicked out as President in 1928 or so. Actually there already was an agricultural slump going on. He was putting substantial amounts of money in farming in the Dakotas. He had a tragic end to his life because he lost their home and everything else. My grandmother stayed with our family a lot, so they did not live much together after they lost their money. She would go out to Billings, Montana or North Dakota where he was trying to get back in the black. But finally that never worked, he could not do it anymore, and one of his sons had to go out and rescue him. They lived in a little cottage for a number of years in northwest Wisconsin. So that was kind of a family tragedy related to the Great Depression.

Paul Samuelson has said that his value judgment ideology has not changed since he was 25. Did the Great Depression have a role in changing your value judgment ideology?
Well, my parents had a big role in that. The Great Depression was just part of the background of which we had applications of value judgments, namely the bad economic and social status of people in our town and in the country was on our mind. Yes, so surely the Great Depression did, I think, for anybody who grew up in those days, shape the way you look at society. The thing about

Hoover was that he seemed to be a cold-blooded fish, not really interested in human problems, even though he had a history of having done good works at the end of World War I. I remember my mother voted for him in 1928 because he appealed to her social work interest. My father voted for Al Smith, of course. That was the only time that they disagreed.

As you look back on this did it not begin to mold you professionally on how you think, would that be fair to say?
I didn't really know what the scholarly or intellectual subject of economics was. I did not have any idea about that. I remember during the campaign of 1932 I was 14 years old and just fascinated by the political campaigning and felt strongly about it. We had a radio, and it was wonderful. The radio gave the political connections the way they were; they were not being staged for the radio audiences. They were just the way they had been when there was not radio. And you just had the good fortune to listen to the connection just the way it was happening. I was a real-time spectator, a listener, just the way it would have been with no microphones. It was fascinating. Every word of every moment of a campaign. One thing I remember is I listened to Ogden Mills, who was Secretary of the Treasury under Hoover, give this scary speech. I heard on the radio during the campaign how Hoover, his President, his boss, has saved us from the most awful event. That event was that we were within, I don't know how many, 12 weeks or something, of having to go off the gold standard.

Horror of horrors!
He made it sound awful scary. It did not impress me.

Victor Zarnowitz has said that the post-war fluctuations have moderated because of profound structural, institutional, and policy changes. What role did the Great Depression play in bringing these changes about?
It brought about a big political change in the United States, as well as in the United Kingdom and other European countries. It was a political revolution not to revert to the unstable high unemployment that preceded World War II. Even politicians who did not understand any economics, what they did understand is that we must not ever let that happen again.

Were they fearful that it might as soon as World War II was concluded?
Yes, a lot of people thought that was what was going to happen as soon as the War concluded, we would have reversion to the 1930s.

Let me follow up. Did the Great Depression lay the foundation for the application of post-war demand management policies?

Yes, I think it did. The Employment Act of 1946 was a symbol of that.

Did you and the people you were associated with have the feeling that there was no going back to the old orthodoxy that existed prior to the depths of the Great Depression?
Well, certainly my fellow students and graduate students at Harvard were of that opinion, and took that for granted so to speak. But most of the teachers we had in graduate school and undergraduate school also were not changing. It was fun to be the young rebels against the old orthodoxy.

Did you have good ideas back then about how the post-war economy would shape up, or was this one more step into unknown territory?
Well, I think we did not know quite where we were going, partly because we were not sure about the economy. But also because we were not sure the politicians were going to use the economic knowledge that we thought we had. I was not one who thought we were going to slip back so fast to pre-war status. Part of that had to do with the consumption function, research that I myself did. So a lot of the more extravagant pessimistic fears about the post-war period were based on extrapolation of the apparent consumption–income relation between the two Wars. It became apparent quite early I think. Paul Samuelson appreciated this fairly early and Albert Hart probably too, that the consumption–income scatter diagram was not the function that was going to rule the economy after the War. Alvin Hansen, people thought that he was the most pessimistic person about the post-war economy, but he also appreciated that things were not on that kind of empirical track.

Do you think monocausal explanations of the Great Depression get very far?
Well, probably not. My own view is there certainly was a fantastically big error made by the Federal Reserve. The failure to increase the supply of high-powered money to offset the drain of reserves from banks to currency holdings, those are terrible errors. A good bit of the American economics profession, some big names, put out a petition in those days opposing any kind of public works, any kind of extraordinary open market operations to remedy the shortage of bank reserves. This is really a terrible disaster in the profession. It was said Fisher believed in the substance of the petition, but he did not go along with that. He was not for public works but he was for pumping up the supply of bank reserves. But that all has to do with what happened in 1931 and thereafter. It seems to me that up to most of 1930 we were still in a business cycle that was similar to previous business cycles and the stock market crash did not result in the Great Depression. Actually most of the value of stocks in October 1929 was recovered in 1930. The expectations of people were still rather resilient in 1930. It is a business cycle

like what we experienced in the 1920s a couple of times, so it is not a great big disaster. When you go on into 1931 and the British devaluation, I think that expectations changed in a very pessimistic direction. People began to think that this is not something temporary, that is going to reverse itself the way previous downturns did. This is the way it is going to be. As soon as people thought they could not make economic decisions on the basis of things getting better, but they make economic decisions based on things continuing the way they are and worse, then it is a whole new ball game.

That was going to be one of my questions. What turned a recession into the Great Depression, and that's your answer, a change in expectations?
Expectations change and the British devaluation led to the type of reaction that was just mentioned. And it leads to the Federal Reserve being unwilling, because of its worry about gold, to do what they would do now for sure if we were faced with that kind of situation. I don't think there is a cut and dried answer to the question. I am a great admirer of Alvin Hansen. I don't think that we were the beneficiaries of more observation than he had. But I don't think that we were doomed to have a depression because of "the ended frontier."

You don't think it was an overinvestment type of result?
No.

Or an over-consumption type of model?
No. I think that both monetary and nonmonetary/expectational theories are reasons for what happened.

I agree, let me follow up.
One thing I think is the change in the leadership of the Federal Reserve was an unfortunate accident of the history of that disaster.

So you agree with Friedman and Schwartz then?
On that point, yes.

Do you agree with Samuelson that the Friedman and Schwartz story is "unfair hindsight?" The supply of high-powered money never did fall during the Great Depression and it is unreasonable to expect the Federal Reserve to do something that had no historical precedent. When I talked to Samuelson he said he sticks to that. Is it unfair hindsight? Do you buy that?
Well, I don't think so, because I think these were economists who realized that there was a draining of money into currency, public currencies, away from bank reserves. There is no good if a dollar of high-powered money has only

the potential of a dollar of low-powered money if it is in currency. It has a lot more potential if it is in reserves. Taken away as it was, banks had problems due to bank runs. That was not something unclear back then, at least not to Fisher.

I was going to ask you what explanations you find do the best job accounting for the Great Depression, as far as the depths to which the economy plunged and you have done that. Do you have an angle on what caused the initial decrease?
Well, there is nothing particularly unusual about having a recession that was similar to the ones we had earlier in the 1920s. The technicality of the relationship of the money market to the stock market in the 1920s was much different than the way the money market is now. We have a Treasury bills market and a federal funds market. Back then the money market was brokerage loans and banks were making those, so the Federal Reserve was concerned about financing brokerage loans by the discount window. They had this dilemma of raising interest rates. If they tightened up because of speculation, monetary measures would also increase ordinary commercial loans to finance farmers in Iowa. Perhaps they tightened too much at that point. The question occurs all the time. Should the Federal Reserve do something to restrain an asset market boom?

Do you think the Fed should be an arbiter of security prices?
No, I don't think they should be, for the reasons that you and I have just been talking about.

Ben Bernanke has said that modern business cycle models need to explain both the post-World War II and the interwar eras, and that we really should not have two set of models to explain both. What is your reaction to that? Do you think that is an unfair standard?
Having theories is one thing. Having different shocks working through some mechanism is another. I could think there are lots of ways a post-World War II structural model would be different from an interwar model with the role of government in the economy and the size of government built-in stabilizers as examples. A lot of things are quite different in that respect. The monetary system is different and standards are different. No doubt there are some behavioral relationships that should be in the same ball park in the two periods. But I don't think we can repeat a single model for both periods. Certainly not an econometric model. That's asking a lot of empirical economics.

What parallels do you see between the recession of 1921 and the Great

Depression? Do you think policy makers at the time figured the Great Depression would be a repeat of those earlier events and thus did not vigorously attempt to fight the Great Depression?

Yes, I think that is consistent with what I've said earlier, by allowing the business cycle fluctuation to gravitate into something of a different nature, and a much more dangerous nature.

Did the Great Depression change the psychology of the country?

Well, yes. It certainly made lots of people who lived through it much more cautious about their economic behavior. Individuals as well as companies were more risk averse.

How about their view of the role of government?

Well, we already talked about the idea that government has a responsibility to make the economy work. That was a new idea. Hoover did not think that was a responsibility of the federal government. And I think that happened all over the world. Many things that were regarded as matters outside the possibility or desirability of control by government actions in the advanced, capitalist, democratic world are now regarded as government responsibilities. It became politically easy once we had a different understanding of what we should and could do about macroeconomic prosperity. Throughout the nineteenth century and the early part of the twentieth century many things were done without any worry about unemployment or business cycles.

Do you think one of Keynes's objectives was to save capitalism or to save it from itself?

Well, Keynes did not find much wrong with the system as it stood. In a famous passage he says that there is nothing particularly wrong with the way that market capitalism allocates the resources that it does employ. The problem is it does not employ them all.

What ended the Great Depression?

Well, the Great Depression was on the way to being ended by the New Deal in the earlier thirties. A good part of that was done by restoring confidence, to use the word, and by Roosevelt being able to do that by getting the banks open. Then the devaluation of the dollar was a very important step in getting recovery going. So things were going quite well up until the interruption of the recession of 1937–38. That was a real shock to Roosevelt and his people. They had every reason to believe that we were going to go back to 1932 or something like that. Then Roosevelt did take the wraps off of Keynesian policy at that time and so things were doing better in the recovery from that setback. Of course then preparation for the War began and the aid to the allies.

So we had Keynesian fiscal policy without any of the restraints that were put upon it during peacetime. But eventually the War is what got us out of it.

What impact did the New Deal have on you and your thinking?
I was a high school kid and very pro-Roosevelt and not terribly discriminating among the different aspects of the New Deal. I tended to go along with almost everything they were doing when I was in high school. When I got to college I began to realize that the NRA and the AAA were very bad ideas and completely unnecessary for the main purpose and a digression from the kind of policies one would like. I thought both because of my family's interests and concerns and my own that the work relief programs like the WPA, those were the best part of the New Deal. The financial reforms were also a real contribution for the long run. Roosevelt was lucky to get out from under the NRA.

What are some of the lessons of the Great Depression that seem to have been forgotten today or need to be continually relearned?
I was thinking the other day that with all the emphasis on the macroeconomics of the last 10, 15, 20 years, on expectations, rational or not, the main emphasis in the literature is on price expectations. The main emphasis in Keynes is the emphasis on demand quantities, not prices. When he talks about long-run expectations they are long-run expectations about where the demand curve has shifted or likely to be relative to where it is now, not prices alone. I find it difficult to understand the concentration on price expectations only being consistent with a complete pure competition market-clearing model. And yet these people are always talking about how they are looking for theories that use monopolistic competition and imperfect competition. But if that is the case they should be like me, interested in expectations of quantities as well as, or maybe more than, expectations of prices. The biggest thing then that I think is that instantaneous market clearing, continuous equilibrium in that sense, supply equals demand and prices move all the time to adapt to whatever shifts in the curves occur, that is not a good way of going about macroeconomics in my opinion.

Does the memory of the Depression stay with you at all?
Well we've mentioned that and I do think about it. Old men and women think a lot about their lives at this stage of life. I had a very happy time as a kid and as a college student. Even when the world was collapsing around me I had a good time and have fond memories of all that. When I graduated from Harvard, I went to Europe that summer with four of my friends. We went on a bicycle trip around France, we went on an ocean liner and had a good time. We went to Paris and bicycled around Normandy and Brittany. But in August

the world began to fall apart as we observed. Our French contemporaries were being called up and we happened to end up in Geneva and were having a tour of the League of Nations building while Hitler was invading Poland. We had to scurry back home without having any reservations to get home. We planned to stay, each of us in a different way, for a whole year. The most depressing piece of news that we encountered that summer was the pact between the Soviet Union and Germany. So that really made us think that the world was coming to an end.

Robert Lucas has said that the Friedman–Phelps rational expectations school just had plain dumb luck that the 1970s came along when it did because "most samples can't tell you which of the stories about the Phillips curve is the best one." What is your reaction to that?
Most of the things that Lucas and others say about the 1970s I think are misguided because they have conveniently forgotten about the oil shocks. So they interpret everything that happened in the 1970s as having been the result of excessive monetary expansion and so on. The fact that there were big supply shocks is not part of their model.

Are there any alternatives to capitalism?
It doesn't look like it. I was interested to a considerable degree when I was in college in market socialism, the works of Abba Lerner and others. I thought that maybe there is an alternative in the democratic market socialist organization of the economy. It hasn't been tried. I don't think communism was a good try at market socialism as it was practiced. But socialism itself is probably not a viable way to go.

Could it happen again? Could we have another Great Depression?
Well, it is hard to believe that any government of a Western-style democracy and capitalist could be as dumb as to let it happen again. I don't think that this country would. But seeing what is going on in Europe and Japan shakes my confidence in what I just said because Japan right now has succeeded in having a depression. It would look a lot worse if they didn't have disguised unemployment. The unemployment rate doesn't look so high by our measures but that is just a different system of unemployment compensation. Companies keep guys on the job and pay them even if they don't need them.

Like a labor hoarding type of idea?
Yes, it is a different kind of contract. They have succeeded in making the liquidity trap, which we had thought was a curiosity from antiquity, into a current reality. In fact they are perhaps a demonstration of Bernanke's point that you could have nonmonetary/financial contributions to depression and

have that at the same time that you have a liquidity trap. The Japanese have interest rates down virtually to zero on government notes and bonds, I think it is 1.5 percent, but at the same time the banks are so scared of risk that they don't lend to anybody at these low rates. So, from the point of view of risky-type borrowers, the risk premium has become bigger. Monetary policy is completely impotent in Japan as Keynes said it might become in a depression situation and Japan will not take any of the fiscal measures that we learned.

Didn't they just propose cutting taxes last week?
Sixteen billion dollars or something like that.

That's not enough.
It's not enough and only for a year.

Well, for heaven's sake, we know enough to know that is not the way you go about it.
Of course we do.

I heard you mention Europe as well, are you concerned about Europe?
I sure am because of Europe having double-digit unemployment all the time.

That was one of the questions that I wanted to ask you. Samuelson has said that "stagflation is an intrinsic characteristic of the mixed economy and a humane welfare state that has replaced ruthless capitalism." Is stagflation like what is in Europe now too high a price to pay for that welfare state?
First of all, I don't believe that the amount of unemployment they have in Europe is the fault of the welfare state. I believe a lot of that unemployment is not structural in its origins. It may have become structural by not doing anything about it. I think there is a large aggregate demand part of that European unemployment. It is too much to think if you look at France or Germany, where the unemployment rate has risen for quite a number of years now, at each point we were told that is the full employment unemployment rate now, that is the NAIRU or the natural rate. Why is the natural rate always increasing? It is not because the welfare state stuff is becoming worse. In fact, they have reduced the benefits of the welfare state. I don't subscribe to the belief that all of this unemployment is the result of the welfare state.

What is your angle on it then?
It is just bad macro policy.

They are too restrictive?
Yes, they are too restrictive, all the time. They are too persuaded that

unemployment is not a problem, that all they have to do is stabilize prices and the market will get to the right place, given whatever institutions they have.

Is price stability the right focus for current Federal Reserve behavior?
Not by itself, no. It is a question of whether you want price stability or inflation stability. That is one thing. But then the other question, the bigger question, is whether you are aiming solely at one or the other of those things rather than worrying about unemployment and the level of GDP and so on. Our central bank is following a pragmatic balanced policy, I think, and does quite well with it. I think the great mistake is to say price stability means that if you have a supply shock that raises the price level you have to get rid of that bulge in the price level. Whereas a more reasonable policy would say, well, a supply shock happened and that's too bad and the price level is higher. What we want to do is keep the inflation rate stable in combination with having a good, strong rate of growth.

Are they getting lucky then currently with a stable inflation rate and some of the lowest unemployment we have had for the last 30 years?
We are getting lucky and the labor market, in terms of unemployment rates and vacancy rates and other measures of labor market tightness, it looks like the labor market of the 1950s and 1960s.

Do you think there has been a shift in paradigm that Alan Greenspan talks about that has possibly made price stability and full employment now compatible?
What made them not compatible? I think what made them not compatible were supply shocks and some things did happen where we didn't have supply shocks like that anymore. We are lucky in that respect that they went the other way. I think the fact that union strength has declined a lot is an aspect of that situation. I think employers have become tougher in the US under the thrust of competition.

And the penetration of international trade too?
It is not just international competition. After all that is just a small percentage of GDP. It is domestic competition also. I don't think that what has happened means that a cruel anti-welfare state is necessary to have prosperity.

So then you don't see this low unemployment rate resulting from price stability necessarily?
I don't. In some ways it results from the increased competition in both the labor and product markets that also results in price stability or low inflation.

Is it not the case that money stock targeting is dead now once and for all?
Absolutely, yes.

Are you bothered by the trend in the distribution of income?
Oh yes, and wealth. Wealth is worse.

Are income distribution and poverty the same topic or can they rightly be viewed separately?
They are not the same topic by definition but they are certainly connected a lot. When we are talking about the trouble with the distribution of income, the one thing we should be considerably worried about is the plight of people at the low end. But the income distribution, per se, gets us into the question of who's going to pay for redistribution. And for anti-poverty work, who is going to shoulder the tax burden? I still believe in progressive taxes. I'm not begrudging Bill Gates his fortune any more than I begrudge Thomas Edison or any other great inventor making money from their inventions. But that is consistent with having progressive income and wealth taxation. At the same time, I think that one of the big problems we have is anti-tax sentiment in this country. We are in danger of having a tax system that leaves high incomes relatively free of taxation.

Do you think poverty can be better understood with the help of anthropologists and sociologists and other social scientists?
Well, I think they can help.

I guess what I'm driving at is isn't poverty more than just the absence of income?
At any moment of time it surely is. But, the question is what were the backgrounds of the evolution of families and the evolution of the education and socialization of children that produced the poverty? My model would be a model in which there certainly are a variety of things that interact. A bad neighborhood, it is hard to say what's a cause and what's an effect. If you have a bad neighborhood with crime and poor housing and poor education, you can be sure that if you made a model of its evolution over time, it would be a vicious circle in which the schools are no good because the families are not very good. And the families are not very good because of drugs and crime and so on. Growing up in that area will put you into that kind of interaction of various things that are related to each other. People say "The key is this or the key is that." I wouldn't deny that the loss of non-economic factors, if you look at the problems of the inner city of New Haven, sure, they are all mixed up together. You can't say "If we just do the one thing, any one thing, that is going to make it better." That any one thing includes just giving money to

people. In the present circumstances, that is not going to be enough, but it is certainly essential to do in one way or another.

Are there any particular trends in economic research or schools of thought that you find disturbing?
Well, we have covered that. I think that although there are some good ideas and some smart people involved in new classical macroeconomics and in rational expectations and all those things, I think what is disturbing is they have become so much of an orthodoxy and so much a, almost a religion.

An ideology perhaps?
And there is some ideology connected with it. Walras was a great economic theorist and so are Gerard Debreu and Ken Arrow. Their welfare theorems connected with general equilibrium are great intellectual achievements. At the same time, they can be used as supporting an ideology. A presumption that that is the way the world is in fact and so the burden of proof is on somebody to say it is not like that in this way or another. It is not saying that Lucas's contributions are all ideological. That is not true. He is a great theorist. But it is saying that people who take some of the propositions that are connected to that and jump to policy conclusions or value conclusions, they are doing ideology.

That's all I have. Thank you so much Professor.

Wassily Leontief

Perhaps no other economist who was interviewed for this book made their reputation by specializing in one topic to the extent that Wassily Leontief did. He was one of the first economists to critique Keynes's *General Theory* and is also considered the father of input–output analysis. The first attempt at an empirical implementation of input–output analysis began with the publication of his book *The Structure of the US Economy 1919–1939*. He continued to focus his career on developing and refining this analytical tool. Its influence was worldwide and it was used as a device for central economic planning. His work earned him many honors including the French Legion of Honor in 1968, the Presidency of the American Economic Association in 1970, and the Nobel Prize in Economics in 1973, among others.

In beginning the search for the leading economists who lived through the Great Depression, Leontief was first on my list, being born in 1905. The interview took place in September 1997 at his home in New York overlooking Washington Square and New York University, where he spent the latter part of his career. When the interview was over, he had to excuse himself so that he could grab a quick lunch in time to make a 2 p.m. lecture he was giving on input–output analysis at the age of 91. He passed away in February 1999.

Can you give me some biographical information about when and where you were born and what you were doing during the Great Depression?
Sit down.

Yes, sir.
I was born in Russia in 1905 and I went to Germany in 1925. I came to the US in 1931, in the meantime I spent a year in China. I was, for a short time, at the National Bureau of Economic Research (*NBER*) and then Harvard for 44 years.

Weren't you at the NBER for the duration of the 1930s?
No, I was just one year there.

Didn't you write The Structure of the US Economy 1919–1939 *during the 1930s?*
Yes, correct.

What were the people at the NBER saying at the time the Great Depression was happening? Did they understand what was going on?
Mitchell already resigned, so it was kind of in between. I had a very short time there really. I wouldn't say it was very interesting, it was kind of disorganized when Mitchell left. And they didn't have any theoretical ideas. As a matter of fact, I organized a secret theoretical seminar at the NBER. The NBER didn't have much theoretical basis and was very much empirically oriented. As you know Mitchell was not a theorist, he was suspicious of theory.

Did you have any interactions with Mitchell?
No. He invited me but he went away when they hired me. The National Bureau was very boring, terribly boring.

Your Structure of the American Economy, *wasn't that the first search for an empirical representation of a general equilibrium model?*
Yes, exactly.

That's what you had in mind?
Yes. It was just my empirical input–output concept.

What do you think the input–output model would have said about the Great Depression? Can you explain that experience within the context of an input–output model?
I do not think it's particularly good. You see the Great Depression, I think, and its explanation, like a business cycle, is really lags. And lags in a multi-sector economy are complicated but I think the spread of the Great Depression from one sector to another would possibly be somewhat clarified by an input–output structure. Otherwise, I think the business cycle is a typical dynamic phenomenon based on lags essentially.

You mean lags of different markets?
Markets and investment and production. I think the lags between investment and production are very important. Investment is generated by changes in demand. But since everybody invests at the same time there is easily overinvestment. Overinvestment, of course, relatively speaking. I think back at that time people who were accustomed to quantitative mathematical thinking could not help but associate the Great Depression with lags, like the solution to a system of differential equations. This is essentially the fundamental theoretical explanation. And in this case it was lags between investment and production or demand. This is, I think, the driving force.

So in the circles you were in that is what the people were thinking?
I think so, I couldn't say, but it was what I was thinking.

Did the Depression shape your life professionally?
No, because you see, I had permanent academic employment. I don't know, you know more about how the Great Depression affected the university. Not too much as it were, you see.

OK then, let me ask you a different question.
Right.

What propelled you into economics and academic life?
Oh, what propelled me is just interest, how an economy works. My interest was only really scientific not pragmatic. I wanted to see how things work. The explanation of why an economy changes must be based more effectively on the study of the structure of the economy. This was always my central interest and of course, I felt always that supply and demand theory was a shaky thing because empirically you didn't know what supply and demand curves are, or at least the derivation of a shape of the supply and demand curves was very shaky statistically. And this drove me toward general equilibrium analysis.

So the economic cataclysm then didn't lead you to the planning agenda necessarily?
No.

Peaked your interest maybe?
Oh yes, but I had that agenda already. You see, at that time the theory of supply and demand was, I think, the dominant element of theoretical analysis. But you cannot observe the supply curve and demand curve separately. So, I started a little already in Germany trying to see how one can determine the shapes of the supply and demand curves which, of course, is very difficult and practically impossible. This drove me, propelled me to think of general equilibrium. I began to think of a general interdependence, and furthermore I was always interested in the implementation of theoretical ideas of empirical analysis. This, I suppose, drove me to analyze the theoretical issues. At the time we spoke about general interdependence, but there were no empirical data. And my attempt to construct an input–output table was essentially an attempt to provide a basis for implementation of general equilibrium analysis. And since nobody was very interested, I began myself to construct an input–output table, which is not easy. But what helped a little was the War and the government asked the Department of Labor, and it was under Roosevelt, to try to provide some idea of what post-war development would be. And

apparently the Department of Labor didn't know how to do it. So they sent somebody, I have forgotten his name, Hutchinson, to talk to me. He was so in despair, he didn't know what to do. He came to me and said, "Weeeee (*that is, Leontief stretched out the sounding of we to indicate trepidation in Hutchinson's voice*) don't know how to answer this letter," he showed me the letter from Roosevelt. And then my book came out. And so he said "All right, possibly you can do it. Construct an input–output table." But in one year's time it was futile. My response was, "It's not so simple to construct an input–output table."And we opened a division of the Department of Labor at Harvard. I hired not so much economists, but engineers and specialists in the market. And we started it, which was the first attempt to construct an input–output table.

Can you talk to me about the article you wrote critiquing The General Theory *that showed up in* The Quarterly Journal of Economics?
Oh, yes, yes. I never became a Keynesian when all my colleagues became Keynesians. I really always felt that Keynes in spirit was essentially a politician. He developed his theoretical structure in order to justify his political advice.

So you were unconvinced by it then?
I was not convinced, no. I mean, everybody was convinced, but I wasn't.

You just thought it was more political than economic?
Exactly. I think Keynes was extremely intelligent, but he was interested in economic policies. And I always felt you have to understand what the structure of the economic system is in order to give some practical advice.

I'm paraphrasing now, but Robert Lucas says he still doesn't understand what The General Theory *is trying to say.*
Yes, he's right (*laughter*). I tried, and this is why I went to input–output analysis. Given an input–output formulation which is simplified, which is based on certain simplifying assumptions, at least it provided two things: it defined exactly what data you needed and then how to use this data. And my feeling is, theorizing is a device to try and interpret information. But if you don't have good information, what is the result? This was my criticism.

Was there ever pressure on you to be a convert to Keynesianism when you were at Harvard?
Not particularly. Practically all economists there became Keynesians, but there was no pressure because I was kind of an exception.

Let me jump ahead to a question I wanted to ask you.
Please.

Is Keynes dead?
His influence is still strong. He was very intelligent and very persuasive. As a matter of fact, I remember once I sent an article to *Economic Journal* and Keynes was the editor. He refused it.

Did the Soviet Union represent the alternative to capitalism back then? What was your sense of how people viewed the alternatives? Back in the 1930s, did people consider communism to be a viable alternative to capitalism?
No, I don't think so. I suppose Sweezy did, but he was not given an appointment at Harvard because of his radical point of view.

What about the public at large? Did they consider socialism or communism to be real alternatives?
I don't think so. I mean obviously there were political extremes but this was not a viable alternative.

But as far as economists are concerned, they never really gave it a second thought?
So far as I know, no. Now, looking at the literature possibly one can find something, but not mainstream economists.

Can you point to one particular contribution in economics, a book, an article or person that did the most in shaping how you think?
Oh, you see, I studied very thoroughly beginning as a student, the history of economic thought. Particularly I read all the economists, beginning with the seventeenth and eighteenth centuries. And I think Quesnay in particular, because he really already had an idea of general equilibrium. Quesnay, he I think had a really good idea, and he was considered a Physiocrat. Of course, the Physiocrats inherited the eighteenth-century theory and interest in theory and in a sense I think, tried to analyze the economy systematically. And in a sense they were very good. In the nineteenth century you had the English and supply and demand, which really doesn't explain much.

So it was Quesnay?
Yes!

and ...
Physiocrats.

and the Physiocrats that influenced you?
Yes, I think so. Those who really used the type of approach which tried to develop their analysis systematically. I don't say that I necessarily agree with them on everything, but this I think was very important.

Did the Great Depression change the psychology of the country?
It certainly changed the psychology of the country.

How?
I suppose it really prepared emphasizing the role of money and consequently prepared the Keynesian approach.

Do you think that people recognized back then that there was a role for money?
Oh, I think so. The Great Depression, after all, was about the breakdown of monetary markets. So my feeling is, you study the literature more than I do, but I think the role of money was already understood. I mean, I don't say interpreted correctly. But the quantity of money simply could be an intermediate factor in changing total demand. Speaking only in relative terms and prices, it was not really important.

Was there anything that happened back then that made you think we were in real trouble, that the recession was turning into the Depression?
My weakness is that I was interested in explaining how a system works, I never really did serious work on policy. I don't say what should be done, I usually try to see how it works. So from this point of view I don't think so. I don't remember having ever written about it. I certainly did not consider a market economy as an ideal arrangement. I think that the explanation of a pure market economy isn't necessarily completely valid. Many other elements enter into the picture. And I should say that even Marxist criticism of this theory was correct. Of course, I consider Marx to be essentially a classical economist who just got particular aspects being a socialist.

Did you have a faith and belief in the inherent stability of the market system and then the Depression shook that?
Oh no. I think that, of course, I was very interested in the mathematical approach. And usually we used differential equations to specify dynamics. And the notion that the solution to differential equations is a terribly complicated thing and it can go either to the ceiling or underground, I think I realized.

Do you think the Great Depression could happen again?

Possibly we will be able to avoid it, to know that something is wrong and try to do something. I think it is very unlikely that such a thing as the Great Depression could happen again.

Do you think we've learned enough to not make the same mistakes?
Yes.

What are your views on our capitalist system? Is it the best there is or are there better alternatives?
I do not know of any better alternative. But of course, I think that the whole problem of the distribution of income is very serious.

That was my next question. Are you bothered by the distribution of income?
I am bothered by it and the distribution of income is changing but this is understandable because of the role of capital.

As well as human capital too.
Yes, as compared to labor. Still labor income is important, but capital and investment increase with changes in technology and what not. I think already government plays a very great role after all. Government already affects the distribution of income very much.

Over half the federal budget is transfers.
Exactly. Already government plays a very great role. Ultimately, I think that the role of government is likely to increase.

To increase?
Yes. In this country, for example, I think we will introduce health insurance pretty soon.

You think that is going to come?
Oh, I know it.

So then government's role will ...
Increase, I believe that in the longer run the role of government will increase, not go down. Already government controls a large part of the allocation of national income.

Forty percent.
Exactly, you see. In Europe it is even higher.

It is even higher in Europe, you're right.

Now you can call it planning, all right call it planning. Call it what you want. But my feeling is that we cannot simply rely on equilibrium being maintained by growth.

Does the memory of the Depression stay with you? Do you ever think about it anymore?
No. But look here, I think very little anyhow. I'm 91 (*laughter*).

I know, but you are still mentally sharp. I think that just about does it. Thank you very much Professor.

Morris Adelman

Morris Adelman was born in 1917. Although he did not contribute to the literature on the Great Depression, he was a student at the City University of New York during the 1930s. It is his experiences there, a hotbed of radical thought at the time, and his insights regarding the Depression's impact on the post-war world that make him an invaluable addition to the list of economists interviewed. Professor Adelman focused his career on studying the economics of the world oil industry and authored the influential 1995 book *The Genie out of the Bottle.*

Professor Adelman received his Ph.D. from Harvard University in 1948. He was an economist at the Federal Reserve Board of Governors in 1946 and is currently a Professor Emeritus at Massachusetts Institute of Technology. We spoke at his office at The Center for Energy Policy Research in Cambridge, Massachusetts in October 1997.

Would you tell me where you were born and what you were doing during the Depression?
Well, I was born in New York. Both my parents were Jews from the Ukraine. I would have said Russia years ago, not any more. And my mother never had a day's schooling in her life and my father got to about the fourth grade. But they both were voracious readers, as that generation was. I went to public school and I went to the City College of New York, which in those days was a damn good school. But it had a lousy economics department. I found this out taking one course and asking around. I was going to major in economics and I didn't. I majored in history instead. This gave me some difficulties in later years, but it was a good choice at the time because the history department was a very good department, it had standards. And I feel like I got a lot out of it, a sense of history that I never lost. It has always been sort of a biggest thing in my mind.

Has that also helped to drive the paradigm of the work you've done as well?
Oh yes, yes. Because I always found it easiest to look at industries in a historical context. Because they never were today what they had been yesterday. That is one reason why I feel particular gratitude to those professors that I had in economics.

Can you name names?
Well yes, let me backtrack for a minute. I majored in history as I say. And I graduated in 1938. And the economics I knew then was a bit of reading I'd done, nothing really that I'd studied in class. I just read in an undirected sort of way. Then I took some graduate courses, this was in 1940–41 at Brooklyn College, in New York because they had a graduate department. They were inexpensive, and what I wanted were some graduate credits because I wanted to take the high school teaching exam (*both chuckling*). Well ... don't laugh, I never qualified on that because I had a decision to make. Whether I'd study hard for that or I'd study hard for the civil service exam coming up for junior economists. And I chose to study for the junior economist. I got a pretty good grade on that, as I was to find out later. But, you know, you "takes your choice," and I was lucky in taking the choice I did. So the vision I had of economics was one, industry was what attracted me, and two, history and development. I had a great admiration, which I retain to this day, for Karl Marx. Not because of his labor theory of value, which I could see and everybody has seen since then, it just isn't any damn good. And the old boy was stubborn and he had his revolutionary vision and he was stuck with it. But as a social analyst, a man who could meld history and economics, he was looking at a particular place at a particular time, he was just masterful.

You have to give him credit for that.
Oh yes. Now, I served in the War, I was a line officer in the navy. You know, when you think of the death and destruction, what was brought by World War II, it's awful to say it was the best thing that ever happened to you. And that unfortunately is so because I was shoved into a job which was the last thing I ever wanted, to be a line officer in the navy. I don't think I was a particularly good one, but I was adequate. I could cope and it was a good thing for me. The second thing was the GI bill and just a prolonged prosperity. In France they call it the *Trente Glorieuses* as the 30 great years after the War. So as I say all the breaks were for me. Starting with ...

*Failing to take the high school test (*laughter*)?*
Yes. I got down to Washington, I did get a job working for the government. And I found it really was my dish, doing economics. And that was interrupted, as I say, by wartime service. But in 1946 I worked a few more months in Washington. There again I was lucky. I worked for the Federal Reserve Board. I had a very good boss, a woman, and women didn't in those days get a fair shake at the Board any more than anywhere else. But at least they were open about it. Women could never get above the job of section chief. And Sue Burr knew this perfectly well and she figured she'd do as well there as she did anywhere else. Well she was just one hell of a good boss. One of these people

who is never in a great rush, always seems to have plenty of time and is on top of everything, and sees everything. She was also a very good economist and had a wonderful sense of English style. And as I have said as a joke that if I had only stuck with her longer I would have made something of myself (*chuckling*). From there I went off to Harvard. I was lucky there too. There are two people to whom I owe the most. The first one is Schumpeter. I was just one student among many. I had read his book just before getting there. And that ...

You mean Capitalism, Socialism and Democracy?
No. Oh I read that yes, but *The Theory of Economic Development* is what I had been looking for. Because he had a theory of markets which embodied the idea of competition as erosion. As always driving all profit rates toward zero. And this promoted, in fact, the eruption of new forms of innovations.

Creative destruction.
Creative destruction. And the more effective the competitive process was, the more it pushed people to doing the only thing they could to escape subsistence wages which is the bare return on investments, and that is doing something else. Now to a man in business, it was all the same. Whether you practiced, as the lawyers would say, tax avoidance or tax evasion, they could avoid subsistence wages by innovating. They could evade them you might say, by getting together to fix prices. One was as good an expedient as the other. So they would always be trying both unless the law frowned upon this. But there you had for the first time a vision of what I thought was really happening in the world. And for that I was grateful, always have been. My esteem for him is much more than of people who knew him much better. Paul Samuelson is one. But again, I got more from him because I was in that position where reading and listening to him gave a lot more to me than it would to somebody else.

The other person to whom I owe the most is Edward Mason. He set an example. He was sort of what I wanted to be. Not remembered any more, and that is inevitable. But he was a man who saw everything and made it all look very simple, but who impressed on my mind indelibly how much you could do with economic principles, often of the simplest kind. In seeing things, he tried to get to the heart of the problem right then and there. He was a man of very striking personality because he didn't seem to have any. Plain as an old shoe to a great extreme. And that was the one fault I could find. He made everything look so simple and commonsensical and didn't realize, not immediately, how much thought there was to what he was saying.

During your student days at CCNY, it was very active in radical economic

thought. What were they saying back then? Can you give me some feeling of the zeitgeist?
Well, I told you I learned to have enormous respect for Karl Marx, for the scholarly and the analytical part of him.

And his appreciation for history.
Yes. City College was a very lively place, it was a great place to be. The radical element came partly from people like myself who were willing to listen to anything and pick what we wanted out of the "cafeteria line."

The Rosenburgs were there at that time weren't they?
Yes, yes, well, he was. He was an engineering major, same graduating class as myself, 1938.

But you never went to that section of the cafeteria line, did you?
No, no. What I still remember was just the clashes you had with ... The one thing I couldn't take either then or now is somebody who knew "the" truth. And that was the thing I couldn't buy very well. You see the leftists, the communists, were what I would call a very high proportion of the student body, by high I mean about 5 percent. That may not sound high to you, but what it means is that of a student body of about 8000, you had 400 people. Four hundred were a lot of people that you could assemble in any one place and they can make a lot of noise. And 400 people are bound to have a lot of bright guys that can argue endlessly. But that doesn't mean you agree with them, in fact if anything it sharpens the disagreements. It makes you see your own beliefs more clearly than you would otherwise.

Did it have any influence on you at all except to say that you got that appreciation for Marx?
Oh, yes. That's been a lifelong thing.

But not necessarily in economics though.
No, no you see, you have to differentiate the economics. In the first place, I should not really say read, I did my best to go through the second and third volumes of *Das Kapital*. I didn't get much out of it, just here and there. The first volume, which was the only one I really finished, a lot of that might be hard going, but I felt like I got a lot out of it. And again it was a great deal of history and that was the thing that impressed me.

So then his dialectical materialism and all that ...
That you learn in the midst of all the clamor. But I just couldn't parse it very well, it seemed to me some of the excess baggage that somebody would have

picked up by being a German student a hundred years earlier. And like a lot of excess baggage you ought to get rid of it. Dump it and get on with your studies. And that's as much as I got out of that part. The revolutionary vision and so on, well that was a vision you might or might not want to get on with it. Politically, the outcome of what was happening in the 1930s was confused and very menacing. It was a great relief, I must confess, when we got into the War because then I knew we would come out of it on the right end. That there would be an end.

So was there then a serious turn of the coin then between communism/socialism in ...?
Yes, well a lot of things were, so to speak, admissible because obviously things couldn't continue as they were going. So all kinds of things could happen and a few of them would. And communism was one of the things that ... what was happening in Russia at the time was one of the things you had to take seriously, it's a funny thing in a way. One of the things that made me most averse to it was what I picked up from another teacher that was at City College, the *Grand Panjandrum* of the student body, the fellow whom we admired most was Morris Raphael Cohen. He was a professor of philosophy and he had been quite prominent in his day. Forgotten now, and I'm sorry about that because what he had to say and what he had to teach is very much alive now. And one of the things I remember reading really hit me. The funny thing is this, I think he'd have appreciated the irony. Cohen called himself a socialist. He knew economics, but he didn't know it very well. He hadn't really appreciated some of the simplicities of it. But I remember reading something he'd written to the effect that the chief defect, he didn't say it was the socialist system, that's the point, he didn't realize what he was saying, but that you couldn't expect liberty under a regime where, like the old mining town, the employer was also the government, the church, the school, and the landlord. If it was everywhere you could never get away from it. All society would be like an old-fashioned mining town. Except people could and did escape from a mining town, but they couldn't escape here. Well I reflected on that and I figured that even a democratic socialist state really couldn't, really was not viable, it would have to be one or the other.

That's an outstanding point.
Yes, well that you see ... it wasn't just a matter of whether you wanted to reach certain ends, by violence or persuasion. But even if you did it by persuasion in a peaceful way it was not a stable or acceptable form of government. As I say, it's rather ironical that you get this from somebody who considered himself a socialist, though he always made that a subordinate part of his beliefs. But that, as I say, impressed me very, very strongly.

It impresses me now having heard you say it.
I remember though, when trying to judge the Soviet regime, we had the big events in those days, the Moscow trials of 1935, 1936, and 1937. Well I was taken in by it. I thought that they were genuinely guilty. But the moral for me was "What else can you expect?" When you have a regime where free discussion was now impossible for anyone in opposition, what recourse does he have but violence and conspiracy? So as I say, I thought, and everybody knows, the trials were show trials.

Who was on trial back then Professor?
Oh, Kamenev, Zinoviev, the early generation of Bolsheviks ...

Oh this is Stalin when he was lopping everybody's head off.
This was the precursor.

There was more to come.
There was much, much more to come, this was the first of it. I think 1937, it was the worst in terms of mass terror. These were the show trials that preceded them. As I say, I figured well, if you have a dictatorship that's what you're asking for. So, I was deceived, but maybe I wasn't altogether deceived, as that was concerned. But anyway that's what made City College a lively place.

OK, but then the McCarthy era went too far on the other side then, didn't it?
Oh yes. By that time I was teaching here, this was a very secure place. It was a wonderful department. I say "was" not because it's gone to the dogs since, it isn't that. It's simply that I don't know the names of half the people, let me backtrack again. We have a weekly department lunch. I never miss it when I have a chance to make it and all the geriatric cases like myself cluster in one corner (*laughter*) and I don't know the names of half the young people there. But you know that's their day and we had ours. But it's a wonderful place.

Paul Samuelson said that he didn't have any experiences during the McCarthy era but he was on Nixon's hate list.
Yes, he was prominent enough to be. I never could understand the distaste a lot of people had for Paul Samuelson unless it was for what he was writing. It couldn't be the man himself, very congenial, you couldn't ask for a better colleague. But why did they take such violent exception to the stuff he was writing? I never could quite understand it, after all these years I still can't. It was the damndest thing.

In 1955 I guess, I was hired to do some work for the law firm that defended Dupont against the charge of monopolizing cellophane. The case became pretty well known in antitrust law at one time. And the lawyer in charge was Gerhard Gesell. It was Judge Gesell at the time of the Pentagon papers. A wonderful lawyer, and a great guy. Anyway, he had decided to hire me to help him with this. And he reported to a Dupont Vice-President and the man we knew was Walter J. Beadle. And when he said he wanted to hire somebody at MIT, to use Gesell's words, this "drilled a small round hole in the ceiling." Beadle was furious at the very suggestion and then he reversed himself almost immediately. He said "If we've hired you to conduct this case then you have to have the freedom you want, do it your way. I still don't like it but you go ahead and retain anybody you want." Well, Gesell told me this sometime afterward and when he mentioned Beadle's name I had the shock of recognition alright, because Beadle was just a, how should I say it, one of the crosses we had to bear. Dupont was, in those days, a name to conjure with MIT. They'd given a lot of money to the institute, they sent a lot of the younger members of the family here, they were very influential. One of the things I remember with much pride is a letter that then President Compton, or maybe by that time he was chairman, wrote to one of the Duponts who was pushing him a bit. And I read the letter with great admiration for a man who could be firm without being abrasive and who could talk back to the Duponts and be respectful of them and say no, and mean it, obviously. But I'm digressing. I told Gesell that Beadle had been a notorious torment to the department. "OK," Gesell said, "but why, what does he have against you guys?" And I said "I can't tell you. I cannot explain this. He's got it in for Paul Samuelson particularly. But I don't know why." Why he's got it in for Samuelson is because he thinks Samuelson is a stand-in for Keynes. What's he got against Keynes? Criticize his ideas, all of them if you like. But there's nothing subversive about him. In fact, quite the contrary. He says very clearly at times in *The General Theory*, he sees nothing wrong with the pattern of expenditures or the composition of the national product or the division of the product. What he says is that the system won't maintain itself in a satisfactory equilibrium. And if you care for the bourgeois order, you better try to keep it functioning and not let it break down. So I said the whole thrust of Keynes and the whole economics profession is to keep the system going. You can call it profoundly conservative. Be that as it may, you can't call it radical, in the sense of the socialists who were aiming to change the established order, in any important way.

Do you think one of Keynes's objectives was to save capitalism or to save capitalism from itself?
Well that was really his only objective.

Didn't Hoover at one time call Keynesians "Marxists," or "Collectivists?" Those two terms were run together, weren't they?

Oh, I'm sure, they were, they were. But it seems just grotesque, that's the best word I would find for it, to couple those two.

Isn't it more demagoging than anything else?
More demagoging. But below the demagoging it is just a basic misconception of what's going on, or who's saying what. When people line up, when they choose sides, then it's no use asking them to compare views. I don't say that's the basic foundation of the McCarthy era. I think that is something different, but it certainly contributed to it. At MIT we never had any of those problems.

This is more of a joke than anything else. There's a professor of mathematics, who by the way is still alive at 102 years old, who made no secret of his sympathies with the communists. What I remember best about him was the chairman of the economics department, a man by the name of Ralph Freeman, a more sweet-tempered man you couldn't hope to meet. And he became furious at the very mention of Struik. That was the math professor's name, Dirk J. Struik. It was something about him that must have been very offensive if he could get Ralph Freeman mad at him. There must have been something poisonous about his personality, as I say, if you could get Ralph Freeman so mad at you. But he was drawn to everybody's attention when a faculty committee questioned him, and I bet this is as close as we ever got to a communist scare. There were grounds to believe that he had lied to them. An ad hoc committee was appointed to look into the matter. One of the members was a member of our department, Charlie Myers, and he told me "OK, I think we got this S.O.B. dead to rights. He can believe what he wants to, but lying to his colleagues is something else." Well, they deliberated and Charlie told me at the end just before they were releasing their findings, "It kills me, but we're recommending that no action be taken, because I don't believe this S.O.B. ever really was a member of the Communist Party. He said he wasn't and I think he was telling the truth. It kills me to vindicate him, but truth is truth and you can't get around it." (*Laughing heartily*) Well this wasn't quite the whole of the story and I'll tell you why not. The thing was initiated by an indictment of Struik. I'm sorry I'm wandering but I haven't thought of these matters in years.

No you are not, please go on.
Struik was indicted under a really stupid law passed by Massachusetts, back in the 1920s or 1919 post-World War I hysteria. And the offense was "criminal syndicalism."

Syndicalism?
Syndicalism. I kid you not. Criminal syndicalism, that was a familiar phrase.

What does it mean?
Well that's a good question. I think it is harboring revolutionary objectives.

I see, OK.
It goes back to the pre-World War I vision of the general strike in Europe. It was most powerful among anarchists and sydicalists and trade unions who would gather together and overthrow the system. That's where they got the name. So the criminal syndicalism statute, as I say it was a stupid thing, nobody had ever been tried under it and here it was being revived in the early 1950s against Professor Struik. And that's what led to the faculty inquiry here. Anyway, since he was under indictment, the institute suspended him *with* pay. Well, the case was never tried. It just dragged on year after year. And the Attorney General of Massachusetts was never willing to either try to bring him to trial, because he knew he'd lose, or to drop the case. And so this suspension lasted for years, I forget how long. And people on the faculty were grumbling, "Can't you arrange to have me indicted for criminal syndicalism?"

Please indict me.
You get leave with pay indefinitely! (*Laughing heartily*) They finally dropped the case. But that was about as bad as the McCarthy era got.

Good work if you can get it?
Good work if you can get it.

OK, can you describe your experiences at the Board of Governors in 1946? What was the sense of how things were going back then and what roles did the Depression and its reoccurrence play in the establishment of the Full Employment Act of 1946?
All I know is what I read about it. The Depression stamped its mark on everybody who lived through it. And, I know before the War was over and when we were visibly heading to the end, there was a catchphrase there ... "golden gate in '48, bread line in '49." That was among the armed services at the time and I don't think it was any different from what was being said elsewhere. Have you seen a television series, I saw just last week, it's a program I should say, on the GI bill?

I have not.
Well, do if you can, try and get to see it. It's really very good from every point of view. But one thing, it brought back things that I have forgotten. It was passed and passed by a very narrow margin in 1944, early 1944, maybe late in 1943. It was passed by a narrow margin, nobody foresaw what the results were going to be. It was basically a scheme of getting some sizeable numbers

of GIs off the street.

And out of the labor force.
Out of the labor force for the time being.

Was that the impetus for why it came about?
Well it was as much of a motive as anybody could see. Of course, things worked out in an entirely different way, as I have told you for me it was the greatest thing that ever happened. But the general expectation or apprehension was of continuing what we had done beforehand.

So was that the sentiment of what the post-war economy was going to shape up like?
Well, I couldn't say it was *the* sentiment, but it certainly was a widespread sentiment. And I for one shared the apprehension, not that I knew this was going to happen, but felt that there was a damn good chance, maybe a predominant chance, that this was going to happen.

What did you say was the luckiest thing that ever happened Professor?
Well, the GI Bill.

OK, OK.
Because I would never had gone to graduate school otherwise. But that is a part answer to your question, what was the apprehension, what was the sentiment at the time? On the Reserve Board, corporate finance was the field in which I was assigned. I was given things to do early on that kept me busy. The thing that struck me was the liquidity of the corporate sector. Does liquidity have anything to do with investment, you know "Did she fall or was she pushed?" There was an awful lot of liquidity to permit investment, whether you thought it was in any sense a cause or not.

So then maybe there was the repressed demand during the War and then when the War was over...
Lots of money to spend. And for business lots to spend it on, they thought the market was there. But it was obvious that far from heading into a depression or a recession, things were really perking.

So the economy was at the starting line ready for the gun to go off?
Well, it was already really moving across the line.

What impact did the Great Depression have on shaping your value judgment ideology?

Well, full employment was the most important thing, even though it was not at the center of my professional preoccupation. Everybody was looking for a niche for themselves and I was looking for mine. But macroeconomics was everybody's second preoccupation. No matter what you were doing everything rested on what the economy generally was going to do.

So then whereas full employment might not have been a concern prior to the Depression ... after?
Well, prior to the Depression I was 12 years old when the stock market crashed. That was the big preoccupation.

So then it moved full employment to the forefront?
Full employment had been at the forefront for well over a decade, ever since the Great Depression began. That was *the* number one question. Now you might be interested in any aspect of economics but that was always a thing at the back of your mind. Well not so far back, everything rested on that.

So the Depression focused a white-hot light on that?
Oh yes. And as I say the very foundations of any kind of democratic society were very much in question. You didn't know what the hell was going to happen and you feared the worst.

What do you think was the initial impetus for the Depression and what accounts for how deep it went?
I don't know what the initial impetus was, and I can't account for how deep it went except I would say that the second question is much more important than the first. And I think that an economy, especially a capitalist economy but not only, was always subject to some kind of internal or external shock. What really matters is whether a shock or downturn, whatever it is, becomes greatly strengthened and amplified.

Propagated.
Propagated, that's the word I want. That is far more important. But I don't think that I understand what happened in the case of the Great Depression. I've seen some plausible explanations, you don't need me to give them, the banking system can be inherently weak and unstable, it's plaguing Southeast Asian governments today. And you could say that of the United States then.

So there's any number of things that perhaps could account for it?
Any number of things could account for it.

But the important point that you want to make is that it's the protracted depth that's much more important.

Yes, the thing that propagated it for so long. And this was the thing that for Keynes became a burning question. Whether you like his answers or not or think they are apropos or not, this was the burning question. Mainly, why did things bump along for so long at such a low level? It's one thing to say there's a shock, there's a propagating mechanism and then things turn around. Well this time there was a shock and a mechanism and you went down and you damn well weren't getting out of it. The worst of it might be over but it was still very bad. And it was only, at the time certainly, the outbreak of war which lifted the system out of the dumps.

What ended the Great Depression?

World War II. You can always argue something else would have done it, or generating forces were there. I never have believed that.

Do you have anything to say about the gold standard and how it functioned back then?

Well, it was universal. It was breaking down of course, at that time. But it had all countries on a currency board regimen, as we would put it today. There was a fixed relationship between the currency and gold and therefore since all currencies had a fixed gold value, all currencies were fixed. And this was OK except when they got out of alignment with each other.

So do you think that part of the responsibility for the transmission of the Depression can be laid at the door of the gold standard?

I had a feeling in those days, yes, that the adjustments were needed. Any rigid system of parities was bad in itself. And I stuck with that belief much longer than I should have. I was all in favor back in the 1950s, 1960s, and 1970s of floating exchange rates. An exchange rate after all is just a price. What good were we at fixing this price more than fixing any other price? Well, I think that was wrong.

You do?

Yes, I think I was wrong at the time. You can't just let them float freely, you generate instability as well as adjust to it.

Like Southeast Asia now for example?

Yes, but that's a mild example because just a few countries have gotten themselves out of whack.

Compared to the Depression?

Compared to the Depression.

OK. So then, more of a managed float you would say would be the way to go?
Well, a managed float or a crawling peg or something like that. You need some kind of fixed relation. It gets fixed, then it becomes also possibly unstable. Because when it is fixed, anybody who speculates is insured. And thereby it is an inducement to speculate. Well, where do you draw some kind of a line or how do you explore the best mechanism for doing that? I don't know, I never got that far, I still have not.

What are some of the lessons of the Great Depression that seem to be forgotten today or that have to be continually relearned?
Disasters can happen. Things accumulate, happenstance and mistakes can happen anytime. The trick is to recognize it in time and not let them propagate as was done then. And that's really all, to be alert, to try to snub these tendencies and try to reverse them.

What are some of the lessons of the energy crises that we've had that have to be continually relearned?
We have never had an energy crisis. All we had was a monopoly which obtained its power in an irregular sort of way. People who did what they thought was good for them, not what was good for the world economy. It's just our misfortune that the people who created the monopoly were poor, undeveloped and ...

Dictatorships?
Well, they were not dictatorships exactly, but all despotic, and undemocratic, largely with the exception of Venezuela, who grabbed too fast and too far for their own good. But I would say they were permitted and even encouraged to do this, by people who really were in the grip of an irrational fear that we were running out of oil.

And that's a fiction.
That's a fiction, and joined to that is the idea that there is a chronic deficit. The notion that the market clears, no matter what happens, the worst is that the price goes up too much and that's bad. But that's the worst that can happen. You can't have a gap. There really was and there still is the belief that there's an energy gap or there will be, or maybe there will be. And if there is, ordinary market processes will never respond. So, you must have access. When you think of the word "access" it packages so nicely the misapprehensions of people because if supply won't equal demand, then of course, you need access. The only way of getting supply is by somebody's grace and favor or making a deal with them. So it's the supposed need for good relations for example, of oil producing countries, which is still alive and well today as any

fallacy could be. It's less urgent, many people are willing to just forget about it. It doesn't seem terribly important for today but it is there.

Why is this a fallacy?
Well, two fallacies are involved. One, no matter what happens, the worst is that demand and supply will be equated at a very high price. But the amount demanded and the amount supplied are going to equate. So the idea that you need some kind of political relation or access, that is purely fiction. But it is very powerful fiction. It does make people do all kinds of weird things.

Like in your book Genie out of the Bottle, *you said that we don't really need or have a special relationship with the Saudis.*
No, you see, we don't need it, but we don't have it either. And we think we have it because it is more than people can bring themselves to admit, that there's nothing they can do, that they have no power, that they have no influence.

That the Saudis don't?
No, that we don't influence them. That we do what we must and they'll do as they jolly well please. To admit to yourself that I have no influence with these people, me, I'm such a big important man, everywhere I go, cameras are pointed at me and people eagerly jot down everything I have to say. To admit that I can't influence these guys is impossible. But that is so. That's one half of it.

The other half is a little more subtle and very seductive. The theory seems to be simple common sense, which allows fascinating and elegant combinations and development as theory. If you have a limited stock, what's the present value of it? Well the stock doesn't exist. Nobody knows how many hydrocarbon molecules exist in the earth. If we did, what we want to know is what is the cost of converting that into usable products? That's a function of technology. So, if you knew today what you know tomorrow then you'd know it all today. And that's why, I still remember this, although I didn't realize then how important it would become in my own work, back in the 1930s when I was told and it was kind of whispered, "Do you realize we have only 10 years' supply of oil left on hand?" I scratched my head and couldn't understand it. Well, it's an inventory and what matters is the terms on which you can add to the inventory, and going from better to the worst means an increasing cost. There's a sort of comfort in that if the slope is flat or declining, for the time being we're doing OK. If you look at other minerals where you have exactly the same conditions, the stinginess of nature and the ingenuity of mankind, where there too the slope is downward, that doesn't prove it will always be downward. Far from it. All it proves is that at the immediate present there are no worries and you know what you ought to look for. Here is where I think I contributed something. What you look for is the investment cost of adding a unit of capacity in what are called crude reserves. Crude reserves or any reserves. What is the cost of creating now the inventory of goods you are going to use up in 5, 10, or 15 years? That's what they wanted, and it was not being done very well, that's the important part.

That's going to tell you what's going to happen to supplies five or ten years from now?
Yes, you can't look very far.

So that's like a marginal cost curve then?
Well that's all it is.

Right. Does the memory of the Depression stay with you, or even have an impact on your thinking today?
Oh sure, nobody ever gets over that kind of experience. When your formative years are spent in the presence of massive unemployment, you don't know what's going to happen to you, your family, your friends, everything else, you are not going to get over that. Even though in my case only the first 20 to 25 years of my life were spent that way and I've lived to a pretty good age. But you never get over it, formative experiences like that, never.

Are there any alternatives to capitalism?
There may be some, I haven't seen them. You see in some sense it goes back much, much longer in the period of time than we tend to think. In the ancient world they had private property and the purchase and sale of almost anything, including human chattel. But they did not have what we call economics. In Schumpeter's *History of Economic Analysis*, he asks "Why is it that the Greeks who contributed so much to our basic thinking in mathematics, the sciences, and history had almost nothing to say about economics?" He was not a historian by trade, just a man of tremendous intellect who could see things. Two esteemed historians picked up on this remark. One is dead now, Sir Moses Finley, and another, an Englishman who teaches at the University of Texas, that's Peter Green. Both of them sort of picked up Schumpeter's remark and in effect they said, "He's letting the Greeks off too easy. Schumpeter said there was almost nothing. Well there was nothing. Why was this so?" The answer they give, I think it convinces me, is that the Greeks had no banking system. They invested in the sense of real investment, after all they were mostly farmers. They invested in buildings and in ships, shipping was very important. But there never was any practice of formally committing money to investment and reckoning that you put down something today for a

series of payments in the future. Of saying you've got to equate these somehow, you've got to reduce them both to present values. That's something you don't find in the ancient code. So they had no idea of investment, no theory of investment. And it's investment which, if there is a thing that makes capitalism, it is the investment process. Now this did, you see, creep into practice and then into some kind of theory in the Italian cities, in the later middle ages around the year 1000. Banking, bills of exchange and double-entry bookkeeping were all Italian inventions. And they were all the inventions of a reviving system of commerce and industry as you found it mostly in northern Italy and southern Germany as well around the year 1000, once mediaeval Europe managed to fend off what was really going to crash the whole place, the Magyars to the east and the Vikings from the north.

And the Orthodox Church split around that time taking Eastern Europe with it.
That's right, and of course, the Muslims from the South and also the East. Who we called Christian Europe around the year 900 was not a good bet. No reasonable man would have offered you much for its chances of surviving and prospering and you see it turned out all wrong. By say the year 1000, the year 1100, the corner had been turned, God knows how. The threat from all these places had stabilized and you had an active capitalist economy in Central Europe. It had that necessary ingredient somehow, namely, banking, formalized investment and money as the investment medium which the ancient world, much larger, more developed and so on, the ancient world lacked. That was the big difference. And if you call that a way of answering your question about alternatives to capitalism, there probably aren't any.

What do you see as the biggest threat from capitalism?
Unemployment, again. You know, 20 years ago you would have said inflation. That probably is lurking still, it's not immediately troubling, it's a long-run danger.

Does the distribution of income bother you?
In the small it does. Why has income become more unequally distributed in the last 20 years? I wish I understood the process. I don't. In the presence of economic expansion it isn't too bothersome because everyone is going to get, I won't say his share because I don't know how much that is. But *the* share, the absolute amount is going to increase. I think that is an essential safety valve.

Well let me ask you a different way. Do you think that income distribution and poverty are separate issues? That we can do something about poverty even if

we can't do much about income distribution?
Or vice versa.

(Adelman is nodding his head) Yes? They are separate?
Yes. I think they're separate, they overlap to some extent, but I think they're separate.

OK, I want to ask you to be a little bit of a visionary now.
Go ahead.

Alrighty, are there any big problems you see confronting us as we turn the corner into the next millennium?
No, you've got the same old problems, and political breakdown.

Political breakdown?
The twentieth century in a lot of ways is the best of times and the worst of times. You have had a tremendous growth in wealth and average income, and a lot of progress that has been allied with this. At the same time there is no century which has been as murderous and brutal as ours. So these things all get mixed up together. Now there was no inherent reason in my opinion why you had to have this kind of a century following on what had seemed to be a long, widely diffused upswing throughout all of the world, with the exception of the less developing nations and there you couldn't say they were much worse than they had been. Why did the Europeans get themselves into such a fix as they did in 1914? Well, I don't see that this was inevitable or ordained, but it's something that can happen again.

You think it could?
Well, there's no such constellation that appears now. But could it appear in the future? Sure. Different groupings, different parts of the world also may be worse. The center was Europe and the United States finally came as the arbiter. But any such clash in the future would be bigger and therefore worse.

What you said strikes me as incredibly insightful, we still have the same problems.
Well yes, sure.

What do you see about the future of oil production and oil shocks?
Oil shocks can come at any time because they have nothing to do with supply and demand.

They have to do with ...

Monopoly and with imperfect monopoly and monopoly by equal but political entities whose behavior is under much more severe constraints. Liquidity constraints particularly.

Because of their spending proclivities?
Yes, many of the countries in the oil cartel will always overspend their incomes and most of them live in bad neighborhoods. You can get mugged or murdered at any time. This makes them prone to sudden and violent actions. That is why you have oil shocks and you're going to have the same possibility in the future. They've been chastened by their experiences, but time goes by and people forget those lessons.

There's a very large stochastic component too, isn't there?
Oh it's stochastic. In a sense everything there is stochastic in what they have done, but it didn't have to evolve that way. The number of actors is small and therefore you don't get the benefit of a stochastic process, that is what a competitive market does for you. In this case, all these things continue to be threatening. It's just a fact that so much originates around the Persian Gulf. It goes out of a narrow waterway, it's a choke point, as the CIA likes to say and that can happen all the time. The big mistake we make and keep making is to suppose oil prices or energy crises have anything to do with supply and demand, especially in the long run. It was our bad luck that the first big oil crisis coincided, I believe, with the Club of Rome and widespread anxiety about running out of everything. Even if you suppose reserves are twice as much as what they are, sure you can take a stock of automobile parts and we're going to run through that in the course of three months. And then, oh, what will we do?

Make more?
Yes, that's what we do with minerals as well, we make more reserves.

OK, we all know about the great productivity slowdown post-1973. Zvi Griliches wrote papers and titled them "Another non-explanation" for the slowdown. What share do you think the oil shocks have to play in this?
They have some, because if you look at the industrial world where you have productivity figures, without exception in 1973–74 you got a down deflection in productivity and it's not negligible. You also get it in 1979–80. So you know it did something to them and it wasn't good. I don't know how big it was, and I just have a feeling, I can't prove it, but if you could allow fully for the oil shock there is something left to explain, maybe a lot.

Any particular trends in our national economy or in economic research or

schools of thought that you find disturbing?
Well, too much uninformed mathematics, people work hard to acquire a technique and they don't know well enough what to do with it.

Do you think the Great Depression changed the psychology of the country?
Oh, it sure did, at least for the time being. I have a feeling now it's relegated to the history books. It's a big event like wars in the past and so on, but it's not a live memory I think. And that's the biggest gap I can see between myself and younger generations. My own children, such feelings my wife and I tried to instruct in them, and I think in this respect we were representative.

The psychology of the role of government, was that the big change?
I'm sure it was a big part of it. But of course, in this country, what we call the welfare state, we were far behind Europe in that respect. So a lot of things that happened here would have come about anyway I'm sure. I think the answer is yes, but the exact changes are harder to point to.

Don't you think the Depression expedited Samuelson's mixed economy model a whole lot faster?
Oh yes, I have no doubt at all that it pushed in that direction. If you take as an index, and it's a good index though it's a limited one, what proportion of national income is channeled through government, it is much larger now than it was before the Depression. Well, you start accounting for the pieces of it and as usual, the causal relation is less clear, but I think it's there.

Leontief thinks it's going to go up even more in the future. He says to look at Europe where it is much more.
He may be right. It would be unfortunate if it did, especially because he used Europe as an example. They have got themselves in a box.

Into a catatonic labor market.
That's the thing. The labor market is allied to the system of pensions, unemployment, and insurance. This is something that is very difficult for me to admit to myself because these were the buffers and safety nets that did not exist during the Great Depression and made it a pretty horrible time. But you can have too much of anything and they have too much of that in Europe.

What really troubles me is that in France, it really doesn't matter what human capital you have, your chances of finding a job are pretty small. It's not just the fact that low human capital people are unemployed, it's people of all levels of human capital are unemployed. And I think that's really pretty pathetic.

Yes, I agree.

Everyone always wants to know when I tell them that I research the economics of the Great Depression, could it happen again?
You can't say that it can't. I think it's unlikely to have the factors there that propagated it so efficiently the last time. In only three years it went down so far, so fast. But to say it couldn't happen is more than I know.

Alright, thanks a lot Professor.

Herbert Stein

Herbert Stein was an economist who wore many hats in his career. He was an academic, an economist working for the government on several tours of duty, the chairman of the Council of Economic Advisors from January 1, 1972 through August 31, 1974, and a frequent contributor to *The Wall Street Journal* and other publications. To me, his writing style and his presentation of economic ideas had an elegant simplicity that I found to be both interesting and enlightening. I wanted him to apply these talents to interpreting the events of the Great Depression as well. Given the high regard in which I held the way and manner in which he expressed his views on social/economic problems and their solutions, I wanted his take on the economics of the interwar era. We spoke in his office at The American Enterprise Institute in Washington, DC in September 1997. He passed away in the fall of 1999.

Would you state where you were born and when and what you were doing during the Great Depression?
Well, I was born in Detroit, Michigan in 1916. So if we start with the Great Depression, from 1929 to 1931 I was in high school in Schenectady, New York. From 1931 to 1935 I was in college at Williams College in Williamstown, Massachusetts, and from 1935 to 1938 I was at the University of Chicago mainly, with some time off. In 1938 I moved down to Washington. So that's my life during the Depression. I was mainly a student. I really went to work in 1938, here in Washington at the Federal Deposit Insurance Corporation.

Did the Depression have anything to do with you going into economics?
I think it probably did. When I came to the end of my sophomore year, I was very uncertain about whether I would major in economics or in English. I was very interested in both and I suppose I was interested in economics because of the condition of the country. But I was also interested in economics because at Williams College there was a $500 prize given for an essay in economics, the David A. Wells prize which is better known at Harvard, but David A. Wells had been a Williams graduate. It had not been given very frequently in the previous 50 or so years. That was an incentive; I could use every dollar. So it was kind of a mixed issue about just why I went into economics. But I

think the fact that this was so much at the center of public attention had something to do with it.

Were you a student of Viner?
As a graduate student, yes. I had two courses with Viner, maybe three.

Did he direct you into employment in Washington after graduation?
No, I came down to Washington in 1938 because that was where people went in those days. Of course, you could not be a perpetual graduate student, as some people are now. Few people had the money for that. In 1938 if you were a person as I was who had finished his preliminary examinations but didn't have his degree yet, Washington was the place to go. So I came here. In fact, most of the people I came to see in Washington were in some way connected with Williams College. But the person with whom I went to work had been a graduate student at Chicago and it was through him and recommendations of the Chicago faculty, especially Lloyd Mints I do believe, that I got my job at the Federal Deposit Insurance Corporation.

Can you give me just a brief rundown of your professional career from there?
Well from 1938 to 1940, I worked at the Federal Deposit Insurance Corporation. In 1940 I went to one of the first of the War agencies, the National Defense Advisory Commission, and I stayed with that through its various metamorphoses into the Office of Price Administration and Control and then to the War Production Board. Then I went into the navy in June or July of 1944 and stayed there until April of 1945, always in Washington working on War economics. Then I came out and joined the Committee for Economic Development for 22 years. That would take me up to 1967. I worked for about a year and a half at the Brookings Institute. Then I went into the government, first as a member, then as chairman of the Council of Economic Advisors. From 1974 to 1984 I was on the faculty of the University of Virginia, from which I retired in 1984. But I would say that beginning in 1977, even while I was at Virginia, I was also connected here with the American Enterprise Institute. And I have been connected here ever since.

Can you remember back when and what happened that made you think that the recession of 1929–30 was changed and that perhaps we were going to go into a depression?
I don't remember thinking anything about it in 1929. I was 13 years old. I knew we were in trouble. My father was unemployed in Schenectady. But as I recall, I remember when I was a junior in college, and that would have been 1933, reading about the history of business cycles. So I knew that there had been a depression in 1873 and a depression in 1893 and something in 1907

and all that. And I don't know when I began to have the idea that this was different, that this was *the* Great Depression distinguished from all the previous depressions. Because at that time we thought of 1873 and 1893 as being pretty severe depressions. Of course we had very little statistics for making the comparison between the 1930s and 1873 and 1893. So I don't really know. I suppose that by 1935 or 1936 we probably knew that this was exceptionally severe. But then it was not very long before we began to have the recovery.

Looking back, in hindsight can you put your finger on one thing that you think, professionally, made the economy turn the corner and fall off the end of the table?
Well, I don't have an independent judgment of that. That is, I rather subscribe to the Friedman–Schwartz view that we were having an ordinary recession which was converted into the Great Depression by the mistakes of monetary policy.

Do you see any parallels between the recession of 1921 and the Great Depression? Do you think that policy makers at the time figured it would be a repeat of the deflation of the recession of 1921 and so they didn't vigorously attempt to fight the Depression?
No, I don't think of that as the problem. I think that they had a number of traditional notions. They had a traditional notion about gold. They had traditional notions about budget balancing. They had traditional notions about the need for occasionally wringing the excesses out of the economy. So I think it took them a while to realize it, like it took everybody. Milton Friedman and Anna Schwartz didn't have this problem of trying to identify what it was like in 1931. They only had hindsight, like all of us.

So you don't think that there is necessarily any connection there at all?
I'm not aware of it.

Do you think the Fed should act as an arbiter of security prices?
No, I don't. I see that Greenspan has said something which indicated he thinks the Federal Reserve should be influenced by asset prices, but I don't think so. In a recent talk at Stanford University he gave the impression, I have not read the text of it but it has been reported in the newspapers, the impression that he thought that the Federal Reserve should be interested in asset prices as well as in the prices of the goods and services. I think that can be very misleading. I think he should keep his eye on the inflation rate.

What do you think was driving the stock market back then?

In 1929?

Yes sir.
I think there was confidence in the continued growth of profits and I guess there was irrational exuberance. There was this belief that things were going up and you better get in before it ended. It was a speculative bubble.

You do think it was a bubble?
Yes.

What do you think explains the difference between 1929 and 1987?
Well, the Federal Reserve provided liquidity.

What do you think is driving the stock market now?
I don't know that either. But I am interested in the notion that was in an article in *The Journal of Economic Literature,* and then my son wrote about it in *Slate* magazine, that we now have a fundamental re-appraisal of the risk of equity investment as compared with the risk of fixed-income investments. It has turned out over the years that the market has overestimated the risk of equity investment and now we are having a new evaluation which would explain the high price–earnings ratios that we now have. But, of course, it wouldn't explain the continuing to go up and up and up. But that is all I have to say about that. I think the market is impressed or has been impressed by the recent stability of the economy, by the fact that we have gotten inflation considerably down and it looks as if it is under control. I think that is a very favorable factor and there is probably more confidence in that now than at any time in a long, long time.

Did the Depression change the psychology of the country?
Oh, yes.

Can you tell me how?
Well, I think it made fear of the Depression a dominant factor of American political life for a long, long time, really up through Nixon's time. That certainly influenced policy and probably had some effect on my generation and the generation of my parents. I think my generation was certainly cautious and had a certain level of anxiety.

What about the increased willingness to accept government in the economy?
Oh, that yes, there was a big change in that. And it's not so much a willingness to accept, but demanding government help and that was perfectly natural, understandable, and correct.

Has the Great Depression shaped your life professionally at all?
Oh, yes, in many ways. I think for a long part of my life, my work revolved around the question of economic stability and the problem of avoiding such depressions. Do you know the story of the Pabst prize?

No sir, I'm afraid not.
Well, in 1944, the Pabst Brewing Company established a contest for essays on "How do we maintain high employment after the end of the War?" There were 36,000 entries, and the essays were no longer than 2,000 words, and I won it. And that, I think ...

How much was that worth?
Well, it was $25,000 at that time, which was a good deal of money in 1944. However, it was in the years of the highest tax rates, so after taxes it was not that great. But still it was a big thing. I think it helped to bring me to the attention of the Committee for Economic Development (CED). It might have happened anyway, because the research director for the CED was a former professor of mine from the University of Chicago, T.O. Yntema. But I think it enabled him to say "Look we got this guy here who just won this contest." So that really shaped my life for a long time. But then it was the subject of a good deal of my writing for the next 20 years or so. Not the Depression particularly, but the instability problem.

Was there something else that occurred in our history that had a bigger impact on you professionally?
The appointment to the Council of Economic Advisors by Richard Nixon had a big effect on me professionally. And I think going to the University of Chicago. It was not inevitable that I would go to the University of Chicago. In fact, most of the faculty at Williams were Harvard people, but there was one who had been a graduate student at Chicago and who encouraged me to go to Chicago. I think that had a big effect on my outlook. I was influenced by the pre-Friedman group, by Viner, Simons, and Knight.

Can you point to one particular contribution in economics, one book, one article, one person that did the most in shaping how you think as an economist?
Well, I would say Henry Simons and his collection of essays called *Economic Policy for a Free Society*. It is one of the few economics books that I ever look back at. Although I don't now agree with everything he said, I like his general attitude and his literary style.

I remember you mentioning some of his ideas in the editorials you wrote for

The Wall Street Journal. *Consumption plus the change in net worth is equal to income. Tax it once.*
But he said a number of other things. For example, that "extreme inequality in the distribution of income, as of power, is unlovely." I think that is a wonderful statement and you see, he was more concerned about inequality, he was more concerned about poor people than I think the latest generation of Chicagoans is. He was more willing to see government action than the latest generation is. Maybe he was too willing. But he was writing, of course, during the Depression and things were terrible and he was looking for strong solutions.

Well, why don't I just jump to that question right now, since we're on it? Does the distribution of income bother you?
Well, distribution does not bother me, poverty bothers me, that's a different thing. That is, I'm not concerned about how rich Bill Gates is or Warren Buffet or even Donald Trump or Michael Jordan. I'm very concerned about a very small group of people who are very poor. For a while I thought of people who were poor by our standard definition of poverty. But I'm now really more concerned with the group that's sometimes called the underclass. Those who are both poor and socially dysfunctional. That is, the number of very young, unmarried girls with children, the crime, the school drop-out rates, the drug abuse and all that kind of thing, that whole syndrome that affects a very small fraction of the American population. It may affect only 1 or 2 percent of the total population. But I think it is a big problem.

Do you think there is much we can do about the distribution of income?
Well, I think we have done a good deal about the distribution of income. That is, for example, we have done a good deal about the income status of the elderly population who have social security. I think you have to look at this in a long perspective, not in a perspective of 5 or 10 years. Free public education in America and very low-cost higher education in America I think have done something to the distribution of income. But I don't know whether there's much more that we can do, or that there's much more that is important to do except for this very low class.

Doesn't over half the federal budget go to transfers in one form or another?
Yes, but it doesn't go to these people, it transfers from and to middle income people.

I guess what I'm driving at is that some people that I talk with make it sound as if we're not hardly doing anything at all. We need to do so much more.
Well, I wouldn't say we need to do so much more. But I would say, that if we

knew what to do about these people, I think it would be desirable and worthwhile to spend quite a lot more money doing it. There are two problems. One is that most of us don't want to spend the money. And second, we don't know what to do with the money if we did want to spend it. But these are people who have problems. They're not just ordinary people who are poor. They have psychological problems, they have family problems and so on. Economists don't know how to deal with these things and I don't know that anybody does know how to deal with them. But I think that we should be willing to spend a lot of money to help them if we can figure out a way that will really help them.

What do you think was effective in ending the Great Depression?
Well, we ended the monetary stringency, we freed ourselves from the gold standard, we created money as was necessary. While fiscal policy in retrospect was very small in the whole picture, I think it was somewhat helpful. Then, of course, the War. There was a case where fiscal policy did help a great deal.

Did you think that the New Deal programs helped at all?
Well, I think they helped lots of people. And that's a different question. They helped a lot of people who could not find work in the circumstances, they provided work for them, provided relief for them. So I think that was certainly a help. Whether on balance the New Deal helped to get us out of the Depression faster than we otherwise would have, is still an open question in my mind and I'm not sure what the answer is yet. So you have to distinguish among the New Deal programs. The WPA and programs such as that were desirable things. They certainly helped a lot of people and helped the country. I think that people don't realize what a condition of despair and revulsion there was in 1933. With all the wild ideas that were floating around about how we needed to change the American economy and American society, I think that the New Deal measures, more or less, put a stop to that and preserved the system.

What are some of the lessons of the Great Depression that seem to be forgotten today or that have to be continually relearned?
Well, if you accept my view that the great problem was the monetary collapse, I don't think that has been forgotten and therefore does not need to be relearned. I am more concerned about another lesson, not from the Great Depression, but from "The Great Inflation." We have serious recessions in this country only after serious inflation. It's very important to avoid inflation and I'm concerned that we will, as a generation that became most aware of that like the generation of Paul Volcker, Greenspan and me (*chuckling*), we'll pass from the scene and we'll get some young people who didn't live through it, for

whom it is not vivid and that we will have another wave of inflation at some point as a result of attempting to pump the economy up too much. That I think is a lesson that needs somehow to be engraved in stone. But I don't think we are likely to go through another deflation.

Well, for what it's worth, Professor, let me make a solemn vow to you that as long as I'm alive I'll continue to shout those same sentiments at the top of my lungs, to whomever will listen.
(*Laughing*) OK, good for you.

Does the memory of the Depression stay with you or have an impact on your thinking?
Well, really not very much. I'm writing a little piece about the history of what has happened during my 81 years. In that piece the Depression does not stand out. There are other, much greater horrors in those 81 years other than the Depression and other greater achievements than getting out of the Depression. So I don't really think of it very much, but I was really in a peculiar situation during the Depression. There I was in Williamstown, in the northwestern corner of Massachusetts, surrounded by mountains in an idyllic circumstance, happy as you can imagine to be there at all. Although I did all kinds of jobs and had very little money and so on, it was a happy time for me. So, when I think about the 1930s, I think about that. And I think about meeting my wife and getting married, so those were golden years despite the Depression.

Any particular trends in economics or economic research that you find disturbing?
Well, I don't understand it (*laughing*), so I can't say it's disturbing. I don't read economics very much. The journals are there (*Stein points to a bookcase*) but I don't read them. They are too mathematical and too technical for me. But I don't find that we've learned very much in a long time. It seems to me almost the last thing we learned was in Friedman's Presidential Address in 1968.

I said to Anna Schwartz that you can take that paper out today and read it, and learn more about stabilization policy in the macro economy than in most of the work that has been done in the last 25 years. That's what I happen to feel.
Well, I think so too. I don't know if we've learned anything since. So, I pretty much have given up economics. I write for *Slate* magazine now, it's on the Internet. I write once a month, but I don't write about economics.

Have you ever looked at the real business cycle literature at all?
Well, the theory, I can't believe it. I can't believe we had 25 percent

unemployment because people didn't want to work.

Or they were making intertemporal substitutions over time?
Yes.

What are your views on our capitalist system? Is this the best going or are there any alternatives?
I don't think there are any alternatives (*laughing*). But you see, the capitalist system covers a very wide range of possible systems. I once wrote a thing called *Triumph of the Adaptive Society*. I guess I wrote that eight or nine years ago. Capitalism has survived and triumphed. But the capitalism that has survived and triumphed is not the capitalism of 1929. And probably the capitalism of 2050 will not be the capitalism of 1997. The main thing is it has certain continuing features but still it adapts and policy has adapted and I think that is what has made it successful and survivable.

What's the major difference in today's capitalism as opposed to 1929?
Well for one thing, what we were just talking about. We do have a positive responsible monetary policy. We have accepted the responsibility for stabilizing the economy through monetary policy. But also we have accepted responsibility for alleviating poverty in a certain fraction of the population. We have accepted responsibility for correcting certain environmental externalities in the system. We have accepted more responsibility I think, for preserving competition than we had in 1929. We are much more open internationally than we were in 1929. So those were some of the adaptions we have made.

Do you think that capitalism has to keep proving it can be economically efficient without being destructive of reasonable equality, like Robert Solow said?
Well I think it does, yes. I think that's right. But I think it has demonstrated that.

What do you see as the biggest threat to capitalism?
The thing I'm writing about the last 81 years shows the world is full of surprises. But I really don't see any threat to capitalism. I can see problems. I can see us having another oil crisis which would be a great big problem for the American economy without a threat to capitalism particularly. But I don't see any competing system out there that is likely to attract people. On the contrary, everyone is being attracted to some version of a free market society.

Are there any threats from capitalism at all do you think, other than the

unlovely distribution of income?
No, but ... capitalism does not define society or our private lives. There is a lot of ugliness in our private lives. There is a failure to appreciate the beauty available in our lives, and in our culture and so on. So those are deficiencies, but they are not particular deficiencies of capitalism. There are some conservative sociologists who have thought that capitalism was really the enemy of culture. I don't think that. I guess this means I'm just old fashioned, but I don't like a lot of things I see in the culture today and I think we are missing a lot of things that are out there.

Do you think we could have another Great Depression?
No. Let me say I think the odds are very, very low.

Do you think that our level of learning and economic sophistication now would preclude that to a large degree?
Well, it didn't require a high degree of sophistication (*laughing*). That is, it's not like learning the results of some big econometric analysis. I think what you had to learn was a very simple thing, and I think we have learned that.

That simple thing being?
Being not to allow the money supply to collapse.

Would you comment on monetary policy today?
Well I think it has been very good. Judging by the results, you'd have to say it is very good. I don't know the system or what is the theory by which Greenspan operates except with a kind of caution and flexibility. That seems to work, but it seems to be a very personal thing. I'm not sure that there is any book that he will hand to his successor that will tell him how to do it.

Don't you think that we're appropriately focusing on the inflation rate now with monetary policy?
Oh, I think we are, I think we are. But that still leaves open the question of people who'll say "Well we can have 4 percent unemployment that's consistent with price stability so let's shoot for the 4 percent." They will say they are aiming at price stability, but that would be a big mistake. I think it would be a big mistake to say we're going to aim at 4 percent unemployment and that will automatically give us price stability. We don't know any rate of unemployment that will give us price stability. So I think we have to focus on price stability, not on the unemployment rate.

So, we're not certain or even reasonably certain about what the natural rate of unemployment is?

That's right.

Thanks so much Professor.

Victor Zarnowitz

If Paul Samuelson is the "Father of Modern Economics," then Victor Zarnowitz easily holds the title of "Mr Business Cycle." In the recent book *Business Cycles and Depressions: An Encyclopedia*, Victor Zarnowitz is the author of the chapter that surveys the field of business cycle research, Q.E.D. No other economist in recent times has done more to sharpen and deepen our understanding of the character of economic fluctuations than Victor Zarnowitz.

Professor Zarnowitz received his Ph.D., summa cum laude, from the University of Heidelberg in 1952. He has been a researcher for the NBER, was a member of the faculty at the University of Chicago from 1959 to 1989, is a Fellow of the American Statistical Association, and currently is a Senior Fellow at The Conference Board. We spoke in New York in December 1997.

I went into the interview pretty much like I did all the others. Professor Zarnowitz indicated he enjoyed the time we spent together and thanked me for being well prepared. I left his office feeling "blown away," if you'll forgive the colloquial term. I'm humbled every time I read the interview that follows. The world would be worse off without Victor Zarnowitz and thinking of him reminds me to be thankful for the many blessings that have been given to me and my family.

Would you please give us a brief rundown of when and where you were born and what you were doing during the Great Depression?
I was born on November 3, 1919 in a little town named Łańcut in southern Poland. It was part of the Austro-Hungarian monarchy before World War I. After World War I, there was an independent Poland, and I was a teenager during the Great Depression. As I recall it, I was not so terribly affected by it because we were in modest but pretty good circumstances. My father died when I was ten, in 1929. He was a teacher in a *gymnasium*, a high school, which was more like lower college here. He taught Greek, Latin, and German. He left a little money to my mother and to us and we moved west to a place called Oświęcim, better known as Auschwitz, where we built a small house. An infamous place today, but at that time it was just a small town like many others. I studied law and economics (economics was a part of law) in Cracow at the Jagellonian University in 1937–39, after graduating from gymnasium in Oświęcim.

Now, coming back to the Great Depression, that hit Poland, as I know now, pretty badly. But we had a pension and some inheritance that my father left the family. I remember that I was tutoring throughout my upper classes in gymnasium and in college, so it helped out. I was a pretty good student with a lot of emphasis on languages, history and so on, not so much on math and economics until much later.

Poland was at that time a poor country, not well organized, the economy was half capitalistic and half just backward. You could see it very clearly in the countryside in particular. And also there was a lot of poverty among the townspeople – both Polish and Jewish, and the town was half Jewish. So the situation was not good. Nevertheless, Poland was better off than it was after the communist rule, there is no doubt about it. It was almost certainly ahead of, say, Korea and right behind Czechoslovakia for example, which was probably the most advanced country in this part of Europe and the most democratic country. But instead of being ahead of such countries as Korea, or some of the poorer ones in Western Europe, now Poland is well behind in the standard of living.

How old were you when you moved from Auschwitz?
My first ten years were spent in Łańcut and my second ten years in Auschwitz and Cracow. When the War broke out, I fled and found myself, eventually, in Russian labor camps where I spent 19 months. My brother died there. I avoided the Nazis in Poland, but my family was essentially destroyed there during the War.

Where did you go to graduate school?
I went to what was called gymnasium, which was set up for eight years at the time. You went at age 10 and left at the age of 18 after taking the *matura* exam. This was a tough exam which was a precondition for getting into the university. The last two years of gymnasium were equivalent, I think, to college studies here.

You spent the better part of your career at the University of Chicago, correct?
Yes, at two places, the University of Chicago and the National Bureau of Economic Research. My wife Lena and I came back from Russia in 1946. (We married in that year in Kazakhstan, Central Asia, and later were able to make a long, slow trip back to the West. Now we have two sons and three grandchildren.) In 1947–51, I studied economics in Heidelberg, the first German university to open after the War, and earned a Ph.D. there. Because of legislation I could not immediately immigrate to the United States until the

McCarran Act was repealed by the Congress. I did not spend the War in Poland or in Germany or in a Nazi concentration camp. I spent it in Russia. Those people who came back from there were restricted from immigration by the Act. After it was revoked by Congress, I came to this country in January 1952. Six weeks later I had a job at the NBER. It was a modest job as a research assistant but I enjoyed it a great deal and I learned a great deal. In 1953–54, I went away for a year to Harvard on a Social Science Research Fellowship. I had a lot to learn. I wrote my first paper in Leontief's seminar on input–output, which was published in *The Review of Economic Studies*. That helped and I came back to the NBER, which meanwhile moved from Columbus Circle to Madison Ave. and 39th street. And there I spent a few more years. In 1959 I moved to Chicago at the invitation that was promoted mainly by George Stigler.

Did you have any contact with Burns and Mitchell?
Oh yes with Burns, not with Mitchell. Mitchell was dead already. But I worked with Burns a lot and mainly with Moore; also with Ruth Mack, Mincer, and Fabricant. To a lesser extent, I had contact with others like Stigler, Friedman, and Kuznets.

You have said that "Post-war fluctuations have moderated because of profound structural, institutional and policy changes." What role did the Great Depression play in bringing those changes about?
A very large, even commanding role. For example, changes in banking, bank deposit insurance, that was all a legacy of the Great Depression. It was very important, I believe, for just about the first half of the post-World War II period, which was the best part of the story. It probably prevented some bad features of the interwar period. We had an earlier period with recurrent bank panics, and the more recent financial crunches are much milder. All of that, I think, was due to the Great Depression. Well, the reforms that I mentioned had some positive and some adverse effects, too, but the former prevailed, since I assume that the avoidance of any depression during the post-war period was due in part to these reforms.

Did policy makers come out of the Depression smarter?
It is hard to say and impossible to answer in a simple way because they may be facing new challenges for which they are not necessarily very well prepared. But I believe the partial answer is yes. They probably learned something that helped us prevent another Great Depression. The fact is that such depressions have not occurred in the form that they have in the past.

However, Europe with its high unemployment and related recent troubles recalls some of the past depressions. One example of ideas that were corrected is that business cycles are strictly a real or nonmonetary phenomenon; this is obviously negated by many of the facts that we observe today.

No doubt about it. Was the Great Depression mainly the result of a series of random shocks or was the downturn mainly endogenous?
I think that a downturn is almost always a combination of the two. The shocks are always with us. But I think that they are not the factors on which we should concentrate as much as recent literature does. I think that this is a misconception and actually it is not an economic explanation of fluctuations, and that is the worst part of it. If we have only fragments and each episode is standing on its own due to some kind of one or more, typically more, shocks of various kinds then we do not advance very much in our explanation of business cycles. It is the endogenous part that calls for explanation, for understanding, more than the exogenous part. The exogenous part, the shocks as I say, are always around. But it is important to know why the economy has different sensitivities over time to these shocks. Why, for example, at certain times these shocks occur and they do not cause a recession or depression, and at other times they do.

Maybe the propagation mechanism is more important to understand?
I think the propagation mechanism is very important. But the whole concept of shocks plus propagation, while today the leading kind of "explanation" of business cycles, is not in my opinion the right way to do it. Actually, more promising seems the way of the old students of the business cycle, such as Mitchell. He understood perfectly well that business cycles are basically a set of endogenous phenomena that are aggravated by various external shocks (or alleviated since some shocks are positive). He studied the data as a long, long prelude to constructing a theory which he never succeeded in completing. But he had the right approach, in my opinion, to study business cycles empirically and helped to derive important elements of theory, notably the role of profits, investment, and credit. (PS: My recent article in the *Journal of Economic Perspectives* follows this line of historical and theoretical research.)

You do not think that all business cycles are alike, isn't that correct?
No, I don't.

So, do you see the Great Depression as of a different character altogether, or does it properly fit the twentieth-century mold?

I think that it was clearly in some ways unique in its length and depth and spread. We have had depressions of various kinds in this country, and in other countries. The 1930s were presumably the worst, but it was not something that was absolutely unique, and it was not the case that there were no predecessors in any sense and no successors in any sense, as some people say. Christina Romer says that the Depression was something unique that has never been before and will never be again. I don't know that I paraphrase her absolutely correctly, but that's the sense I get from reading Romer. I would not subscribe to that view. The Great Depression had its own unique features, there is no doubt about it, but so had many other episodes.

You can always find historical particularities, the story never repeats itself exactly.

But I would not stress those. The important things are – precisely what is in common to many business cycles? For example, the concurrence of declines in profoundly cyclical variables – actual and expected profits, credit, money, plus inventory and fixed investment – was clearly often the main source of trouble. Inventory investment in lighter cycles and fixed investment proportionately more in big cycles. This repeats itself in every cycle including the Great Depression. The interaction among these variables is the most important part of the cycle, it seems to me. So this is not accidental, this needs to be studied as it has been studied intensively by a great many economists. What I am saying is that we should return to that instead of seeking explanations in thinking that it will always be unique causes, like particular technological innovations, that account for business cycles. This factor is probably more important in longer waves but does not furnish as much of an explanation of business cycles as the variables I just mentioned.

So then, qualitatively, can we say that you think the Depression was like other twentieth-century cycles?
No, because the post-Depression cycles did not have what the Great Depression had, so I would not say that they are in the same family of cycles. But the Great Depression was not the first depression. In the nineteenth century and early twentieth century there were several important depressions. For example, the downswings of 1907 and 1921 were short but very severe and deflationary. These contractions had much more in common with the Great Depression of the 1930s than have the post-World War II recessions. (PS: The late 1990s produced depression-like developments in Japan and the Asian 'tigers'.)

Did you have a good idea at the time of what the post-war economy was going

to shape up like?
I can't claim that I did, and at my age then should not be expected to. I think that few people, even very great economists, could see it very clearly. In fact some very excellent economists missed the Great Depression altogether, at least in the early stages. As is well known, Irving Fisher and others did not recognize it as a deep and disastrous event until much later. Then they had much to contribute, for example Fisher had developed the debt–deflation theory. But they were very wrong initially, and it is a well-documented fact that Fisher lost a lot of money in the process. So he can be claimed rightly as one of the greatest American economists, but he certainly was not a great forecaster or prophet. Keynes was better at portfolio management, but there also is no evidence that he foresaw the Great Depression, as far as I know.

Do you think monocausal explanations of the Great Depression get very far?
No, I don't. It is troublesome, but true, that the Great Depression is still not very well explained despite an enormous amount of work that has been done on it. Some explanations, for example, stressing the stock market, are off the mark because the downturn did not start with the stock market. The market collapse was partly a reflection of what was going on, more than a source, but this does not say much. And then the controversy about whether it was consumption or construction or still another part of output, which started the downward spiral, that also did not get very far. It may have been both consumption and investment, and it certainly soon came to involve all of that. At various times different sectors had different impacts. There were outside errors of course, errors in policy and errors in the private sector as well. The Austrians and Swedes had much to contribute with their various overinvestment theories. And then there is a revival of underconsumption as well.

Do you think, as Ben Bernanke has said, that modern business cycle models need to explain both the post-World War II and the interwar eras and we should not have to have two different sets of models to explain both?
I agree with that, in principle. A fully satisfactory model will have to explain all kinds of episodes. There is no single model, to my knowledge, that does that right now. I think that what we need is a kind of synthesis of the theoretical and econometric models. Historical studies, leading indicators, all of these things are complementary rather than competitive, and should be viewed in this light. I called for this synthesis in my *Journal of Economic Literature* survey of business cycle theories, and I still think that this is the right way to go. But since multi-causal explanations are called for and since

I also believe that different factors will play different roles in the different episodes, the same factors that I already mentioned, profits, investment, and money, will reappear but with different weights. The weights will differ over time and across countries.

That is kind of a tough standard to present for any model isn't it?
Very, very tough. I am afraid that we are not yet there, we simply do not have the capability to explain it all with a single model. But, in principle yes, such a model is precisely what is needed.

You have said, "Business cycles are not mere transitory deviations from long-term growth trends."
They are not.

Is output mean reverting, and was it mean reverting during the Great Depression?
Well, it was mean reverting in a very weak sense. Normally, say, in the post-war period, it is true that deviations in the downward direction will be followed by a process of re-approaching an upward moving equilibrium. The plucking model of Friedman has something to recommend itself. If you pluck a string, it vibrates and comes back to you. So if you pluck it from below, it springs upward. And it is a fact that after a big deviation downward that is a severe recession or depression, you will often have a strong rebound, that is to say a strong recovery and expansion. Whereas the opposite is not true: an expansion could be strong or mild and it could be followed by a mild or severe recession. There is no clear correlation between the amplitude of expansion and the amplitude of the following recession, but there is much more correlation between the amplitude of a recession and the amplitude of the following expansion.

Asymmetric behavior of the business cycle?
Oh yes. It is definitely asymmetric and, I believe, essentially nonlinear.

Do you think like Nelson and Plosser (1982), and Beaudry and Koop (1993) that there is a permanent component to the recessionary behavior of the business cycle?
Yes, I think that there is probably something right about it, and that this work on the mix between transitory and permanent components is revealing something true. Business cycles are not mere transitory short-term effects without any longer-term effects. They can affect the growth trend. And vice

versa, it is also true that growth affects business cycles. There is no doubt that the Great Depression had strong long-term effects.

What parallels do you see between the recession of 1921 and the Great Depression? Do you think policy makers at the time figured that the Great Depression would be a repeat of the successful deflation that they had and so didn't attempt to vigorously fight the Depression? Do you think that holds any water?

Perhaps it does, but I would not emphasize this so much. I see little evidence that the 1920–21 contraction and the whole deflationary decade of the 1920s produced many real economic successes. I don't think that the onset of the Great Depression can be mainly attributed to errors of policy.

You don't think that?

No, I do not. I think policy errors probably contributed much to the later worsening of the situation, but it is not easy to imagine that politicians could take the right steps in time to avert the downturn. The old monetarist idea was to emphasize the money supply and to show that the Depression was essentially a matter of monetary policy. I don't subscribe to that. I see very important endogenous elements in the money supply.

Paul Samuelson has said that it is unfair and hindsight to say that the Fed should have increased the monetary base by whatever was necessary to avert the Depression.

That is true. It is very easy to be wise so long after the event. We know all about it. We do not understand fully what caused the Great Depression, but we certainly know the events that happened rather well. So we know a lot that these guys in 1929–30 did not know and could not have known. On the other hand, it is also true that Friedman and Schwartz have shown that this was not the first episode of this kind, so there should have been some learning process involved. The learning process is very slow, two steps forward and one back at the best. Recently, so many people at the Fed have almost forgotten all the troubles that the Fed has caused time and again in the past. They think that what has happened in the last few years is somehow decisive. I am very skeptical about that.

Then let me ask you a related question. Do you agree that the Fed should act as an arbiter of security prices?

No, I don't. I think that is a misplaced role that gives them too much power. However, they should not close their eyes to the fact that occasionally we have money creation that leaks mainly into the market, so that there is little inflation in goods and services but a lot of inflation in security prices. They ought to be aware of it, and study it. But I would not give them a regulatory role in securities markets which anyway is already in existence and given to other authorities. I am all for cooperation between the authorities, but not for centralization of all power in the Fed's or anybody else's hands.

What explanations do you find most compelling and think do the best job accounting for the Great Depression? What in your judgment was the initial impetus and what accounts for the protracted depth to which the economy plunged?

Well the depth, let me put it in this order because it is easier. There, the policy mistakes and what happened with the Smoot–Hawley Act, the beggar-thy-neighbor policies which were unopposed and ill-conceived as such, all of that was bad and contributed to the length and severity of the Depression. Events in the foreign trade area, events in monetary policy, of course. It was wrong to place the maintenance of the gold standard ahead of a stabilizing, countercyclical monetary policy. But none of this caused the Great Depression. What was the original set of factors? That is still not clear and you can see the divergence of opinion in the literature. That in itself is evidence that we don't fully understand what happened. I think we had a decade in the 1920s, with its deflation, with its troubles in agriculture and construction, that prepared the way to the downturn in 1929. But it is certainly true that the downturn need not have led to such a disaster. So on how to precisely apportion the blame, so to speak, between the various sectors of the economy, I must pass. I'm not prepared to explain it and it is a matter for much additional study, even now. It should be possible to reach a better conclusion than we have. I think what is preventing us from a better consensus on these matters is a lot of pure assumptions and simple ideology. This is not conducive to good objective research.

Did the Depression change the psychology of the country?

Oh yes. For example, without the Depression we would most likely not have as much government interference as we have had in our economic affairs, some of it good, some of it bad. Some of the New Deal-style legislation and reforms were prompted by the Great Depression directly. So the Great Depression had a profound impact on economic policy and economic ideas and the thinking of people in general. It also had much to do with purely political but very important developments, such as the rise of the left in intellectual circles and other places both here in the US and to a much larger extent in Europe.

How did the Great Depression shape your life professionally? Was the Depression the biggest single event that shaped you professionally or has something else occurred in our history that had a bigger impact?
Well personally, the biggest impact, no doubt, on me was what happened in the 1930s. Not so much the Great Depression, but the rise of fascism and national socialism in Europe and the persecution the Nazis unleashed all across Europe. Being Jewish, I was their direct target and intended victim. On the other hand, I also realize that the rise of Nazis itself was due, in part, to the Great Depression and to earlier events, especially the great inflation in Germany. The economic histories of Europe, especially Germany, and the United States are enormously important for what happened later. The interwar period was a disaster in an economic and in a political sense. It was a global, enormous and, I hope, unique catastrophe. You cannot abstract from economics as most people do. It is not just plainly a moral issue, although it is that as well. What happened was a mixture of various political as well as economic factors. It is one chain that indeed goes all the way back to the Franco-Prussian war of the 1870s and the defeat of Germany in World War I that led to World War II.

Would you place the blame for World War II on the Great Depression's doorstep?
No, I would not, that goes again too far. It was not the single cause. But no doubt the Great Depression played a major role and so, as I already said, did other events, the great inflation and the 1920s in general, a very miserable period in Germany.

The Treaty of Versailles and the whole thing.
Right, all of that is well understood. Now, none of that explains why Hitler came to power and why the excesses and atrocities followed. That is not fully explained. One must not abstract from things that reveal human nature at its worst; that is how it is.

Do you think one of Keynes's objectives was to save capitalism or save capitalism from itself?
I think so. It may have been misguided (*chuckling*), but that was his objective, yes. He certainly did not see much merit in socialism, as far as I know. He was bored to death by reading Marx. I understood some of my friends say the same thing about Keynes. Bob Lucas, he does not think much about Keynes, as you

know, and says he never understood him.

I told that story to Leontief and he laughed and said, "He's right. I still don't understand it."
Leontief was one of the best critics of Keynes. *The General Theory* is not very well written. It proved to be very important but it is not clear.

Is Keynes dead?
No, he is not. Neither is Mitchell and neither is Schumpeter and a number of many other great economists. They are not "dead" for they continue to be very influential.

What about as far as practical policy making is concerned?
I think many economists overreach, by thinking that they can shape policy and that they can foresee events that will shape policy. That has been found to be wrong, so far. But one can do very important things in economics without accomplishing all of that. I think we are much better in simply trying to understand the economy, its interactions and dynamics. To affect policy is not yet the first line of our business. We claim too much if we think that we can indeed act very well as policy advisors. A very large part why we cannot is that we are so poor as forecasters.

What ended the Great Depression?
World War II ended it. There was a relapse in 1937–38 that was short but very bad, coming as it did at the end of a long and incomplete expansion. At the end of 1937 we still were not, in many ways, where we were in 1929. That was unique. Usually it is in a year or two that a recovery is completed, that is, the previous peak is regained and the next growth phase begins. Here we had a period from 1929 to 1937 and a recovery had not been accomplished. The disaster ended very slowly and with another setback. Finally, the impetus that brought us out of the Great Depression was World War II.

What impact did the New Deal programs have on your thinking?
Well, I'm not an activist for I feel we are not particularly qualified for that yet. We are better qualified than most people who are non-economists, but we have not reached the stage in which we can confidently shape policy and believe that we can avoid recessions. There are strong forces out in the economy and abroad that are difficult to deal with. But, of course, in principle we want to move in this direction, to become efficient policy advisors and forecasters. I believe that this is really the proof of the pudding. We will not really be valued

until we prove to be better at forecasting and policy advice given to elected officials.

What is your view on the role of the gold standard in the international transmission mechanism of the Depression?
Recent work by Eichengreen and others shows well the importance of the gold standard in this regard, I believe.

What are some of the lessons of the Great Depression that seem to be forgotten today or that have to be continually relearned?
One lesson that is very important is that not all elements of the Great Depression are a matter of the past that will never come back. In his most recent interview in *Fortune* magazine, Friedman says that he sees no reason to change anything in his statement of several years ago where he said that the Depression will never reoccur. I agree that it will certainly not reoccur the way it did in the 1930s, but serious troubles can and are likely to happen in different forms. The high unemployment in Europe is a very serious matter: although quite different from the Great Depression, it is still very bad.

Does the memory of the Depression stay with you and have an impact on your thinking?
I can't claim that I go to bed and that I wake up with thoughts of the Great Depression. Almost every day makes me think of what happened in Europe during World War II and this is not true of the Great Depression, but that is personal. As I have said before, there is a chain of events from the Great Depression to these disasters and wartime events and that should not be forgotten either.

But the chain of events, you keep going back to it.
I keep going back to it. It is very important generally and to me personally as well.

Here is a silly question.
OK.

What would you have done to prevent it from happening if you knew then what you know now?
Well, I don't know that I would be able to do anything to prevent the downturn from happening. But I think I would have some knowledge on what to do and what not to do. The what not to do was the most important thing at

the time. We now do know much about what to do to avoid a repetition of the Great Depression as it happened in those times. An overly restrictive monetary policy for example. That does not mean that I believe it's time to forget about all and any depressions that might come. They come in different forms. They have in the past and may in the future.

Robert Lucas has said that the Friedman–Phelps rational expectations school just had plain dumb luck that the 1970s came along when it did because of the fact that "most samples cannot tell you which of the stories about the Phillips curve is the best one." What is your reaction to that?
I never put much stock in the Phillips curve. It was pretty clear from the 1970s on that it's shaky as an empirical regularity. There were all kinds of ways, some more successful than others but none fully successful, to "fudge" it up. Lucas is probably right, in principle. They were lucky in that the word spread and was widely acknowledged in the economics profession; personally I think, much too fast and much too much. Moreover, I'm skeptical of rational expectations as such. In studying forecasting, I see that there is a lot of bias in actual economic forecasts which should not be there if rational expectations were to apply 100 percent seriously.

And the empirical evidence for it is also shaky.
Very shaky.

Is the Phillips curve dead?
Well, its original formulation, yes. But it is capable of being re-formulated and has reinvented itself time and time again in the past (*chuckling*). I would not pronounce it as absolutely dead and buried. It is not a very exploitable relationship and certainly not policy-exploitable. The Phillips curve is not dead if you admit all of its reincarnations for better or for worse, and I believe largely for worse. Nothing is pretty much dead in economics. A good science ought to bring about the death of certain relationships that are proven to be empirically unsound. But in economics it is so difficult to prove or disprove certain things. They live the cat's nine lives (*chuckling*).

How do you explain the behavior of real wages in the Great Depression?
Again, that is something that is not consistent, clearly, with a simple view of the economy as fully competitive with fully flexible prices and wages. All of these axioms are not really that at all. You cannot build an empirically successful macro model on these assumptions, and you should not try.

What is your take on the apparent stabilization of the business cycle and the work of Christina Romer?

I think that the idea that there is no moderation and perhaps no difference at all in the business cycle after World War II is wrong. There has been some moderation and there is a difference. Pre-World War I we had a number of depressions which we did not have in the US after World War II. That has been enough for me to say there has been an important change over time. But recessions became again more frequent and more severe in large parts of the world since the 1970s when compared with the earlier part of the post-war period. And recent developments in Europe's high unemployment and East Asia's severe contractions have something in common with past depressions.

What is your take on the recent literature regarding whether prices are procyclical or countercyclical?

No, they are not countercyclical. I think this is a mis-measurement. When you measure inflation and business cycles properly, you find that inflation is lagging and procyclical, and so it has remained. There are some exceptions here as there are on virtually anything. An exception that is very important is the 1970s, the inflationary recessions of that decade. These were to a large extent a matter of oil price hikes. Here you had cases of countercyclical price behavior, indeed. There was not just inflation, but increased inflation during these recessions of the 1970s. But that's about it. That is not the decisive story over time. The prevailing pattern is procyclical prices that are lagging.

Could you comment on recent Fed behavior?

I think the Fed was successful partly because of luck and partly because of good management. But that is a short-run story not a long-run story. For example, all this stress on how long and how great this expansion was misses the fact that the first two or three years of this expansion were exceptionally sluggish. Recovery was disappointingly slow in 1991–92. Unemployment was still increasing, employment was stagnant. This was very different from typical cycles where the recovery is the time of the highest growth rates. So the good times started only in 1993. Slowly 1994 led to premature fears of inflation and the moves of the Fed against the inflation which turned out to be alright but could have been bad as well. Over time, if they are repeated, they may prove adverse. Anyway, 1995 was another slowdown. The years 1996 and 1997 are very, very good years in all respects, no doubt about it. Low inflation, low unemployment, everything is just fine, but people forget that these are just two or three years. (PS: 1998 and 1999 proved highly prosperous overall as well.)

Is price stability the right focus for the Fed in your mind?
Well in some ways, yes, because they can do more about it than about other things. But somebody, presumably the Treasury, should take care of fiscal policy as well; it is not something to be forgotten or written off. The elimination of federal deficits, with its presumed downward effects on interest rates, has clearly been a welcome success in which Treasury and Congress both share.

Has there been a shift in paradigm that Alan Greenspan keeps talking about that makes price stability and full employment compatible now?
There have been changes. Probably there is more technological progress than is shown in our statistics.

Because of productivity being mis-measured and slippery?
Yes, it is very difficult to measure productivity, particularly in services. We don't quite know what the advances in productivity in services have been. We don't fully know how the computer works, it is not yet like the car where everybody knows how to use it, far from it. That is probably part of the story why it does not show up so strongly in the statistics. It is simply too early to tell and we know too little about it.

And a large part is going to be unmeasurable.
That's right.

Do you think that fiscal policy should be used for growth and not for stabilization purposes?
It should be used for stabilization purposes, to the extent it can. But the results have been very disappointing in the past, both because of errors and policy ideology. But people who blame Keynes or Keynesians for that are not entirely right. Keynes certainly did not advocate deficits in expansions, only in recessions. But there is no doubt that some Keynesians and post-Keynesians went simply astray.

Are you bothered by the trend in the distribution of income?
Yes I am, to the extent that it is valid and true. But it is a measurement problem again.

Do you know what to do about income distribution?
It is hard to tell. I am very uneasy about it. I am uneasy with forgetting about it and thinking it will take care of itself.

Leontief alerted me to some good thinking. He said this is where anthropology and sociology and economics need to come together because you are not going to find the answer to this just from economics.
I agree with that.

Are income distribution and poverty the same topic, or can they rightly be viewed separately?
No, poverty is the main thing. Even without poverty, inequalities in income distribution create resentment which has adverse effects, it makes people uncomfortable. So the distribution problem remains, even if somehow one could say that poverty is taken care of. Of course, one cannot say that anywhere, including the US.

But poverty is the bigger issue though.
Poverty is the bigger issue.

Are there any alternatives to capitalism?
Well, the only feasible alternative is more or less of what we have, namely, some mixture of capitalism and government interventions. It is still a mixed economy, although the mixture itself is shifting and I think it is shifting toward the market and away from the government sector. So it is not pure capitalism that we have, and some sort of "corrections" are probably unavoidable. I don't believe, for example, that people will voluntarily take care of the poorest of the poor by voluntary contributions if the government is somehow taken out of the business of redistribution through taxes and spending. So some moderate redistribution seems to me alright. I think without it we would have a less just and less tranquil society. But I don't like to see too much of it.

You mean too much government?
Yes, I mean it's well intentioned perhaps, but when it is growing we don't exactly know what is going on or how much. We never know exactly what the optimum is here. The result of too much government and too much redistribution is reduced incentives and growth, hence also more cyclical and other instability.

What do you see as the biggest threat to capitalism?
Well, the biggest threat has been temporarily and perhaps for a long period of time, abolished. That is, the threats first from fascism and then from communism. We buried them and not they us, as Khrushchev predicted. So we are free of those threats. I think capitalism has triumphed, but in a particular

form, after long periods of various reforms. And that probably was in part the contribution of moderate or democratic socialism, these reforms that happened. And they happened not only without the blessings of the radical left, it was against their strenuous opposition. They claimed that it never can happen, capitalism can never come to grips with poverty and inequality. Well it has to a very large extent.

Are there any particular trends in economic research or schools of thought you find disturbing?
Well yes, for example, emphasis on efficiency to the detriment of all distribution. On growth versus instability of business cycles, I think growth is a major, perhaps the major, problem. But instability of business cycles remains important as well. Less growth often means more instability, too. Elimination of depression and poverty is as high as you can put it on my agenda. So economists have social, and indeed even moral and ethical, objectives. That should not detract in any way from the objectivity of their research, quite the contrary. But there is nothing wrong with an economist who is socially conscious.

Then we all have a lot to do, don't we? There is still a lot to know.
Some people go along on this. The late Bill Vickrey, he is an interesting case of an exceedingly socially conscious economist.

Everyone wants to know, could it happen again? Could we have another Great Depression?
I cannot say it could never happen again, but it will not happen again in the same form, this I know. So, if it comes at all, it will be very different and will be unexpected. Most downturns come unexpectedly and are not forecasted. They are not even recognized promptly despite the fact that we have good tools in leading indicators. This is partly because we do not want to see them. A lot of people in business make forecasts that don't make much sense. For the next year or two, or even three or four years ahead, they don't recognize that recessions exist and will return.

Like the Hoover administration of the 1930s. They did not want to recognize that they had a problem.
And we still don't recognize it. We have official forecasts without recessions. I gave a paper at the Congressional Budget Office at their invitation on their assigned topic "Has the business cycle been abolished?" I answered in the negative. They say that they do take recessions into account, but not formally,

because they are not able to forecast the timing of the next recession cycle. And I agree with that, you cannot do it well, but you still must take it into account.

Thanks so much Professor.

Concluding Remarks

This book has endeavored to provide a record of the reflections on the Great Depression of a small sample of economists from the interwar generation. I hope it has succeeded in that endeavor. But more than this, I would also like for this book to be considered another chapter of the legacy of the interwar generation of economists and in some manner to be a small part of the many ways in which they will be remembered. The conversations show just how different the Great Depression was in our economic history. Assembling a complete understanding of the economics of the interwar era has been, and remains, a daunting task that is as yet unfinished. However, the economics profession has advanced a great deal in the almost 70 years since March 1933.

It seems to me that the economics profession owes the economists of the interwar generation a large debt of gratitude for what they have done. The research that they have conducted has allowed our level of understanding to be where it is currently. This has been made possible by the very people interviewed for this book and their contemporaries. The interwar generation has passed the torch to a new generation to see if the puzzle of the Great Depression can have all of its pieces put together. The next generation, the post-World War II generation of Bernanke, Calomiris, Eichengreen, Hamilton, and Romer, has pursued a research agenda that continues to produce advancements in our understanding. I will state with great confidence that the profession is much closer to a consensus on the causes for the impetus, depth, protracted length, and worldwide spread of the Depression than at any time you care to mention. It is the economists of the interwar generation who have made this possible. It is the economists of the interwar generation who have provided the opportunity for a new generation of economists, with different life experiences, to look at the Depression in a fresh way to find new answers and new interpretations. There is still much to learn, but we have come a long way in our understanding of the Great Depression. To the economists of the interwar generation, may God bless you and I offer you a humble and cordial "thank you" for all you have done.

Glossary of Names

The following is an extensive, but not exhaustive, selection of the individuals whose names are mentioned in the 11 interviews. The information below is contained in numerous sources such as *The Encyclopedia Britannica*, *The Columbia Encyclopedia*, *Great Economists before Keynes*, *Great Economists after Keynes*, *Who's Who in Economics*, The History of Economic Thought web site (http:cepa.newschool.edu), and other sites on the internet too numerous to mention. Quotations are the words of the Royal Swedish Academy of Sciences, indicating the motivation for awarding the Nobel Prize.

Angell, James W. (1898–1986), Born: Chicago, IL. A predecessor of the monetarist school of thought. His books *Theory of International Prices* and *The Behavior of Money* are Angell's major contributions. However, being published during the Depression, and in the same year as Keynes's *General Theory*, resulted in little attention being paid to his book *The Behavior of Money*. *Who's Who in Economics*, pp. 10–11.

Arrow, Kenneth J. (1921–), Born: New York, NY. Professor Arrow is known for his research in theories of justice, equilibrium under monopolistic competition, collective decision making, and shifts in income distribution. He was the past President of the American Economic Association, the Western Economic Association, and the International Economic Association. Arrow received the John Bates Clark medal in 1957 and shared the Nobel Prize in Economics with John Hicks in 1972 "for their pioneering contributions to general economic equilibrium theory and welfare theory." *Who's Who in Economics*, pp. 12–13.

Bagehot, Walter (1826–77), Born: Langport, Somerset, England. One of the first economists to stress the connection between credibility and the central monetary authority. His writings also stressed the need to incorporate social and cultural factors into economic analysis. *Who's Who in Economics*, p. 17.

Becker, Gary (1930–), Born: Pottsville, PA. Professor of Economics and Sociology at the University of Chicago. He received the 1992 Nobel Prize in Economics "for having extended the domain of microeconomic analysis to a wide range of human behavior and interaction, including nonmarket behavior." *Who's Who in Economics*, p. 29.

Bernanke, Ben S. (1953–), Born: Augusta, GA. Professor Bernanke was raised in Dillon, SC, attended Harvard College in 1971, and graduated in 1975 summa cum laude. After Harvard, Dr Bernanke went on to graduate school at MIT, and completed his Ph.D. in 1979. His first job was at the Stanford Graduate School of Business. In 1985 he accepted a tenured professorship in the Woodrow Wilson School at Princeton University. Dr Bernanke's research interests include macroeconomics, monetary economics, and economic history. He recently co-authored the book *Inflation Targeting: Lessons from the International Experience.* Dr Bernanke has held many advisory and visiting positions with the Federal Reserve System, but has never held a government position. He is a research associate of the NBER, a Fellow of the Econometric Society, and editor of *The American Economic Review.*

Boulding, Kenneth E. (1910–93), Born: Liverpool, England. President of the American Economic Association in 1968 and winner of the John Bates Clark medal in 1949. Boulding conducted research to synthesize Keynesian and neoclassical macroeconomics. He also stressed the importance of incorporating more normative evaluations of economic policy. *Who's Who in Economics*, p. 45.

Bradley, Omar N. (1893–1981), Born: Clark, Randolph County, MO. Graduated from West Point in 1915 and served in World War I. Bradley was the commander of the 2nd Corps in World War II, was active in the North African and Sicilian campaigns, and led the 1st Army in the invasion of Normandy. Later he commanded the US 12th Army Group in the battle for Germany. *The Columbia Encyclopedia*, p. 261.

Bronfenbrenner, Martin (1914–97), Born: Pittsburgh, PA. His interests varied widely from macroeconomics and international trade to the economics of the Japanese economy, which was his area of specialization. *Who's Who in Economics*, p. 50.

Brown, E. Cary (1916–), Born: Bakersfield, CA. Professor Brown wrote the definitive assessment of the impact of fiscal policy during the Depression. He worked at the US Treasury during World War II and his academic career focused on the topic of the history of fiscal policy.

Buchanan, James M. (1919–), Born: Murfreesboro, TN. Professor Buchanan developed public choice theory, essentially the application of economic principles to the analysis of political and bureaucratic behavior. He received the 1986 Nobel Prize in Economics "for his development of the contractual and constitutional bases of the theory of economic and political decision making." *Who's Who in Economics*, p. 52.

Burns, Arthur F. (1904–87), Born: Stanislau, Austria. Burns was instrumental in the promotion and growth of the NBER. His research was centered on macroeconomics: the study of economic growth, causes of business cycle fluctuations, and the effectiveness of stabilization policies. He was President of the NBER, Chairman of the Council of Economic Advisors for President Eisenhower, Economic Advisor to Richard Nixon, chairman of the Federal Reserve Board (1970–78) and Ambassador to Germany. *Who's Who in Economics*, p. 54.

Calomiris, Charles W. (1957–), Born: Washington, DC. Professor Calomiris is Paul M. Montrone Professor of Finance and Economics at Columbia University, a Research Fellow at the NBER, and is also Director of the American Enterprise Institution's project on financial regulation. He is a leading authority on the economics of financial institutions and has written extensively on the economics of the Great Depression.

Clark, John B. (1847–1938), Born: Providence, RI. Founder of the American Economic Association in 1888. The medal, presented by the American Economic Association every two years, given to the best economist under age 40 bears his name. Originally a critic of capitalism, his work evolved over time and he became a staunch supporter of capitalism. His later career was spent trying to move from static to dynamic analysis. *Who's Who in Economics*, pp. 70–71.

Clark, John M. (1884–1963), Born: Northampton, MA. Clark's father was John Bates Clark, the namesake of the medal awarded by the American Economic Association. An eclectic economist that wrote widely on many topics. *Who's Who in Economics*, p. 71.

Cohen, Morris R. (1880–1947), Born: Minsk, Russia. An American philosopher and a graduate of College of the City of New York. Cohen received his Ph.D. from Harvard in 1906. He came to the United States in 1892. Cohen began as an instructor in mathematics at the College of the City of New York, and then he transferred to the department of philosophy, where he taught from 1912 until 1938, becoming famous for his use of Socratic irony. Cohen is rated as one of the most important American philosophers. *The Columbia Encyclopedia*, p.446.

Coughlin, Charles E. (1891–1979), Born: Hamilton, Ontario, Canada. Father Coughlin was a US Roman Catholic radio priest who expressed his economic and political views to his growing mass audience. He was a supporter of President Franklin D. Roosevelt during the 1932 election. He later turned on Roosevelt, and expressed his anti-New Deal views. He founded a magazine, *Social Justice*, which attacked communism, Wall Street, and Jews. The magazine was barred from being mailed in the US and Father Coughlin halted his broadcasts by order of the Catholic hierarchy. *The Columbia Encyclopedia*, p. 500.

Currie, Lauchlin (1902–93), Born: West Dublin, Nova Scotia, Canada. Currie received training at both the London School of Economics and Harvard and was an early adherent of monetarism. Currie was an advisor to Roosevelt during World War II, where he was involved with the Lend–Lease Program with China. He was later targeted by McCarthyites, and lost his US citizenship in 1954, thereafter moving to Colombia.

Debreu, Gerard (1921–), Born: Calais, France. Professor Debreu is currently a faculty member at the University of California at Berkeley. He provided one of the first simple proofs of the existence of a competitive equilibrium and introduced the concept of a quasi-equilibrium. Debreu was awarded the Nobel Prize in Economics in 1983 "for having incorporated new analytic methods into economic theory and for his rigorous reformulation of the theory of general equilibrium." *Who's Who in Economics*, pp. 88–89.

Donovan, William J. (1883–1959), Born: Buffalo, NY. "Wild Bill" Donovan was Director of the Office of Strategic Services (OSS) and a veteran of World War I. Left the army a major general in 1945 and was also Ambassador to Thailand between 1953 and 1954. *The Columbia Encyclopedia*, p. 587.

Douglas, Paul H. (1892–1976), Born: Salem, MA. Douglas was the developer, along with Charles W. Cobb, of the famous Cobb-Douglas production function. Douglas represented Illinois and served in the US Senate for almost 20 years. *Who's Who in Economics*, p. 98.

Eccles, Marriner S. (1890–1977), Born: Logan, UT. An unorthodox banker, Roosevelt appointed him to the Board of Governors of the Federal Reserve System in 1933. Eccles served as chairman of the Board of Governors from 1936 to 1948. *The Columbia Encyclopedia*, p. 620.

Eichengreen, Barry (1952–), Born: Berkeley, CA. Dr Eichengreen is the George C. Pardee and Helen N. Pardee Professor of Economics and Political

Science at the University of California at Berkeley. He is also a research associate at the NBER and also was a visiting scholar at the International Monetary Fund. He has written extensively on a variety of economic issues. His current research topics include European monetary unification and the economics of currency crises and capital flows.

Fischer, Wolfram (1928–), Born: Weigelsdorf-Tannenberg, Germany. Research focuses on economic history of industrialization and the economic history of the twentieth century. *Who's Who in Economics*, p. 115.

Fisher, Irving (1867–1947), Born: Saugerties, NY. Milton Friedman claims Fisher is the best economist America has ever produced. His contributions on index numbers, real versus nominal interest rates, debt deflation and many other topics are all notable advancements in economics. *Who's Who in Economics*, p. 116.

Gayer, Arthur (1903–51), Born: Poona, India. Gayer worked for the Roosevelt administration during the Depression on the Commission on Economic Reconstruction. An early advocate of Keynesian economics. *Who's Who in Economics*, p. 130.

Gerschenkron, Alexander (1904–78), Born: Odessa, Russia. Gerschenkron wrote on Soviet economics but later moved into other research areas, such as the convergence hypothesis in economic growth. *Who's Who in Economics*, p. 132.

Graham, Frank D. (1890–1949), Born: Halifax, Nova Scotia, Canada. Served on the special US War Department Commission in 1945 and also as an economic advisor to the US. Served on the Federal Farm Board from 1930 to 1931. His works include *The Golden Avalanche*. *Who's Who in Economics*, p. 140.

Grange, Harold "Red" (1903–91), Born: Forksville, PA. Grange was a highly publicized collegiate and professional football player. He entered the University of Illinois in 1922, and in a total of 20 varsity games he scored 31 touchdowns. He earned the nickname "the Galloping Ghost" through his amazing feats as a running back. He left college three years later to play professional football with the Chicago Bears.

Greenspan, Alan (1926–), Born: New York, NY. Greenspan has served in many capacities under several Presidents. He was chairman of the President's Council of Economic Advisors under Gerald Ford from 1974 to 1977. From

1981 to 1983, he served as chairman of the National Commission on Social Security Reform for Ronald Reagan. Greenspan was appointed to the Federal Reserve Board in 1987 by Reagan, who made him chairman in 1988.

Hamilton, James D. (1954–), Born: Denver, CO. Professor Hamilton is currently the Chair of the Economics Department at the University of California, San Diego. He received his Ph.D. in economics from the University of California, Berkeley in 1983, and previously was on the faculty at the University of Virginia. His primary fields of research are in macroeconomics and econometrics. He is a Fellow of the Econometrics Society and a research associate at the NBER. His 1994 book *Time Series Analysis* sets the standard for the profession.

Hansen, Alvin H. (1887–1975), Born: Viborg, SD. One of the first, if not the first, prominent orthodox economist to convert to and promote the Keynesian school of thought in the US. *Who's Who in Economics*, p. 154.

Hardy, Charles O. (1884–1948), Born: Island City, MO. Hardy's research focused on mathematical economics and questions concerning gold flows. *Who's Who in Economics*, pp. 156–57.

Hawley, Willis C. (1864–1941), Born: Monroe, OR. US representative from the 1st Congressional district in Oregon from 1907 to 1933. Co-sponsor of the Hawley–Smoot tariff legislation at the beginning of the Depression.

Hawtrey, Ralph (1879–1971), Born: Buckinghamshire, England. Hawtrey was responsible for the "overconsumptionist" monetary theory of business cycles. Hawtrey also conducted research on monetary issues with a distinct "Cambridge" approach. *Who's Who in Economics*, p. 160.

Hayek, Friedrich A. von (1899–1992), Born: Vienna, Austria. Hayek's book *The Road to Serfdom* was a devastating critique of socialism and government intervention in economic affairs. Hayek shared the 1974 Nobel Prize in Economics with Gunnar Myrdal "for their pioneering work in the theory of money and economic fluctuations and for their penetrating analysis of the interdependence of economic, social, and institutional phenomena." *Who's Who in Economics*, pp. 160–61.

Henderson, Hubert D. (1890–1952), Born: Beckenham, England. Professor at Oxford, public official and contemporary of Keynes. *Who's Who in Economics*, p. 165.

Hicks, John (1904–89), Born: Warwick, England. One of the most prolific research economists in history. Hicks wrote on many topics from consumer theory to economic growth. Hicks was knighted in 1966 and shared the 1972 Nobel Prize in Economics with Kenneth Arrow "for their pioneering contributions to general economic equilibrium theory and welfare theory." *Who's Who in Economics*, p. 167.

Higgins, Benjamin H. (1912–), Born: London, Ontario, Canada. Macroeconomist and advisor to many different governments. *Who's Who in Economics*, pp. 167–68.

Hoover, John E. (1895–1972), Born: Washington, DC. Director of the Federal Bureau of Investigation from 1924 to 1972. During the 1930s he sought to publicize the work of the agency in fighting organized crime, and participated directly in the arrest of several major gangsters. After World War II, Hoover focused on the threat of communist subversion. In office until his death, he became a controversial figure. His many critics considered his anti-communism obsessive. He served under eight Presidents. *The Columbia Encyclopedia*, p. 969.

Hopkins, Harry L. (1890–1946), Born: Sioux City, IA. President Roosevelt named Hopkins head of the Federal Emergency Relief Administration and the Works Progress Administration. Hopkins favored the idea of producing jobs instead of giving direct financial relief. He served as the Secretary of Commerce from 1938 to 1940. Hopkins also sat on the War Production Board and the Pacific War Council and began the Lend–Lease Program. *The Columbia Encyclopedia*, p. 970.

Hotelling, Harold (1895–1973), Born: Fulda, MN. Early proponent of the use of statistics and mathematics in economic analysis. Hotelling's research areas included the economics of renewable resources, welfare economics, and the incidence of taxation. *Who's Who in Economics*, pp. 177–78.

Ickes, Harold L. (1874–1952), Born: Frankstown Township, PA. Ickes began as a newspaper reporter and switched to practicing law in 1907. He was active in municipal reform politics and civil liberties, and helped develop the Progressive Party. He was the campaign manager for Republican candidate Charles Hughes in 1916, thus rejecting the nomination of Warren Harding in 1920. He supported Franklin D. Roosevelt in his 1932 election, and was later named Secretary of the Interior and the head of the Public Works Administration. *The Columbia Encyclopedia*, p. 1001.

Johnson, Harry G. (1923–79), Born: Toronto, Canada. A prolific researcher, Johnson made important contributions to the fields of international trade theory, the monetary approach to the balance of payments, the economics of R&D, and the economics of higher education. *Who's Who in Economics*, pp. 189–90.

Jones, Homer (1906–86), Born: Ainsworth, IA. Jones played a major part in developing the St. Louis Federal Reserve Bank as a leader in monetary research and statistics. Jones served as Research Director and Senior Vice-President at the Bank. During his tenure, the Bank earned the reputation as a maverick in the Federal Reserve System. Jones was a major mentor of Milton Friedman. A group of articles praising Jones's work and the impact he had on economics was published in the *Journal of Monetary Economics* in 1976.

Kamenev, Lev B. (1883–1936), Born: Moscow, Russia. Russian communist leader. Kamenev sided with the Bolshevik wing of the Socialist Party when the party split (1903). Kamenev was banished (1915) to Siberia, and returned after the Revolution of 1917 and became a member of the first Politburo of the Communist Party. When Lenin died in 1924, he formed a triumvirate with Stalin and Zinoviev that excluded Trotsky, Kamenev's brother-in-law, from power. In 1925 the Stalinist majority in the party wrested power from Kamenev and Zinoviev. They both joined the opposition organized by Trotsky. Kamenev, Zinoviev, and 13 others were tried for treason in the first big public purge trial; they confessed and were executed. *The Columbia Encyclopedia*, p. 1109.

Keynes, John M. (1883–1946), Born: Cambridge, England. Arguably the most important economist of the twentieth century. His 1936 book *The General Theory* set the course for the development of macroeconomics for the remainder of the century. *Who's Who in Economics*, pp. 202–03.

Khrushchev, Nikita S. (1894–1971), Born: Kalinovka, Ukraine. Russian communist leader and statesman. He became ruler of the Soviet Union after the death of Stalin. During a speech to the UN, used his shoe to bang the podium claiming that socialism would triumph over capitalism and that "we will bury you." He also was Premier of the Soviet Union during the Cuban missile crisis. *The Columbia Encyclopedia*, pp. 1130–31.

Knight, Frank H. (1885–1972), Born: White Oak Township, McLean County, IL. Considered to be one of the founders of "the Chicago School" during the 1920–40 era. Knight was also a colleague of Aaron Director, Charles Hardy, Lloyd Mints, Homer Jones, Beardsley Ruml, and Henry Schultz during this period. Influential mentor of Milton Friedman and his contemporaries. *Who's Who in Economics*, pp. 208–09.

Kuznets, Simon (1901–85), Born: Kharkov, Russia. Conducted research on measuring economic activity and the composition of national income. Received the Nobel Prize in Economics in 1971 "for his empirically founded interpretation of economic growth which has led to new and deepened insight into the economic and social structure and process of development." *Who's Who in Economics*, p. 216.

LaFollette, Robert (1855–1925), Born: Primrose, WI. LaFollette was a political leader known for being the founder of the Progressive Movement. He served as a Republican in the House of Representatives and was elected to the Senate in 1905. He founded *LaFollette's Weekly Magazine* and the National Progressive Republican League. When war broke out in Europe in 1914, he completely opposed President Wilson's support of the allies. In 1924, he ran for President in an independent campaign and gathered 17 percent of the vote. He was active in stands on labor and civil liberties. *The Columbia Encyclopedia*, p. 1163.

Langer, William L. (1896–1977), Born: Boston, MA. Received his Ph.D. from Harvard in 1923. Professor at Harvard from 1927, Langer, together with Ed Mason, was instrumental in forming the research and analysis branch of the Office of Strategic Services. Langer also was assistant to the Secretary of State in 1946. His studies of the diplomatic climates preceding World Wars I and II are masterly factual surveys. He was one of the first to urge that historians make fuller use of related disciplines, especially of psychology.

Lenin, Vladimir I. (1870–1924), Born: Simbirsk, Russia. Organizer of the Russian Communist Party, and leader of Russia after the 1917 Revolution. *Who's Who in Economics*, pp. 228–29.

Lerner, Abba P. (1903–82), Born: Bessarabia, Russia. Lerner studied economics at the London School of Economics in order to find out why his printing business had failed. Lerner is best known for his work in international trade, Keynesian economics, welfare economics, and macroeconomics, in which he created the concept of functional finance. *Who's Who in Economics*, pp. 229–30.

Long, Huey P. (1893–1935), Born: Winnfield, LA. Long, nicknamed "the kingfish," was a populist Senator from Louisiana and sought national power with a "Share-the-Wealth" program. He proclaimed to make "every man a king." During the Depression and its economic desperation, Long's message drew some public attention. Long would have received substantial votes in the election of 1935 and could have been a power broker between Democrats and Republicans. It is said that Long and Douglas MacArthur were the two men Roosevelt feared the most. Long, however, was assassinated at the height of his power. *The Columbia Encyclopedia*, pp. 1238–39.

Lucas, Robert E. Jr. (1937–), Born: Yakima, WA. Principal contributor to the development of rational expectations and the refutation of Keynesian econometrics. Lucas won the 1995 Nobel Prize in Economics "for having developed and applied the hypothesis of rational expectations, and thereby having transformed macroeconomic analysis and deepened our understanding of economic policy." *Who's Who in Economics*, pp. 242–43.

Marshall, George C. (1880–1959), Born: Uniontown, PA. Marshall, a graduate of the Virginia Military Institute, served as the chief of operations during World War I and then was placed in charge of instruction at the infantry school in Fort Benning, GA. He was the chief of staff of the US Army the day World War II began in September 1939. He was responsible for raising and equipping the largest ground and air force in the history of the US. This feat earned him the nickname of "the organizer of victory" by Winston Churchill. He served as Secretary of State in 1947 and later proposed the Marshall Plan for the rebuilding of the European economies. In 1953 he was awarded the Nobel Peace Prize. *The Columbia Encyclopedia*, p. 1316.

Mason, Edward S. (1899–1992), Born: Clinton, IA. Mason was instrumental in forming the research and analysis branch of the Office of Strategic Services. Mason also held numerous positions throughout his career, including Dean of what is now the Kennedy School of Government at Harvard University, and also was President of the American Economic Association. *Who's Who in Economics*, pp. 254–55.

Mayer, Thomas (1927–), Born: Vienna, Austria. One of the first economists to refute the findings of Temin in his 1976 book *Did Monetary Forces Cause the Great Depression?* Also has written extensively about monetarism and its empirical foundations. *Who's Who in Economics*, p. 255.

McCarthy, Joseph R. (1908–57), Born: Appleton, WI. "Tail gunner Joe" McCarthy was a Marine during World War II and a Republican Senator beginning in 1946. He systematically sought persons whom he suspected of having communist sympathies and led a nationwide anti-communist crusade. The pervasive and persistent persecution that resulted became known as

McCarthyism. The crusade was dealt a serious blow when one of the individuals called to testify before his hearings asked McCarthy "at long last Senator, have you no decency ... simple human decency?" The era of McCarthyism ended in 1954 when he was officially censured for his conduct by other Senate members. *The Columbia Encyclopedia*, p. 1265.

Meade, James E. (1907–95), Born: Swanage, Dorset, England. Received the Nobel Prize in Economics in 1977 "for his pathbreaking contribution to the theory of international trade and international capital movements." *Who's Who in Economics*, p. 261.

Mellon, Andrew W. (1855–1937), Born: Pittsburgh, PA. Secretary of the Treasury (1921–32) for Presidents Harding, Coolidge, and Hoover. One of the richest men in the US in the 1920s, Mellon became unpopular during the Depression. He resigned from the Treasury to become Ambassador to England. *The Columbia Encyclopedia*, p. 1346.

Mills, Ogden (1884–1937), Born: Newport, RI. Secretary of the Treasury under Hoover from February 1932 until March 1933. Advocate of "sound money" policies that followed balanced budgets and strict adherence to the gold standard. *The Columbia Encyclopedia*, p. 1379.

Mincer, Jacob (1922–), Born: Tomaszow, Poland. Professor Mincer is the Buttenwieser Emeritus Professor of Economics and Human Relations at Columbia University. His research has focused on labor economics, and he is responsible for introducing the concept of human capital. His work also extended to the areas of female labor force participation, fertility, and demographics. *Who's Who in Economics*, p. 270.

Mises, Ludwig von (1881–1973), Born: Lemberg, Austro-Hungary. He was the founding father of the Austrian school of economic thought. Mises was also a main critic of central planning and socialist economies. *Who's Who in Economics*, p. 271.

Mitchell, Wesley C. (1874–1948), Born: Rushville, IL. One of the most important individuals in the founding of the NBER. Mitchell was a pioneer in business cycle measurement and research. *Who's Who in Economics*, p. 272.

Morgenthau, Henry, Jr. (1891–1967), Born: New York, NY. Chairman of the Federal Farm Board and Governor of the Farm Credit Administration. He was Under-Secretary of the Treasury in 1933 and became Secretary when William H. Woodin resigned. He remained Secretary of the Treasury until 1945. *The*

Columbia Encyclopedia, p. 1420.

Okun, Arthur (1928–80), Born: Jersey City, NJ. He is the namesake of the famous "Okun's Law" regarding the empirical relation between changes in the unemployment rate and economic growth. Okun served on President Kennedy's Council of Economic Advisors and was the chairman in 1968–69. Thereafter he was a Senior Fellow at the Brookings Institution for the remainder of his life. *Great Economists since Keynes*, pp. 188–89.

Olson, Mancur (1932–98), Born: Buxton, ND. Olson is best known for his book *The Rise and Decline of Nations* and his research on economic growth. Olson stressed that the key to understanding the growth process lies in examining the quality of the institutions and the policies of a country.

Phelps, Edmund S. (1933–), Born: Evanston, IL. Along with Milton Friedman, Phelps was the first to argue that the Phillips curve was not exploitable by policy and was not a stable relation. He also conducted research on the non-accelerating inflation rate of unemployment, or the so-called NAIRU. *Who's Who in Economics*, p. 304.

Phillips, Alban W. (1914–75), Born: Te Rehunga, Dannevirke, New Zealand. Phillips pioneered the application of optimal control and engineering techniques to econometric models. He is the individual from whom the Phillips curve derives its name. Phillips also developed econometric estimation techniques for models with autoregressive, moving average errors. *Who's Who in Economics*, p. 305.

Quesnay, Francois (1694–1774), Born: Méré, France. French economist, founder of the physiocratic school. A physician to Louis XV, his chief work was the *Tableau Economique* (economic table), said to have been printed by the King's own hands. The natural laws of the economy were thought to be summed up in his *Tableau*. *Who's Who in Economics*, p. 312.

Robbins, Lionel (1898–1984), Born: Sipson, Middlesex, England. Influential professor who took over the chair at the London School of Economics in 1929 and built the reputation of the department of economics. *Who's Who in Economics*, pp. 320–21.

Romer, Christina D. (1958–), Born: Alton, IL. Dr Romer is the Class of 1957 – Garff B. Wilson Professor of Economics at the University of California at Berkeley. Her main fields of research are economic history and macroeconomics. She has researched the business cycles of the late nineteenth and early twentieth centuries, the causes of the Great Depression, the effects of monetary policy, and the reliability of historical macroeconomic data.

Rosenburg, Nathan (1927–), Born: Passaic, NJ. Fairleigh S. Dickenson Professor of Public Policy, Stanford University. Rosenburg's research interests include the economics of technological change, the economic role of science, and economic history and development.

Rostow, Walt W. (1916–), Born: New York, NY. Economic historian who focused on British economic history and the stages of economic growth. Rostow was later a close advisor to Robert McNamara during the Vietnam war. *Who's Who in Economics*, pp. 326–27.

Say, Jean-Baptiste (1767–1832), Born: Lyons, France. Say began his career as a businessman, and switched his interest to economics in the early nineteenth century. He was a member of the French Tribunate from 1799 to 1806. Through his works, he introduced the ideas of Adam Smith to France and other European countries. His law of markets stating "supply creates its own demand" was long thought to be one of the foundations that ensured full employment equilibrium and the absence of overproduction. *Who's Who in Economics*, p. 335.

Schumpeter, Joeseph A. (1883–1950), Born: Triesch, Austro-Hungary. A most influential and important economist of the twentieth century. Schumpeter had much popular success with his book *Capitalism, Socialism and Democracy*. In this book, Schumpeter rejected Marx's claims of the imminent downfall of capitalism. Instead, Schumpeter asserted that capitalism, by its own internal forces, would ultimately be transformed into socialism. *Who's Who in Economics*, p. 342.

Simons, Henry C. (1899–1946), Born: Virden, Illinois. A student of Frank Knight, Simons was an early promoter of monetarism and the desirability of adhering to rules in the conduct of monetary policy. Simons also wrote extensively on tax policy. Milton Friedman credits Simons as a major influence on his career. *Who's Who in Economics*, p. 354.

Smith, Adam (1723–90), Born: Kirkcaldy, Scotland. Adam Smith is regarded as the founder of modern political economy. His book *The Wealth of Nations* set laissez faire economics off as its own academic discipline. Smith attended Balliol College at Oxford. After graduating, in 1751, he was made the chair of moral philosophy. *Who's Who in Economics*, p. 356.

Smith, Alfred E. (1873–1944), Born: New York, NY. Smith was the first Roman Catholic to run for the office of President in 1928. He had served in the state assembly, and advanced to the office of speaker due to his intelligence, dedication, and genial manner. While serving as a four-time Democratic governor of New York, he fought for social issues such as adequate housing, improved factory laws, proper care of the mentally ill, child welfare, and state parks. *The Columbia Encyclopedia*, p. 1977.

Smoot, Reed (1862–1941), Born: Salt Lake City, UT. US Senator (1903–33). Smoot was the first Mormon to be elected to the Senate. He was a member of the so-called "irreconcilables" in opposing the League of Nations and was one of the group that worked for Warren G. Harding's nomination. In his later years in the Senate he was chairman of the finance committee. He was the co-author of the Hawley–Smoot Tariff Act of 1930. *The Columbia Encyclopedia*, p. 1980.

Solow, Robert M. (1924–), Born: New York, NY. Solow made major contributions to the theory of capital and growth in the 1950s and 1960s. He won the John Bates Clark award in 1961 and was President of the American Economic Association in 1979. He won the Nobel Prize in Economics in 1987 "for his contributions to the theory of economic growth." *Who's Who in Economics*, p. 358.

Stalin, Joseph (1879–1953), Born: Gori, Russia. Real name was Dzhugashvili, but adopted the name Stalin meaning "man of steel" in 1913. Leader of the Soviet Communist Party after the death of Lenin and throughout World War II. *Who's Who in Economics*, p. 362.

Stigler, George J. (1911–91), Born: Renton, WA. Received the Nobel Prize in Economics in 1982 "for his seminal studies of industrial structure, functioning of markets and causes and effects of public regulation." *Who's Who in Economics*, p. 364.

Struik, Dirk J. (1894–2000), Born: Rotterdam, Netherlands. Struik attended the Hogere Buger school, which was a school designed for children of middle class parents who were aspiring to better their status. He then attended Leiden University by commuter train and never was involved in student life. He ultimately was a faculty member of the Department of Mathematics at MIT. By this time he was well known for his left-wing views. In 1951, he was charged with teaching Marxism and being part of the Communist Party.

Sweezy, Paul M. (1910–), Born: New York, NY. Sweezy was a Harvard economist well known for his concerns on analyzing monopolistic competition and updating Marxian thought into neo-Marxian thought. He is responsible for the discovery of the kinked demand curve for oligopoly. He is also known for his study on the English coal industry. He helped found the publication *Monthly Review* in 1949. Sweezy openly defied the Attorney General of New Hampshire's inquiry into his alleged "subversive activities," and was jailed for "contempt" in 1953. This conviction was overturned by the Supreme Court in 1957. *Who's Who in Economics*, pp. 367–68.

Tarshis, Lorie (1911–93), Born: Toronto, Canada. A Guggenheim and Ford Fellow, he was the author of several books and dozens of journal articles and served stints as chairman of the Economics Department at Stanford University. Tarshis was one of the first followers of Keynes and wrote one of the earliest textbooks on Keynesian economics.

Taussig, Frank W. (1859–1940), Born: St. Louis, MO. Editor of the *Quarterly Journal of Economics*, and also influential in the development of the careers of many economists. *Who's Who in Economics*, pp. 368–69.

Temin, Peter (1937–), Born: Philadelphia, PA. Temin is the Elisha Gray II Professor of Economics at MIT. An economic historian who has made major contributions to our understanding of the economics of the interwar era, and the role of the gold standard in particular. *Who's Who in Economics*, p. 370.

Thomas, Norman (1884–1968), Born: Marion, OH. Thomas was known as one of the founders of the American Civil Liberties Union. During World War I, he became a pacifist and opposed the US participation in both World War I and World War II. In 1918 he joined the Socialist Party and was the Party's candidate for President in 1928 and many times thereafter. *The Columbia Encyclopedia*, p. 2128.

Thornton, Henry (1760–1815), Born: Clapham, England. Early monetary economist who studied money, velocity, prices, and employment. Thornton's research went largely unnoticed until it was re-discovered by Viner and Hollander. *Who's Who in Economics*, p. 372.

Tinbergen, Jan (1903–94), Born: The Hague, Netherlands. Tinbergen shared the very first Nobel Prize in Economics with Ragnar Frisch in 1969 "for having developed and applied dynamic models for the analysis of economic processes." *Who's Who in Economics*, p. 373.

Vickrey, William (1914–96), Born: Victoria, British Columbia, Canada.

Vickrey is best known for his progressive taxation reform proposals on issues such as power succession, tax, and taxable tax credit for government interest. He received the Nobel Prize in Economics in 1996 "for his contributions to the economic theory of incentives under asymmetric information." *Who's Who in Economics*, p. 385.

Viner, Jacob (1892–1970), Born: Montreal, Quebec, Canada. Full Professor on the faculty of Chicago in 1925 and the editor of the *Journal of Political Economy* beginning in 1928. Viner worked for the government extensively during the Depression and was a consistent advocate of deficit spending and public works to ease the distress of the time. *Who's Who in Economics*, pp. 386–87.

Volcker, Paul A. (1927–), Born: Cape May, NJ. He divided the earlier part of his career between the Federal Reserve Bank of New York, Chase Manhattan Bank, and the Treasury Department. Volcker served as the President of the Federal Reserve of New York from 1975 to 1979 and was chairman of the Board of Governors of the Federal Reserve System from 1979 to 1987.

Warburton, Clark (1896–1979), Born: Shady Grove, NY. Warburton was one of the earliest contributors to the modern literature on the quantity theory of money. He was also one of the first economists to investigate the behavior of the money supply during the Great Depression. He spent most of his career at the Federal Deposit Insurance Corporation. *Who's Who in Economics*, pp. 391–92.

Wells, David A. (1828–98), Born: Springfield, MA. Wells originally began his career as a geologist and chemist. He turned to economics in mid-life and later became a determined free trader. His interests were mainly concentrated on tariffs, currency, theory of money, and taxation. *Who's Who in Economics*, pp. 396–97.

Wicker, Elmus (1926–), Born: Lake Charles, LA. Emeritus Professor of Economics at Indiana University. Wicker has written extensively on monetary issues during the Depression. His recent book *The Banking Panics of the Great Depression* presents an alternative interpretation to that of Friedman and Schwartz regarding the economic impact of the bank panics.

Yntema, Theodore O. (1900–85), Born: Holland, MI. Yntema received his Ph.D. from the University of Chicago and was a faculty member there for many years. He also worked for the National Recovery Administration during the Depression, and was Director of the Cowles Commission and the NBER. He was also appointed Vice-President of Finance for the Ford Motor Company in 1949 and remained there until he retired in 1965.

Zinoviev, Grigori E. (1883–1936), Born: Yelizavetgrad, Ukraine. A Bolshevik leader after 1903, Zinoviev was forced to flee abroad in 1908. He was Lenin's main collaborator from 1909 to 1917, and returned with Lenin after the February Revolution of 1917. Zinoviev, Kamenev, and Stalin fought for control of leadership after the death of Lenin. Stalin turned against Zinoviev and Kamenev, defeating them and other opposition from the left. Zinoviev was tried for treason along with Kamenev and 13 other members of the Bolsheviks in 1936 and was executed by Stalin. *The Columbia Encyclopedia*, p. 2383.

Zuckerman, Solly (1904–93), Born: Cape Town, South Africa. Research anatomist who served in many capacities throughout his career. Valuable advisor to the military from 1939 to 1946. Was originally called upon to examine the effects of bomb blasts on the human body. He was knighted in 1964.

Zuppke, Bob (1879–1957), Born: Berlin, Germany. Zuppke was an American college football coach credited with the introduction of the offensive huddle. He emigrated to the US with his family in 1881. Zuppke graduated from the University of Wisconsin, and coached high school football until 1913. He then became the head football coach at the University of Illinois.

References

Abramovitz, M., undated, 'The monetary side of long swings in US economic growth', Stanford University Center for Research in Economic Growth, Memorandum No. 146.

Abramovitz, M. (1977), 'Determinants of nominal-income and money-stock growth and the level of the balance of payments: two-country models under a specie standard', unpublished, Stanford University.

Abramovitz, M. (1986), 'Catching up, forging ahead and falling behind', *Journal of Economic History*, June.

Abramovitz, M. (1989), *Thinking About Growth and Other Essays in Economic Growth and Welfare*, New York: Cambridge University Press.

Abramovitz, M. (1993), 'The search for the sources of growth: areas of ignorance, old and new', *Journal of Economic History*, June.

Abramovitz, M. and P. David (1996), 'Convergence and Deferred Catch Up', in R. Landau, T. Taylor and G. Wright (eds), *Mosaic of Economic Growth*, Stanford, CA: Stanford University Press.

Adelman, M.A. (1995), *The Genie out of the Bottle*, Cambridge, MA: MIT Press.

Anderson, B.L. and J.L. Butkiewicz (1980), 'Money, spending and the Great Depression', *Southern Economic Journal*, October.

Angell, J.W. (1926), *The Theory of International Prices*, Cambridge, MA: Harvard University Press.

Angell, J.W. (1936), *The Behavior of Money*, New York: McGraw-Hill Co.

Bagehot, W. (1867), *The English Constitution*, London: Chapman and Hall.

Bagehot, Walter (1880), *Economic Studies*, London: Longmans, Green.

Balke, N.S. and R.J. Gordon (1986), 'Historical Data', in R.J. Gordon (ed.), *The American Business Cycle: Continuity and Change*, Chicago: University of Chicago Press.

Beaudry, P. and G. Koop (1993), 'Do recessions permanently change output?', *Journal of Monetary Economics*, April.

Bernanke, B.S. (1983), 'Nonmonetary effects of the financial crisis in the propagation of the Great Depression', *American Economic Review*, June.

Bernanke, B.S. (1986), 'Alternative Explanations of the Money–Income Correlation', in K. Brunner and A. H. Meltzer (eds), *Real Business Cycles, Real Exchange Rates and Actual Policies*, Amsterdam: North-Holland.

Bernanke, B.S. (1995), 'The macroeconomics of the Great Depression: a comparative approach', *Journal of Money, Credit, and Banking*, February.

Bernanke, B.S. (2000), *Essays on the Great Depression*, Princeton, NJ: Princeton University Press.

Bernanke, B.S. and H. James (1991), 'The Gold Standard, Deflation, and Financial Crisis in the Great Depression: An International Comparison', in R.G. Hubbard (ed.), *Financial Markets and Financial Crises*, Chicago: University of Chicago Press.

Bernanke, B.S. and K. Carey (1996), 'Nominal wage stickiness and aggregate supply in the Great Depression', *Quarterly Journal of Economics*, August.

Bernanke, B.S., T. Laubach, F.S. Mishkin and A.S. Posen (1999), *Inflation Targeting: Lessons from the International Experience*, Princeton, NJ: Princeton University Press.

Blaug, M. (1985), *Great Economists since Keynes*, Totowa, NJ: Barnes and Noble Books.

Blaug, M. (1986), *Great Economists before Keynes*, Atlantic Highlands, NJ: Humanities Press International.

Blaug, M. and P. Sturges (1983), *Who's Who in Economics*, Cambridge, MA: MIT Press.

Bridgewater, W. and S. Kurtz (1963), *The Columbia Encyclopedia*, 3rd edition, New York: Columbia University Press.

Brown, E.C. (1956), 'Fiscal policy in the thirties: a reappraisal', *American Economic Review*, December.

Brown, W.A. (1940), *The International Gold Standard Reinterpreted, 1914–1934*, New York: National Bureau of Economic Research.

Card, D. and A. Krueger (1995), *Myth and Measurement: The New Economics of the Minimum Wage*, Princeton, NJ: Princeton University Press.

Cecchetti, S.G. (1992), 'Prices during the Great Depression: was the deflation of 1930–32 really anticipated?', *American Economic Review*, March.

Cecchetti, S.G. (1998), 'Understanding the Great Depression: Lessons for Current Policy', in M. Wheeler (ed.), *The Economics of the Great Depression*, Kalamazoo, MI: W.E. Upjohn Institute for Employment Research.

Cecchetti, S.G. and G. Karras (1994), 'Sources of output fluctuations during the interwar period: further evidence on the causes of the Great Depression', *Review of Economics and Statistics*, February.

Choudri, E.U. and L.A. Kochin (1980), 'The exchange rate and the international transmission of business cycle disturbances', *Journal of Money, Credit, and Banking*, November.

Clark, J.M. (1934), *Strategic Factors in Business Cycles*, New York: National Bureau of Economic Research .

DeLong, J.B. and A. Shleifer (1991), 'The stock market bubble of 1929: evidence from closed-end mutual funds', *Journal of Economic History*, September.

Eichengreen, B. (1986), 'The Bank of France and the sterilization of gold, 1926–1932', *Explorations in Economic History*, 23.

Eichengreen, B. (1992), *Golden Fetters: The Gold Standard and the Great Depression, 1919–1939*, New York: Oxford University Press.

Eichengreen, B. and J. Sachs (1985), 'Exchange rates and economic recovery in the 1930s', *Journal of Economic History*, December.

Evans, M. and P. Wachtel (1993), 'Were price changes during the Great Depression anticipated? Evidence from nominal interest rates', *Journal of Monetary Economics*, October.

Fackler, J.S. and R.E. Parker (1994), 'Accounting for the Great Depression: a historical decomposition', *Journal of Macroeconomics*, Spring.

Fackler, J.S. and R.E. Parker (2001), 'Was debt deflation operative during the Great Depression?', East Carolina University working paper.

Fisher, I. (1933), 'The debt–deflation theory of great depressions', *Econometrica*, October.

Fisher, I. (1934), *Stable Money: A History of the Movement*, New York: Adelphi Co.

Flacco, P.R. and R.E. Parker (1992), 'Income uncertainty and the onset of the Great Depression', *Economic Inquiry*, January.

Friedman, M. (1953), *Essays in Positive Economics*, Chicago: University of Chicago Press.

Friedman, M. (1956), *Studies in the Quantity Theory of Money*, Chicago: University of Chicago Press.

Friedman, M. (1957), *A Theory of the Consumption Function*, Princeton, NJ: Princeton University Press.

Friedman, M. (1962), *Capitalism and Freedom*, Chicago: University of Chicago Press.

Friedman, M. (1968), 'The role of monetary policy', *American Economic Review*, March.

Friedman, M. (1987), *The Essence of Friedman*, Kurt R. Leube (ed.), Stanford, CA: Hoover Institution Press.

Friedman, M. and S. Kuznets (1946), *Income of Independent Professional Practice*, National Bureau of Economic Research.

224	*Reflections on the Great Depression*

Friedman, M. and A.J. Schwartz (1963), *A Monetary History of the United States, 1867–1960*, Princeton, NJ: Princeton University Press.

Friedman, M. and R. Friedman (1980), *Free to Choose: A Personal Statement*, New York: Harcourt, Brace, Jovanovitch.

Ginzberg, Eli (1939), *The Illusion of Economic Stability*, New York: Harper and Brothers.

Gordon, R.J. (1998), *Macroeconomics*, 7th edn, New York: Addison Wesley.

Graham, F.D. and C.R. Whittlesey (1940), *The Golden Avalanche*, Princeton, NJ: Princeton University Press.

Hamilton, J.D. (1987), 'Monetary factors in the Great Depression', *Journal of Monetary Economics*, March.

Hamilton, J.D. (1988), 'Role of the international gold standard in propagating the Great Depression', *Contemporary Policy Issues*, April.

Hamilton, J.D. (1992), 'Was the deflation during the Great Depression anticipated? Evidence from the commodity futures market', *American Economic Review*, March.

Hamilton, J.D. (1994), *Time Series Analysis*, Princeton, NJ: Princeton University Press.

Hart, A.G. (1938), *Debts and Recovery*, New York: The Twentieth Century Fund.

Hart, A.G. (1948), *Money, Debt and Economic Activity*, New York: Prentice-Hall.

Hayek, F.A. von (1956), *Road to Serfdom*, Chicago: University of Chicago Press.

Henderson, H.D. (1932), *Supply and Demand*, Cambridge, UK: London, Nisbet and Co.

Hoover, H. (1952), *The Memoirs of Herbert Hoover: The Great Depression 1929–1941*, New York: Macmillan.

Hoyt, Homer (1933), *One Hundred Years of Land Values in Chicago*, Chicago: University of Chicago Press.

Keynes, J.M. (1930), *A Treatise on Money*, New York: Harcourt, Brace and Co.

Keynes, J.M. (1936), *The General Theory of Employment, Interest, and Money*, London: Macmillan.

Kindleberger, C.P. (1973), *The World in Depression 1929–1939*, Berkeley: University of California Press.

Kindleberger, C.P (1989), *Manias, Panics and Crashes*, New York: Basic Books, Inc.

Kindleberger, C.P (1991), *The Life of an Economist*, Cambridge, MA: Basil Blackwell.

Kindleberger, C.P. (1992), *Mariners and Markets*, New York: Harvester Wheatsheaf.

Kindleberger, C.P. (1993), *A Financial History of Western Europe*, New York: Oxford University Press.

Laidler, D. (1999), *Fabricating the Keynesian Revolution*, Cambridge, UK: Cambridge University Press.

Leijonhufvud, A. (1968), *On Keynesian Economics and the Economics of Keynes: A Study in Monetary Economics*, London: Oxford University Press.

Leontief, W. (1941), *The Structure of the US Economy 1919–1939*, Cambridge, MA: Harvard University Press.

Marx, K. (1936), *Das Kapital*, New York: The Modern Library.

Mayer, T. (1978), 'Consumption in the Great Depression', *Journal of Political Economy*, February.

McCallum, B.T. (1990), 'Could a monetary base rule have prevented the Great Depression?', *Journal of Monetary Economics*, August.

Meltzer, A.H. (1976), 'Monetary and other explanations of the start of the Great Depression', *Journal of Monetary Economics*, November.

Mishkin, F.S. (1978), 'The household balance sheet and the Great Depression', *Journal of Economic History*, December.

Moggridge, D.E. (1993), 'Review of *Golden Fetters:The Gold Standard and the Great Depression, 1919–1939*', *Economic Journal*, May.

Moreau, E. (1991), *The Golden Franc: Memoirs of a Governor of the Bank of France*, Boulder, CO: Westview Press.

Nelson, C. and C. Plosser (1982), 'Trends and random walks in macroeconomic time series: some evidence and implications', *Journal of Monetary Economics*, September.

Nelson, D.B. (1991), 'Was the Deflation of 1929–1930 Anticipated? The Monetary Regime as Viewed by the Business Press', in Roger L. Ransom (ed.), *Research in Economic History*, Greenwich, CT: JAI Press.

Neumark, D. and W. Wascher (1995), 'Minimum wage effects on school and work transitions of teenagers', *American Economic Review*, May.

Olson, Mancur (1982), *The Rise and Decline of Nations*, New Haven: Yale University Press.

Peppers, L. (1973), 'Full employment surplus analysis and structural change: the 1930s', *Explorations in Economic History*, Winter.

Persons, C.E. (1930), 'Credit expansion, 1920 to 1929 and its lessons', *Quarterly Journal of Economics*, November.

Polenberg, R. (2000), *The Era of Franklin D. Roosevelt, 1933–1945: A Brief History with Documents*, Boston: Bedford/St. Martin's.

Quesnay, F. (1972), *Tableau Economique*, London: Macmillan.

Raynold, P., W.D. McMillin and T.R. Beard (1991), 'The impact of Federal Government Expenditures in the 1930s', *Southern Economic Journal*, July.

Romer, C.D. (1988), 'World War I and the postwar depression: a reappraisal based on alternative estimates of GNP', *Journal of Monetary Economics*, July.

Romer, C.D. (1990), 'The great crash and the onset of the Great Depression', *Quarterly Journal of Economics*, August.

Romer, C.D. (1993), 'The nation in depression', *Journal of Economic Perspectives*, Spring.

Samuelson, P.A. (1938), 'A note on the pure theory of consumers' behavior', *Econometrica*, February.

Samuelson, P.A. (1939), 'Interactions between the multiplier analysis and the principle of acceleration', *Review of Economics and Statistics*, May.

Samuelson, P.A. (1947), *Foundations of Economic Analysis*, Cambridge, MA: Harvard University Press.

Samuelson, P.A. (1948), *Economics*, New York: McGraw-Hill.

Samuelson, P.A. (1966–77), *The Collected Scientific Papers of Paul A. Samuelson*, J. Stiglitz (ed.), vols I–V, Cambridge, MA: MIT Press.

Samuelson, P.A. and R.M. Solow (1960), 'Analytical aspects of anti-inflation policy', *American Economic Review*, May.

Schumpeter, J.A. (1934), *The Theory of Economic Development*, Cambridge, MA: Harvard University Press.

Schumpeter, J.A. (1950), *Capitalism, Socialism, and Democracy*, New York: Harper and Row, Inc.

Schumpeter, J.A. (1954), *History of Economic Analysis*, E.B. Schumpeter (ed.), New York: Oxford University Press.

Schwartz, A.J. (1981), 'Understanding 1929–1933', in K. Brunner (ed.), *The Great Depression Revisited*, Boston: Martinus Nijhoff.

Simons, H. (1948), *Economic Policy for a Free Society*, Chicago: University of Chicago Press.

Smith, A. (1937), *An Inquiry into the Nature and Causes of the Wealth of Nations*, New York: The Modern Library.

Snowdon, B. and H.R. Vane (1999), *Conversations with Leading Economists: Interpreting Modern Macroeconomics*, Cheltenham, UK: Edward Elgar.

Soule, G. (1947), *Prosperity Decade, From War to Depression: 1917–1929*, vol. III, *The Economic History of the United States*, New York: Rinehart and Co., Inc.

Stein, H. (1989), *Triumph of the Adaptive Society*, Memphis, TN: Rhodes College.

Temin, P. (1976), *Did Monetary Forces Cause the Great Depression?*, New York: W.W. Norton.

Temin, P. (1989), *Lessons From the Great Depression*, Cambridge, MA: MIT Press.

Thernstrom, S. (1973), *The Other Bostonians: Poverty and Progress in the American Metropolis, 1880–1970*, Cambridge, MA: Harvard University Press.

White, E.N. (1990), 'The stock market boom and crash of 1929 revisited', *Journal of Economic Perspectives*, Spring.

Wicker, E. (1965), 'Federal reserve monetary policy, 1922–33: a reinterpretation', *Journal of Political Economy*, August.

Wicker, E. (1996), *The Banking Panics of the Great Depression*, New York: Cambridge University Press.

Zarnowitz, V. (1985), 'Recent work on business cycles in historical perspective: a review of theories and evidence', *Journal of Economic Literature*, June.

Zarnowitz, V. (1992), *Business Cycles: Theory, History, Indicators, and Forecasting*, Chicago: University of Chicago Press.

Index

229